Women, Culture and Morality
Selected Essays

American University Studies

Series XI
Anthropology and Sociology

Vol. 10

PETER LANG
New York · Bern · Frankfurt am Main · Paris

Women, Culture and Morality

Selected Essays

edited by

Joseph L. DeVitis

PETER LANG

New York · Bern · Frankfurt am Main · Paris

Library of Congress Cataloging-in-Publication Data

Women, culture and morality.

(American university studies. Series XI, Anthropology
and sociology ; vol. 10)
Includes index.
1. Women—Psychology. 2. Moral development.
I. DeVitis, Joseph L. II. Series: American university
studies. Series XI, Anthropology/sociology ; vol. 10.
HQ1206.W8745 1987   305.4'2   87-3638
ISBN 0-8204-0447-0
ISSN 0740-0489

CIP-Kurztitelaufnahme der Deutschen Bibliothek

Women, culture, and morality : selected essays /
Joseph L. DeVitis. – New York; Bern; Frankfurt
am Main; Paris: Lang, 1987.
(American University Studies: Ser. 11,
Anthropology and Sociology; Vol. 10)
ISBN 0-8204-0447-0

NE: DeVitis, Joseph L. [Hrsg.] ; American University Studies / 11

Printed by Weihert-Druck GmbH, Darmstadt, West Germany

DEDICATION

To two women who nurtured my development toward caring and independence: Mary Romaniello DeVitis and Lena Romaniello Franklin

TABLE OF CONTENTS

ACKNOWLEDGMENTS

The interdisciplinary channels of this collection run deep and wide, created in dialogue with many colleagues in social and humanistic foundations of education and psychology. For introducing me and countless others to the rich tapestry of women's moral development, I owe an original debt of gratitude to Carol Gilligan. For further fueling and focusing that interest, I wish to thank numerous collegial sisters and brothers: Kenneth Benne, Robert Deluty, Michael Littleford, Jane Roland Martin, Nel Noddings, Madhu Suri Prakash, Kingsley Price, John Martin Rich, and Betty Sichel. Special appreciation is due Ralph Page, editor of **Educational Theory**, for pointing me in the direction of several essays which made their way into the volume. In addition, I gratefully acknowledge the care and generous attention given the manuscript by the Office of Faculty Research at The University of Tennessee at Martin, especially the kind and diligent assistance of Linda Davis and Phillip Miller. Finally, I commend Jay Wilson, of Peter Lang, for having the courage and conviction to publish this work in the hope that it might help women and men speak with each other--in more deeply felt tones--for their mutual benefit.

FOREWORD

Madhu Suri Prakash

The Pennsylvania State University

Some rise by sin, and some by virtue fall," Shakespearean irony reminds us. The essays in Joseph DeVitis's **Women, Culture and Morality** open our eyes to the fall that comes from settling exclusively for the dominant virtues of patriarchal societies. Taking us into the heart of the "culture of silence", it also invites us to appreciate the values and virtues of the "second sex." We reconnoitre "the dark continent", look back at the other continent (of light?) through the eyes of feminists, unabashedly questioning what The Establishment, governed by our Patriarchs-- intellectuals from Aristotle to Freud and Rousseau, and others less known--has taught us to accept as obvious or well-established truth.

Dissuading us from assent, **Women, Culture and Morality** reveals how these "Truths" are part of the "social construction of reality" by patriarchs over the long span of human history. We see how these "Truths" help oppressors maintain control over the oppressed. We join in committing "the sin" of challenging "approved" maps--of history and psychology, of sociology, morality and ethics--that have been used to direct men and women for centuries.

Among other elements of our morality and culture, we confront the hollowness in the "ideal of the educated person," held up for emulation in the past and even today by noted educators:

The Peters-Hirst educated person will have knowledge about others, but will not have been taught to care about their welfare, let alone to act kindly toward them. That person will have some understanding of society, but will not have been taught to feel its injustices or even to be concerned over its fate. The Peters-Hirst educated person is an ivory tower person: a person who can reason yet has no desire to solve real problems in the real world; a person who understands science but does not worry about the use to which it is put; a person who can reach flawless moral conclusions but feels no care or concern for others.

Simply put,... Peter's ideal of the educated person is far too narrow to guide the educational enterprise. Because it presupposes a divorce of mind from body, thought from action, and reason from feeling and emotion, it provides at best an ideal of an educated **mind**, not an educated **person**. To the extent that its concerns are strictly cognitive, however, even in that guise it leaves much to be desired.[1]

Following "the sin" of declaring that the prevailing truths are tarnished, the feminists writing in **Women, Culture and Morality** help us "rise" to a fresh and rich understanding of the denigrated "feminine virtues."

We come to appreciate the virtue of gentleness--for both men

and women, and not merely as something that the "weaker sex" must
accept as its lot in life. Other relocations include a respectable role for the processes and activites of "reproduction."
These no longer compete with "production", taking place as a low
second in books of history and sociology. The feminist map of
moral education puts an end to the belittling of the moral development of half the human race. The feminine ethics of care and
responsibility is appropriately established in import side by side
with the masculine ethics of justice and rights. In short, we
find a redefinition of all the academic disciplines. Even medical
"facts" are reinterpreted impartially. With new lenses, we study
the misunderstood "hysterical" woman: earlier, the bane of her
pre-Freudian physican for failing to have "regular" straightfor-
ward masculine problems; and later, mis-diagnosed by post-Freudian
psychologists for suffering penis-envy.

By "reclaiming the conversation," the feminists in **Women,
Culture and Morality** are not merely setting right past wrongs.
Their concerns about oppression help bring us in touch with the
inhumanities presently practiced or condoned in "the global
village."

Our prevailing social norms support modes of production,
redistribution and consumption reminiscent in some ways of those
of the Roman elite. While some of us--the yuppies, muppies, and
other privileged groups in the economically (and, morally?) developed world--are "getting into gourmet food," 35,000 people die
each day as a consequence of hunger--24 people every minute, 18 of
them children. But do we, with our well stocked refrigerators,

have a moral obligation to alter our daily menu? Should each of
us radically alter our patterns of acquisition and consumption to
benefit one or more hungry within our own political territory--the
starving Mexican across the sacrosanct national boundary line, or
the faceless Asian across the blue seas? Do we need to change our
norms, our social ethic? Or, is Dr. Brown in Vonnegut's **God Bless
You, Mr. Rosewater** right in concluding, after "a deeply upsetting
investigation of normality of this time and place," that it is
apparent

> a normal person functioning well on the upper levels of
> a prosperous, industrialized society can hardly hear his
> conscience at all[?] . . . [S]amaritrophia is only a
> disease, and a violent one, too, when it attacks those
> exceedingly rare individuals who reach biological matu-
> rity still loving and wanting to help their fellow men.
> I have treated only one case. I have never heard of
> anyone's treating another.[2]

Hungry for Profit[3], a study of international agri-business,
goes beyond Dr. Brown's diagnosis of moral apathy condoned by our
social norms. It reveals that global hunger is exacerbated by
"the hunger for profit" of international food businesses like
Dole, Purina, and Roy Rogers (to mention only a few) in their efforts to feed the hunger for "good food deals" within affluent
nations. Small farms supporting subsistence farming in the Third
World are usurped from powerless peasants and turned into

gigantic farms for cash crops which add only to the quality of life of the privileged. We trample to death thousands of mute peasants so we can improve the quantity and quality of our own meals.

Starvation is not the only evil that attends the formation of such conglomerates. The agricultural plunder for quick profits leaves nature ravaged. The results: eroded top soil and denuded forests; fertile land turned into desert; polluted seas and skies; and the fast extinction of innumerable plant and animal species. In **Declarations of a Heretic**, Jeremy Rifkin notes: "Our species has become expert executioners. We now can boast of killing off one of God's creatures every sixty minutes. Between now and the year 2000 A.D., we will have exterminated nearly 20 percent of all the remaining species left on the planet."[4]

Greedily guzzling our way through the non-renewables that took millions of patient centuries to form and build, we have scant time to express the maternal thought: And what will we leave for future generations? Like the Romans whose culture and morality brought about the burning of Rome, we are too busy sating our desires to seriously consider such questions. And to defend ourselves against any threats to this way of life, we continue to arm our way towards complete annihilation. One wishes in this case that the statistics lied; for the truth they tell is simply awesome, grotesque: "If we spent one million dollars **every day** since the birth of Jesus, we would have spent **half** of what the administration wants to spend on the U.S. military in the next five years--or 1.5 trillion." Representative James Jones brings

home to us our death-wielding extravaganza by translating figures
most of us have difficulty comprehending. Stock-piling feverish-
ly, by some simple error of judgment we could blow away all living
creatures into extinction in defending our position of global
privilege.

If not now, when do we face the imperative to re-examine the
culture, the morality, the education, the virtures that have
occasioned such "a fall"? The feminist voices in **Women, Culture
and Morality** confront this challenge. While lamenting the rape
and carnage that continues, they gently remind us about maternal
thinking:

> "[M]aternal" is a social category: Although maternal
> thinking arises out of actual child-caring practices,
> biological parenting is neither necessary nor suffici-
> ent. Many women and some men express maternal thinking
> in various kinds of working and caring with others. . .
> . It is an attitude elicited by the work of "world-pro-
> tection, world-preservation, world-repair."[5]

In radical contrast to the social virtues promoted within our
"progressive" and "powerful" societies, "maternal thinking" calls
for the virtue of humility, which is a "selfless respect for
reality"; the virtue of clearsighted cheerfulness, which is a
"willingness to continue, to give birth and to accept having given
birth, to welcome life despite its conditions"; and last, it
demands the "capacity of attention" and the virtue of love for

invigorating preservation and enabling growth:

> The recognition of the priority of holding over acquir-
> ing once again distinguishes maternal from scientific
> thought, as well as from the instrumentalism of techno-
> cratic capitalism. In recognizing resilient good humor
> and humility as achievements of its practices, maternal
> thought takes issue both with contemporary moral theory
> and with popular moralities of assertiveness.[6]

Unfortunately, the maternal perspective has its "degenerative forms":

> the cheery denial that sometimes passes for cheerful-
> ness. Preservation can turn into the fierce desire to
> foster one's **own** children's growth whatever the cost to
> other children. Holding--world-preservation and world-
> repair--can turn into frantic accumulating and storing,
> especially under the pressures of consumerism. . . .

> [I]t would be foolish to believe that mothers, just
> because they are mothers, can transcend class interest
> and implement principles of justice. All feminists must
> join in articulating a theory of justice shaped by and
> incorporating maternal thinking. Moreover, the gener-
> alization of attentive love to all children requires
> politics. The most enlightened thought is not enough.[7]

In **Women, Culture and Morality**, feminists pave the way for other heretics to work towards cracking oppressive class structures. They lend support not to violent revolution, but to the loving, patient, non-violent ways of the universal mothers: Mother Theresa, Dorothy Day, Winnie Mandela, Dorothy Soelle, among others[8]; and to the maternal thinking of the gentle warriors: Gandhi and King, Mandela and Berrigan, Tutu and Walensa. I hope the reader of this volume takes heart and joins the **politics** of these universal mothers and gentle warriors.

FOOTNOTES

[1] Jane Roland Martin, "The Ideal of the Educated Person," **Educational Theory** 31 (1981): 104.

[2] Kurt Vonnegut, **God Bless You, Mr. Rosewater** (New York: Dell, 1965), p. 43.

[3] **Hungry for Profit**, Directed by Robert Richter (New York: Robert Richter Productions).

[4] Jeremy Rifkin, **Declarations of a Heretic** (Boston: Routledge and Kegan Paul, 1985), p. 108.

[5] Sara Ruddick, "Maternal Thinking," **Feminist Studies** 6 (1980): 350.

[6] Ibid.

[7] Ibid., 354-361.

[8] These are the well-known universal mothers. There are hundreds of "ordinary" mothers and fathers doing extraordinary work. My own life has been made rich by Darlene Large, mother to over a hundred handicapped children abandoned by their natural parents, and more recently, to raped, pregnant teens. See Madhu Suri Prakash, "Proof That One Woman Can Make a Difference," **Centre Daily Times**, April 22, 1986.

This research was supported by a Spencer Fellowship Grant awarded by The National Academy of Education.

INTRODUCTION

Christopher Lasch has characterized the "art of social survival" as the capacity to "transform myths" in any embedded social
structure--a "long-term development arising not from particular
historical events but from general [cultural] changes."[1] However,
processes of socialization--the transmission of cultural configu-
rations from one generation to the next--do not yield readily to
those who seek to generate new attitudes, beliefs, values, and
behaviors. This is particularly evident when scholarly criteria
are drawn along narrow, disciplinary-protective lines, as appears
to be the case in the empiricist-positivist tradition. Thus
recent interest in feminist thought--a long overdue element on the
research agenda--has been deluged by controversy and criticism.
Much of this debate has focused on charges of intellectual uneven-
ness, dilettantism, and even outright ideology. A central objective of this book is to show that such charges are far from being
fully defensible. More importantly, this collection of essays
will attempt to make clear that domains of knowledge teach must
systematically, effectively, and endurably when they are broadly
conceived, interlacing connections and cross-connections from
among many areas of study.

The weaving of culture is, by nature, a grand trans-gener-
ational undertaking; as such, it necessitates personal as well as
social piece work. As Suzanne K. Langer once put it, the imaginative power of symbol-making, the inner domain of any culture,
is really our own "web of ideas, a fabric of our own making."[2]

Walter Feinberg has similarly dissected the interconnected domain of "educational understanding:"

> . . . Society itself is continually re-created (but not exactly or always in the same way) through a shared understanding in which all of its members, to one degree or another and within different frameworks, participate.[3]

It can be safely claimed that women have been largely denied full and equal access to the re-creation of those "shared understandings" within the "different frameworks" of our cultural domains--from the assumed "destiny" of biology, through the blind spots of psychology in general, to the core institutions which serve to canonize, as it were, the internal strata of any society, i.e., its moral foundations. As a consequence, feminine dimensions on the construction of power, personality, socio-economic change and morality itself have been viewed myopically--sometimes darkly, through stained glass or rigid, noncrystalline prisms. On other occasions, feminine perspectives have been summarily submerged or lost altogether.

A concomitant effect of such submersion has been to place feminine visions on the underside of the history of ideas, thereby relegating to subterranean levels some significant philosophic opposition to dominant paradigms of culture and morality. Indeed, any dominant "construction of cultural reality implies posing certain types of questions about the basic problems of human existence . . . as well as a range of permissible answers, thus excluding other possible questions and answers."[4]

The primary task of this interdisciplinary volume of essays is to bring to light that submerged side of human discourse, namely **feminine** discourse, so that important facets of culture and morality may be approached with a sense of freshness, vitality, and reasoned sensibility for **both** men and women. Accordingly, these essays are written for neither the "strong" nor the "weak." Nor are they composed in a totally "tough" or "tender"-hearted fashion. Above all, they are likewise neither strictly "empirical" nor always precisely "logical." Nor are they based on presumed "cold facts" or "raw data." Instead, they reflect a **tentative** domain of discourse, yet one which lends a powerful lens of interpretation and normative analysis to critical social theory. Perhaps one of the contributing writers best describes the tenor and tapestry of the selections:

> It is a language that attempts to capture what Wittgenstein advised we "must pass over in silence." But if our language is extended to the expressive--and, after all, it is beautifully capable of such extension--perhaps we can say something in the realm of ethical feeling, and that something may at least achieve the status of conceptual aid or tool if not that of conceptual truth. We may present a coherent and enlightening picture without **providing** anything and, indeed, without claiming to present or to seek moral **knowledge** or moral **truth.**[5]

Each of the essays in this anthology contributes to a subtle kind of personal and social dialectic. The order of the readings permits a fairly free-flowing, discursive dialogue among partici- pants in the history of ideas. Critical social and psychological theory forms the basis for much, but not all, of the analysis--one which weaves a critique that cuts underneath appearance to eluci- date actual social realities. Transcendence and praxis compose the end-points of the dialogue--one which is yet to be spoken or written in complete form.

Susan Moller Okin begins the dialectic by arguing that sexism and inequality have been part of the defining features of Western political theory. Functionalist social analysis has provided a scholarly foundation for innumerable social theorists from Emile Durkheim to Talcott Parsons. According to Parsons, for example, "the significance of the concept of function implies the concept- ion of the empirical system as a 'going concern.' Its structure is that system of determinate patterns which empirical observation shows, within certain limits, 'tend to be maintained' or . . . 'tend to develop' according to an empirically constant pattern."[6] To the contrary, Okin attempts to show that conventional funct- ionalist translations of role-distribution and role-patterns are not necessarily basic and imperative for the ongoing survival and growth of civilized social and political life. She clarifies how certain given assumptions have served to solidify sexism and inequality within functionalist paradigms: (1) the premise of "familial primacy," which has tended to link state and family interests; (2) gender dualism, with its attendant unequal differ- entiations in sex roles and political participation; and (3) the

centrality of patriarchy, which has extended unequal sexual differentiation to the legal and social disfranchisement of women.

In her ironically titled paper, "'The Disorder of Women',"
Carole Pateman traces some dominant ethical conceptions of justice
which run through the works of other central figures in Western
thought, focusing primarily on Rousseau and Freud. She analyzes
the role of theories of the "state of nature" and "social contract" as well as distinctions between "private" and "universal"
spheres of interest. Each of these developments serves to illustrate how women have been misplaced in that "scheme of things"
which constitutes civilization. In terms of contemporary culture,
Pateman is especially interested in how given ideologies, particularly capitalism and "liberal individualism," have set certain
limitations on the scope of public discourse.

The socio-cultural stereotyping of women is placed in stark
perspective in Carroll Smith-Rosenberg's "The Hysterical Woman."
In the history of medicine and psychiatry, the term "hysteria" has
been specifically and peculiarly applied to feminine experience,
with accompanying pejorative and destructive connotations. Smith-
Rosenberg demonstrates that inquiry into hysteria has focused on
"individual psychodynamics and relations within particular families" rather than on those larger social structures which may lie
at the root of more decisive causal relationships. The social
milieu for Smith-Rosenberg's study is 19th-century America--a
patriarchal society with structural social and familial role
patterns which were hardly conducive to healthful feminine expression and interaction.

The dark lens through which Freudian psychoanalysis has

viewed women is highlighted in Joseph L. DeVitis' essay, "Freud, Adler, and Women: Powers of the 'Weak' and 'Strong'." An inter-disciplinary excursion in the history of ideas, it seeks to eluci-date the cultural underpinnings of Freud's thought while juxta-posing Adlerian perspectives alongside the master psychologist's teachings. Adler, of course, shared roughly the same cultural background as Freud. However, as DeVitis' argument makes evident, the two analysts came to radically different conclusions on the questions of women, particularly on the matter of moral and social development. These divergent strands of thought also have much to say about how human beings, male and female, interact in the soc-io-political world and how conceptions of human development become propagated or submerged in the history of psychology.

That submergence of socio-political connections, the lack of thoroughgoing dialectic, in psychological thought is ably brought to light in Edward Jones' "Critique of Empathic Science: Sexism and the Hidden Society." While analyzing Kohut's work on nar-cissism as background for his wider discussion, Jones surveys how the social and political dimensions of feminine psychology need to be structurally unearthed. First focusing on issues of gender and self-development, he outlines Nancy Chodorow's influential theory of the "reproduction of mothering." Then Jones demonstrates how Chodorow's internal and external psychological linkages might be brought to bear on the largely internal parameters of empirical, psychodynamic, and "empathic" social science. Without such dia-lectical thinking, psychology, claims Jones, is unable to observe or explain women's development in a genuinely critical and con-structive fashion.

Sara Ruddick's now classic "Maternal Thinking" seeks to extend the definitional powers of feminist discourse in order to appropriate explicit identities of public power, culture, tradition, and scholarly inquiry for women. Transcending accepted narrow boundaries of disciplinary analysis, Ruddick views "maternal thinking" as, **suis generis**, a social category and insists that it exists for women in vastly different ways than are "normally" conceived in most social-science discourse. Such notions as class, ethnicity, and sex-gender systems are incorporated into Ruddick's new definition. A boldly interdisciplinary critic, Ruddick does not hesitate to use such rich literary resources as the works of Simone Weil and Iris Murdoch in making her case. She also relies on recent reformulations of feminine psychology by Jean Baker Miller.[7]

Since education reflects so much of what is culturally transmitted to the young of any society, Jane Roland Martin's "The Ideal of the Educated Person" offers a particularly pointed challenge. In her own discipline of educational philosophy, Paul Hirst's analytic treatment of liberal education as "a form of education knowing no limits other than those necessarily imposed by the nature of rational knowledge" has been widely acknowledged and accepted.[8] At the same time, R. S. Peters, another highly respected analytic philosopher, has persuaded many of his colleagues to accept certain educational "aims" as well-nigh self-evident and beyond reasonable debate.[9] Yet Hirst and Peters also leave other critics to wonder whether their educative goals and objectives are as "obvious" as they would make us believe.[10] Martin is a direct critic of both Hirst and Peters. She broadly questions the whole

notion of liberal education as developed in the tradition of
Western political thought from Plato to Rousseau. Sensing a "male
bias" in the treatment of educational aims, Martin calls for a
"gender-sensitive" and "gender-just" ideal which might yield more
equitable, and thus identical, educative results. Martin's argument has engendered a new controversy among her brethren in analytic educational philosophy--over issues which had been seemingly
long laid to rest by Hirst and Peters.[11]

There have been few contributions to social science research
over the last several decades which have drawn as much attention
as Lawrence Kohlberg's theory of cognitive moral development--a
model which has had significant influence in developing practical
rationales for moral education as well. However, the longitudinal
studies on which Kohlberg bases his original research are singu-
larly devoid of reference to female samples.[12] A colleague of
Kohlberg in Harvard's Center for Moral Education, Carol Gilligan
has challenged his theories in light of her own pioneering research on women's psychological development.[13] While Gilligan's
work is not in finished form and still needs to be further tested
(with larger, more diverse, samples of its own), it nonetheless
counterposes a rich tapestry of **particular personal and social
context** alongside Kohlberg's more abstract, contemplative universe
of discourse. The basic thrust of Gilligan's findings underscore
a language of care, responsibility, and not wanting to hurt others
in women's presumably unique and different moral thema. According
to Gilligan's thesis, Kohlberg's dialectic (largely a **male** dialectic despite his more recent samples of "mixed" male and female
subjects) seems to be focused in terms of individual rights,

liberties, duties, and their attendant protection. The essay in this book, "New Maps of Development: New Visions of Maturity," represents Gilligan's views immediately following the release of her widely acclaimed and much discussed **In a Different Voice.**

Betty Sichel's trenchant review and comparison of competing findings in cognitive moral development theory more clearly focuses the debate between Kohlberg and Gilligan. In precise analytic terms, Sichel's critique of each paradigm pinpoints strengths, weaknesses, and limitations in the overall research design and specific samples constructed by Kohlberg and Gilligan. Sichel also alludes to some "current dominant views" in political theory and public discourse which may have lent support and sustenance to the Kohlberg–Gilligan controversy. Parenthetically, Sichel introduces Lawrence Blum's argument in **Friendship, Altruism and Morality** as an aid in articulating a dual portrait of morality: one of Kantian rights and impartiality (Kohlberg), the other one of primary human feeling (Gilligan). As Sichel implies, the morality of interaction which Gilligan and Blum seek is principally one "that is prerequisite to the fulfillment of . . . individual goals."[14] That is, neither seems to have successfully developed a social dialectic in its fullest sense.

Repercussions from Gilligan's studies on morality have only recently begun to generate sustained dialogue and reaction.[15] Nel Noddings' philosophical argument in "An Ethic of Caring" is based on principles of "natural caring," as in the case of a mother's concern for her child. An artful weaving of both classical philosophy and linguistic analysis, Noddings' thesis maintains that the powerful stream of "natural caring" has been largely neglected in most traditional philosophic approaches to ethics. By positing such an ethic as foundational, Noddings' wider task is to build a future agenda for moral education--one which she contends would benefit men as well as women.

To conclude this introduction on another sobering, but still hopeful note, the editor has included George Sher's "Our Preferences, Ourselves." This paper points to some important open-ended moral questions which must be addressed more directly by social philosophers and other interested investigators. Sher claims that public philosophy and social policy have begun to recognize that women "should have as much opportunity to realize . . . preferences as men." Nevertheless, he argues that there has been inadequate inquiry into the nature of women's "traditional" preferences (i.e., those which are undergirded by social conditioning) by both mainstream and feminist scholars. In this assessment, Sher implies the need to alter dominant social circumstances which impede the understanding of women, culture and morality. The essays in this volume admirably elucidate some of those understandings which would make us all--women and men--more fully human if and when we learn to share them in our everyday thought and action.

FOOTNOTES

[1] Christopher Lasch, **The Culture óf Narcissism: American Life in an Age of Diminishing Expectations** (New York: Warner Books, 1979), p. 122.

[2] Suzanne K. Langer, **Philosophical Sketches** (Baltimore: Johns Hopkins University Press, 1962), p. 147.

[3] Walter Feinberg, **Understanding Education: Toward a Recon-struction of Educational Inquiry** (Cambridge: Cambridge University Press, 1983), p. 157.

[4] S. N. Eisenstadt, "Intellectuals and Tradition," **Daedalus** 101 (1972), 5.

[5] Nel Noddings, **Caring: A Feminine Approach to Ethics and Moral Education** (Berkeley: University of California Press, 1984), p. 3.

[6] Talcott Parsons, **Essays in Sociological Theory**, rev. ed. (New York: Free Press, 1954), p. 217.

[7] Jean Baker Miller, **Toward a New Psychology of Women** (Boston: Beacon Press, 1976).

[8] Paul Hirst, in R. D. Archambault, ed., **Philosophical Analy-sis and Education** (London: Routledge and Kegan Paul, 1965), p. 127.

[9] R. S. Peters, **Authority, Responsibility and Education**, 2d ed. (London: Allen and Unwin) ch. 7.

[10] See Clive Beck, **Educational Philosophy and Theory: An Introduction** (Boston: Little, Brown, 1974), ch. 1.

[11] For example, see James McClellan, "Response to Jane Mar-tin," **Educational Theory** 31 (1981): 111-114; and Eleanor Kallman Roemer, "Harm and the Ideal of the Educated Person: Response to Jane Roland Martin," **ibid.**, 115-124. Also see Harvey Siegel, "Genderized Cognitive Perspective and the Redefinition of Philos-ophy of Education;" Jane Roland Martin, "Taking Sophie Seriously"; and Donald Arnstine, "Siegel's Arguments, Martin's Sympathies, and the Rest of Us Poor Folk," in **Philosophy of Education 1983**, ed. Robert E. Roemer (Normal: Illinois State University, 1984). For a more recent synthesis of Martin's ideas, see her **Reclaiming a Conversation: The Ideal of the Educated Woman** (New Haven: Yale University Press, 1985).

[12] Lawrence Kohlberg, **The Development of Modes of Moral Think-ing and Choice in the Years Ten to Sixteen**, unpublished doctoral dissertation (Chicago: University of Chicago, 1958). Jean Piaget, who directly influenced Kohlberg's cognitive structural-ism, also conducted experimentation on moral development with a small sample of young male children. See Piaget, **The Moral Judg-**

ment of the Child, tr. Marjorie Gabain (New York: Harcourt, Brace and World), 1932.

[13]Carol Gilligan, In a Different Voice: Psychological Theory and Women's Development (Cambridge, Mass.: Harvard University Press, 1982).

[14]Lawrence A. Blum, Friendship, Altruism and Morality (London: Routledge and Kegan Paul, 1980).

[15]For a recent empirical analysis which disputes Gilligan's findings, see Lawrence J. Walker, "Sex Differences in the Development of Moral Reasoning: A Critical Review," Child Development 55 (1984): 677-691.

CHAPTER 1

WOMAN'S PLACE AND NATURE IN A FUNCTIONALIST WORLD*
Susan Moller Okin

Aristotle's philosophy is strikingly different, in its aim
and in its entire tone, from that of Plato. Whereas Plato,
throughout the dialogues, is essentially critical, radically
questioning the most sacredly held conventions of the world around
him, Aristotle sets out to acquire knowledge of the way the world
is, and, moreover, to explain why it is the way it is. There is
probably no other philosopher, not even Hegel himself, whose work
better fits the definition that Hegel gave to philosophy--that it
is "its own time apprehended in thoughts."[1]

On the subject of scientific knowledge, Aristotle says: "We
all suppose that what we know is not even capable of being otherwise . . . Therefore the object of scientific knowledge is of
necessity. Therefore it is eternal."[2] He sees the object of
scientific inquiry as not simply correct observation of the world,
but demonstration of why it is that the world and its constituent
parts are, and must be, the way they are. This approach, moreover, is not peculiar to his natural philosophy, but deeply pervades his ethical and political writings also. He does not, like
Plato, attempt to set out from a rational and autonomous base to
examine and criticize prevailing modes of behavior, opinions and

standards. Aristotle's very different method of inquiry into these areas of thought is clearly described in the **Nichomachean Ethics**, at the outset of his discussion of one of the virtues. He states:

> We must, as in all other cases, set the observed facts
> before us and, after first discussing the difficulties,
> go on to prove, if possible, the truth of all the common
> opinions about these affections of the mind, or, failing
> this, of the greater number and the most authoritative;
> for if we both refute the objections and leave the com-
> mon opinions undisturbed, we shall have proved the case
> sufficiently.[3]

He perceives his task as moral philosopher, then, as that of redeeming prevailing moral views and standards from whatever inconsistencies or vaguenesses might mar them. The assumption is that they are far more likely to be right than wrong.[4] Aristotle's ethic is, to a large extent, traditional ethics, clarified and justified. Unlike Plato, he does not argue, in dealing with ethics any more than with biology, that the world should be different from the way it is, but starts from a basic belief that the status quo in both the natural and the social realm is the best way for things to be.

This conservative approach, however, is not simply assumed dogmatically, but has its own rationale. Things are the way they are, Aristotle argues, because of the function each of them performs, and their survival is proof that they perform their functions well. He asserts, at the beginning of the Politics, "All things derive their essential character from their function and their capacity; and it follows that if they are no longer fit to discharge their function, we ought not to say that they are still the same things."[5]

Aristotle's functionalist outlook is very clearly illustrated by the account he gives of the nature of the soul. Although psyche, soul or essence, is a characteristic found only in living beings, it is defined in reference to two things that are clearly instrumental or functional -- an axe and an eye. First Aristotle asserts, "If some utensil, for example an axe, were a natural body, then 'being-an-axe' would be its substance, and this would be its soul. Apart from this, it would no longer be an axe, save equivocally." Then he adds, "If the eye were an animal, sight would be its soul."[6] Clearly, in Aristotle's view, the soul of a thing is its capacity to fulfill its function, and while this seems reasonable enough when applied to artefacts or organs of the body, he extends it further, stating, "What, therefore, holds of a part, we ought to apply to the whole living body."[7] There is obviously no recognition by Aristotle of the significant distinction between natural beings and either artefacts or the component parts of natural beings. Not only does he perceive the relationship between soul and body as an instrumental one, as when he says that "each art must use its tools, and the soul its body,"[8] but he also perceives the entire living creature in an instrumental or functional manner.

Certain prerequisites, however, are necessary, for beings to be perceived in terms of their functions. Clearly, a thing can be thought of as having a function only in relation to some other thing or things. This is why tools and parts of the body are archetypal examples of things that are thought of functionally. In order to postulate that living beings, in a manner parallel to artefacts or organs, have functions, they must be viewed in relationship to each other and to the world as a whole, in a particular kind of way. Aristotle provides such a world view.

While acknowledging that the earlier natural philosopher, Democritus, had recognized that natural phenomena are necessary, Aristotle criticized him for having omitted the concept of "final cause" or purpose. "It is of course true," Aristotle agrees, "that (all the things which Nature employs) are determined by necessity, but at the same time they are for the sake of some purpose, some Final Cause, and for the sake of that which is better in each case."[9] The last clause of this assertion points us to the crucially important fact that Aristotle's view of the world is completely hierarchical. His entire universe, from the lowliest plant to the human race, and beyond the human race to the heavenly bodies and the gods, is arranged in a strict hierarchy, and it is this that enables him to say, "In the world of nature as well as of art the lower always exists for the sake of the higher."[10]

Thus, frequently stressing that "nature makes nothing in vain," Aristotle argues that plants exist to give subsistence to animals, and animals to give it to men. Since man is clearly at the top of the scale of mortal beings, "all animals must have been made by nature for the sake of men."[11] The vision is not just an anthropocentric one, however. While all human beings are the highest of animals, within the human race, too, the hierarchical ordering is maintained. When Aristotle approaches the study of society, he arrives quickly at some fundamental and very firmly held premises, which are to function as the bases of his ethics and politics. These are that the Greek **polis** is the natural, and therefore best, form of political association, and that the Greek family -- with its subordination of wife, children and slaves--is the natural, and therefore best, form of household and family structure. In order to see how he arrives at these beliefs, which of course gain a large part of their strength from the fact that these institutions **were** the Greek world of Aristotle's time, we must examine what he conceives the function of man to be.

Near the beginning of the **Nichomachean Ethics**, Aristotle determines that happiness is the final and self-sufficient end of human activity, and sets out to give an account of what this happiness consists in. "This might perhaps be given," he says, "if we could first ascertain the function of man."[12] Significantly, the function that is peculiar to man, unlike the functions of the lower members on the scale of being, is not found to be some purpose he serves for a being higher on the scale. While man shares some characteristics, such as nutrition, growth and sensation, with the lower animals, Aristotle concludes that what is peculiar to him alone is his reason. Since this is his distinguishing feature, man's highest good is the "active life of the element that has a rational principle."[13] Man's relationship to those above him in the hierarchy is not that of serving some purpose of theirs; though his reasoning power makes him akin to the gods, whose whole existence is spent in rational contemplation, it is clearly for his own sake, not theirs, that he emulates them. His objective is his own happiness, not the fulfillment of the needs of another. In fact, Aristotle is well aware that the gods, anthropomorphic as they are, are the idealization of the highest human virtues, reason and self-sufficiency. The gods are the way they are because man imagines them thus: "We make the lives of the gods in the likeness of our own--as we also make their shapes."[14] It is therefore hardly coincidental that man's highest virtue is also the defining characteristic of the gods, or that the gods are depicted as perpetually engaged in that activity which man has decided on as the most worthwhile for himself.

Thus, whereas most beings serve a function in relation to some higher being, and whereas most activities have an end which lies outside the activity itself and to which it is subordinate, man's proper end is his own happiness, and "the activity of reason, which is contemplative, seems . . . to aim at no end beyond itself, and to have its pleasure proper to itself."[15] The proper activity of man alone among mortals has no end or aim outside the actor himself.

The word for "man" that Aristotle uses throughout his arguments about the nature of man, and man's highest good, is **anthropos**, the Greek word meaning "human being." It soon becomes very clear, however, that only a small minority of one sex of the human race is to share in what have been characterized as the human virtues and man's highest good and happiness. For "man" requires not only his reason, but also certain essential external goods, if he is to live the good life. He cannot be happy, Aristotle tells us, without assets such as riches, friends, many and good children, leisure, noble birth, and beauty. Some of these clearly depend on the service of other people. Thus, in accordance with his characteristic teleology, Aristotle argues that not only the entire animal kingdom, but the vast majority of humans as well, are intended by nature to be the instruments which supply to the few the necessities and comforts that will enable them to be happy in their contemplative activity. Thus, women, slaves, and artisans and traders are all subsidiary instruments for the achievements of the highest happiness of "man." "In the state," Aristotle asserts, "the conditions which are necessary for the existence of the whole are not organic parts of the whole system which they serve."[16] Human good and human happiness have been defined in such a way that the vast majority of the human race is necessarily excluded from the achievement of either.

From time to time, presumably to make his functionalism appear more palatable, Aristotle argues that the relationships between those whom he perceives as naturally ruling and naturally ruled, such as husband and wife, or master and slave, are good for both parties because the capacities of these are very different. This kind of reasoning forms a substantial part of his argument for slavery. Although the slave is characterized as an instrument or tool, we are told that "the condition of slavery is both beneficial and just" for him, that the relationship between him and his master is "for the preservation of both," and that the two of them "have an identical interest."[17] Moreover, Aristotle argues that in the relationships between soul and body, craftsman and tool, and master and slave, "the latter in each case is benefited by that which uses it."[18] In a parallel manner, he argues, first,

that husband and wife have a mutually beneficial relationship--
that "they help each other by throwing their peculiar gifts into
the common stock," and, second, that it is in fact the woman who
is the beneficiary, and the man the benefactor of their relationship.[19]

As we might expect, however, given the hierarchical structure
of Aristotle's world, these illusions of mutuality and of benefits
accruing to the inferior party are not consistently maintained.
With regard to slaves, they very soon disappear, We are told that
the relationship is primarily in the interest of the master and
only incidentally in that of the slave, "who must be preserved in
existence if the rule itself is to remain."[20] In general, moreover, speaking of all such pairs of the ruling and the ruled,
Aristotle asserts, "Nor is the good divisible between them but
that of both belongs to the one for whose sake they exist."[21]
Again, in a context which explicitly includes reference to the
rule of men over women, he says that "the ruled may be compared to
flute-makers: rulers are like flute-players who use what the
flute-makers make."[22]

Aristotle asserts that women are "naturally" inferior to men,
and that they are therefore "naturally" ruled by them. However,
his use of the word **physis** (nature) and its derivatives is at
least as complex and ambiguous as Plato's.[23] Sometimes, clearly,
he uses "natural" to refer to innate as opposed to acquired characteristics.[24] At times, again like Plato, he acknowledges that
very little clear distinction can be made between the nature of a
mature being and the habits it has acquired throughout its life.[25]
Aristotle's most usual use of the word "nature," however, is

intimately connected with his functionalist approach to the world. I have already pointed out that he considered the "essential character" of a thing to be derived from its function, and the soul of each thing to be its capacity to function. Thus, when he tells us at the beginning of the **Politics** that "what each thing is when its growth is completed we call the nature of that thing, whether it be a man or a horse or a family,"[26] we must not fail to take into account the essential connection which exists in his mind between the way a thing should grow and develop, and its function. It is noteworthy that when he first introduces the three basic relationships that exist within the household, he states his intention to examine "the nature of each and the qualities it ought to possess."[27] It is clear that, in Aristotle's world, these two factors are virtually synonymous. Thus, when he makes the extraordinary statement that "dealing with . . . . animate beings, we must fix our attention, in order to discover what nature intends, not on those which are in a corrupt, but on those which are in a natural condition,"[28] it is necessary to perform a substitution of the two equivalents--the nature of a thing, and the goodness pertaining to that thing--in order to give the proposition any content. We must acknowledge Aristotle's normative use of the word "natural," and give the "natural" at the end of his sentence a distinct moral connotation. In order to be meaningfully contrasted with "corrupt," it must mean "well-ordered" or "good," and Aristotle's statement is no longer value free, as it at first appeared. Moreover, as the above discussion of his functionalism indicates, nothing is well-ordered or good unless it can perform and does perform the function ascribed to it within

Aristotle's hierarchical world. Thus Aristotle has established a philosophical framework by which he can legitimize the status quo. For the conventional function of any person determines that person's goodness, and a person's nature, or natural condition, is also equated with his or her goodness. Every person, therefore, is naturally suited to his or her existing role and position in society.

Aristotle's arguments about the nature of things and beings, especially of those within the human social realm, are virtually unintelligible unless one continually recognizes his esoteric use of the term. The family exists "by nature"; the **polis** exists "prior in the order of nature to the family and the individual."[29] By saying that the family is natural, Aristotle by no means intends to imply that it has always existed, but rather that its existence is necessary for the well-ordered life of man. The reason that the **polis** is prior in the natural order is, likewise, not that it is more original or basic than the family. It is because, while the family exists "for the satisfaction of daily recurrent needs" and sustains mere life, the **polis** is the only association within which man can enjoy that self-sufficiency which enables him to live the rational life, the highest life to which he can aspire. The **polis** is more natural, in other words, because of the superiority of its aim or object, which makes it a better institution than the family.

Similarly, Aristotle's arguments about the naturalness of slavery are incomprehensible unless one recognizes his totally teleological version of the natural. For his attempts to convince us that some people are by nature slaves are most unpersuasive if we rely on his claims that natural slaves are those men "who differ from others as much as the body differs from the soul, or an animal from a man."[30] It is only if we accept the premises that society is most properly structured when it enables the privileged few to spend their lives in rational activity, and that the functions and therefore the nature of all others must be fixed accordingly, that we can accept Aristotle's justification of slavery as natural.

The same considerations apply to Aristotle's conclusions about the nature and the natural position of women. These can be understood only by reference to the function the female sex is perceived as fulfilling in the stratified society he assumes to be the best for man. At the beginning of his discussion of the household, Aristotle informs his reader that, contrary to what the barbarians think,

> the female and the slave are naturally distinguished from one another. Nature makes nothing in a spirit of stint, as smiths do when they make the Delphic knife to serve a number of purposes: she makes each separate thing for a separate end; and she does so because each instrument has the finest finish when it serves a single purpose and not a variety of purposes.[31]

As the context makes very clear, the slave's function is the provision of the daily needs of subsistence, whereas the female's primary function is reproduction.

On the subject of woman's function, which is on the whole

implicit in the **Politics**, we must turn to Aristotle's biological writings for clarification. Reproduction was a subject in which he had an intense interest, since he regarded it as the "most natural" of the operations of mature living beings.[32] In fact, however, compared with the astounding accuracy and originality of his biological findings as a whole, Aristotle's "observations" about sexual reproduction contain a number of serious errors, of which virtually all are attributable to his basic assumption that the male is always and in every way superior to the female.

The reason for the very existence of the sexual form of reproduction in most animals, Aristotle argues, is the superiority of form over matter. His "observations" of sexual reproduction informed him that the male, via his semen, always provides the form or soul of the offspring, while the female, via her menstrual discharge, provides the matter. Since "the Form, is **better** and more divine in its nature than the Matter, it is **better** also that the superior one should be separate from the inferior one. That is why whenever possible and so far as possible the male is separate from the female."[33]

Thus Aristotle explains the need for sexual reproduction in terms of his hierarchical view of the world. Indeed, he argues that it was only the need for this higher form of reproduction that made nature stray from the generic type of each species, which is clearly perceived by him as that embodied in the male. Immediately prior to explaining the appearance of "monstrosities" in nature, he accounts for the "first deviation," which occurs "when a female is formed instead of a male." This deviation from the norm, we are told, "is a necessity required by Nature, since the race . . . has got to be kept in being." Altogether, he concludes, "we should look on the female as being as it were a deformity, though one which occurs in the ordinary course of nature."[34] Even with respect to reproduction, the only reason she exists at all, the female is characterized as inferior and disabled. It is the male who performs the active role, whereas the female merely acts as a passive receptacle for the new life. It is he who provides the new life with its soul, which is after all the raison d'etre of the body that she furnishes. "A woman," Aristotle concludes, "is as it were an infertile male," and even in regard to reproduction, "a male is male in virtue of a particular ability, and a female in virtue of a particular inability."[35] In all this, moreover, "what happens is what one would expect to happen," and "in all her workmanship herein Nature acts in every particular as reason would expect."[36]

The proposals made in the **Politics** for the regulation of marriage and breeding clearly reflect these biological beliefs and Aristotle's perception of woman as fundamentally an instrument for breeding men. Marriage is regarded solely as an institution for "the provision of a stock of the healthiest possible bodies (for) the nurseries of our state,"[37] and the age of marriage should therefore be when both partners are at the height of their procreative powers, with the woman in her late teens, and the man in his late thirties. Following the oracle, Aristotle recommends that the citizens "plough not the young fallow"; when mothers are too young they have great difficulty in childbirth. In keeping with his general theory of reproduction, since the mother provides only the matter for the child and the father its rational soul, it is only the father's mental prime that is taken into account, and while the mother is advised to exercise and eat well while pregnant, since the growing foetus draws on her body, her mind should be kept idle, in order that more of her strength be preserved for the child's growth. Since the child is in no way perceived as drawing on the mother's mind, the development of her mind is quite needless.[38]

In spite of her widespread inabilities, then, woman is necessary for the reproduction of man, and this is therefore seen by Aristotle as her natural function. After all, if it were not for the requirements of sexual reproduction, this particular "deformity in nature" would never have existed. Within the well-ordered society, however, reproduction is not woman's only function. Unlike the other animals, man does not couple by chance and temporarily, since he "is not only a political but also a householding animal." For "human beings live together," Aristotle argues, "not only for the sake of reproduction but also for the various purposes of life; for from the start the functions are divided, and those of man and woman are different." While it is the man's function to acquire, it is the woman's "to keep and store."[39] The necessity of all the things and services provided by the household for daily life, taken together with the assumption that all other classes of people are intended by nature to enable the few to pursue their truly human activities, leads Aristotle to regard the entire conventional division of labor between the sexes as strictly in accordance with nature.

Aristotle's reaction to Plato's radical proposals about the family and women is extremely illuminating in this context. In

Book II of the **Politics**, Aristotle argues at great length against Plato's proposal to abolish the family. He voices three major objections. First, he maintains, though not very convincingly, that the unity which Socrates regards as the supreme good for the **polis**, and which he aims to ensure by abolishing the private family and making the guardians into one big family, will have the effect of destroying the **polis**. "It is obvious," he argues, "that a **polis** which goes on and on, and becomes more and more of a unit, will eventually cease to be a **polis** at all." Rather, it will tend toward being a household, or even an individual.[40] Too much unity, or sameness, is very bad for a **polis**, which "by its nature is some sort of aggregation." Secondly, and, it seems, contradictorily, he argues that Plato's proposed extension of the bonds of kinship would have the effect of weakening them so much that they would be worthless. Since men care most for what is their own, Aristotle claims, the result would be the general neglect of people by each other, since no none would have any relatives who cared exclusively for him. Finally, it concerns Aristotle immensely that not knowing who one's relatives are would lead to an increase in breaches of "natural piety," in the form of such crimes as incest, parricide and fratricide. These arguments against Plato are not compelling. The first can be combated by reference to the fact that there were to be other types of diversity within the ideal state, so that the abolition of the family would by no means result in excessive sameness. Besides, Aristotle's first two arguments seem to be mutually inconsistent; if doing away with the family would severely dilute the bonds of kinship, how could it at the same time lead to much unity? The third argument seems no more convincing than Plato's contrary assertion that the formation of all the guardians into one family would result in the extension of the traditional kinship loyalties and taboos throughout the entire ruling class.

However, Aristotle certainly considers himself to have demolished Plato's case, and continues to regard the private family and household as the only, natural and necessary basis for social life. As was mentioned earlier, it was a central aspect of his philosophical method to begin by discussing previous and especially authoritative views on the subject at issue. Since Book II of the Politics is in large part taken up with the survey of previous writers' ideas about the abolition of the family, the equalization or communalization of property, and other such radical reforms, it is conspicuous that Aristotle has almost nothing to say about the extremely radical and unorthodox proposals of Book V of the Republic regarding equal education and opportunities for women. Apart from a fleeting reference, he merely comments on Plato's analogous reference to male and female dogs, which, he had claimed, are an example to humans because they do not adhere to rigid sex roles. Aristotle's answer, moreover, is virtually unintelligible unless it is recognized that both for him and for Plato, once the issue of the family is settled, that of the role of women is not an independent one. For Aristotle asserts, puzzled by Plato's ignorance of the obvious, that the analogy is quite unsuitable, since "animals, unlike women, have no domestic duties."[41] It is quite clear that, since he considers himself to have refuted the idea of the community of women and children, he does not even consider it necessary to argue against Plato's wild ideas about women and their potential as individual persons. Given the family and the private household, women are private wives with domestic functions, and there is no more to be said on the subject.

Aristotle's assumption that woman is defined by her reproductive function and her other duties within the household permeates everything he has to say about her. Indeed, Aristotle's entire moral philosophy is much affected by the existence of the hierarchy which he considers to be natural because it is necessary for the attainment of the proper objective of human life. First, all the basic relationships discussed in the **Ethics**, such as friendship and justice, are perceived as differing radically in their natures, depending on the relative positions in society occupied by the two or more persons involved. Second, none of the basic moral terms, such as virtue, temperance, and courage, are held to be universally applicable, since a person's position in the human hierarchy, and consequent function, determine the particular type of virtue, temperance, or courage that will be required of him or her. I will discuss each of these two issues in turn.

Because he perceives woman as naturally inferior to man, Aristotle asserts that all relationships between them must acknowledge and, insofar as possible, compensate for this inequality. Political justice, which he regards as the only type that genuinely deserves the name of justice, can exist only between equals, between those who have an equal share in ruling and being ruled, as fellow citizens do. In such a case, it is unjust for equals to be treated in any way other than equally. Where such parity between persons does not exist, however, justice is an entirely different matter, and can only metaphorically be called justice at all. Aristotle seems, however, to have been unsure as to the type of "metaphorical justice" that is properly applied to women. At first, he says that "justice can more truly be manifested toward a wife than toward children and chattels, for the former is household justice; but even this is different from political justice."[42] Subsequently, however, he appears to retract even this concession, comparing justice between husband and wife to that between master and slave (who is certainly a chattel) and to that between the rational and irrational parts of the soul.[43] Since he implies at times that a slave is not a human being at all, and he parallels the relationship between him and his master to that of despot and subject, we are left with the impression that, so far as justice is concerned, Aristotle has relegated woman to an altogether subhuman position.

Like the other moral relations, friendship, too, varies in accordance with the respective status of the friends in Aristotle's social hierarchy. Whereas there can be no friendship at all between a man and a slave **qua** slave (though paradoxically a man can be friends with the same individual **qua** man), the friendships between father and children and between husband and wife are categorized as friendship between benefactor and benefited. "The friendship of man and wife . . .," Aristotle asserts, "is the same that is found in an aristocracy; for it is in accordance with virtue--the better gets more of what is good, and each gets what befits him; and so, too, with the justice in these relations."[44] The difference between various types of friendship depends both on the respective virtues and functions of the two persons and on the reasons for which they love each other. In all friendships in which the friends are not equal, the love should be proportional to the merit of the two parties, for only if the better is loved more than he loves, will equality be restored.[45] In marriage, the husband is, of course, by virtue of his superiority always the benefactor and the more useful partner. As Aristotle's disciple argues in the **Oeconomica**, one reason that a wife must obey her husband and serve him sedulously is that "he has indeed bought her with a great price--with partnership in his life and the pro-creation of children; than which things nothing could be greater or more divine."[46] There is no emphasis placed, in such a con-text, on the fact that the woman's entire life is defined in terms of the function she performs for man. And thus Aristotle con-cludes that it would be ludicrous for a wife to expect her affec-tion to be returned in a similar way, just as it would be ludi-crous for man to expect the same of God; "for it is the part of a ruler to be loved, not to love, or else to love in another way."[47] Friendship and marriage are no exception to the basic principle that relationships must always reflect the respective merits and functions of those who are party to them.

The second relevant phenomenon of Aristotle's ethics--the variable application of terms and standards--was by no means new at his stage of Greek thought. As A. W. H. Adkins has demonstrat-ed in his illuminating book, **Merit and Responsibility**, the Greeks from the time of Homer to that of Aristotle, with the notable exception of Plato, had no concept of a single standard of human morality or excellence which might be applied to anyone, regard-less of his or her role or position in society.[48] Their word of highest praise, **arete** (excellence or virtue), originated in the commendation of an entirely masculine, noble, and leisured way of life, and could only be used of those who had the wherewithal, in terms of both high birth and their command of material goods and other people's services, to pursue such a life. . . ."Woman's **arete**" was a relative term, consisting of a set of qualities entirely different from those of men, who alone could achieve absolute excellence. This was the immense weight of custom and opinion that Socrates was combating, both in the **Meno**, in claiming the irrelevance of sex to **arete**, and in the **Republic**, in implying that sex is no more related to the soul than baldness is. The importance of these passages in the gradual universalizing of ethical values must not be underestimated.

In his ethical and political writings, Aristotle reacts against these heresies of Socrates, and both consolidates and justifies the traditional way of thinking. Having defined the highest human virtue as reason, he constructs a functionalist rationalization of a society in which this highest virtue can be shared in only by those at the top of the class- and sex- determined hierarchy. As Adkins asserts, "Thus Aristotle leaves no hope of establishing any standard for the whole community."[49] Even free males whose work is considered menial are excluded from the possibility of participation in the higher things of life, and what is the case for artisans is, of course, even more the case for slaves, and for women of any class at all. Women's work is clearly regarded as in no way compatible with the life of excellence.[50]

What Aristotle does, therefore, is to define the goodness of each thing and each person according to its function; "let it be

assumed as to goodness," he says, "that it is the best disposition
or state or faculty of each class of things that have some use or
work."[51] His examples extend from a coat, a ship, and a house, to
a soul.   While it is quite easy for us to accept this functional
characterization of the excellence of artefacts, and to agree with
Aristotle that "what is healthy or good is different for men and
for fishes," it is jarring to the modern ear to hear the
adjectives of commendation which we are accustomed to think of as
constant in their meanings, applied differently to different
classes of human beings. But for Aristotle, human beings have
functions just as much and in the same way as artefacts do, and
only those at the very top of the hierarchy have a function which
is defined only in relation to themselves and not to others.
There are two fundamentally different orders of human goodness.
The goodness of the leisured and fully rational men is something
absolute, while all the others can achieve only forms of goodness
that are relative and inferior.   Their goodness is determined
entirely by their respective functions, and all these functions
are inferior to that of those at the top. Thus, although they
cannot attain the higher form of goodness, "even a woman is 'good'
and so is a slave, although it may be said that a woman is an
inferior thing and a slave beneath consideration."[52]

Even in the case of the free male citizen, it is "his good
discharge of his function" which determines his excellence,[53] and
in the good **polis** he will have two sorts of goodness, since because of his constitutional equality with his fellow citizens he
must rule and be ruled in turn. He must therefore have "one sort
[of excellence] which fits him to act as a ruler, and one which

fits him to act as a subject."[54] Women, however, together with all the other persons who are necessary conditions but not parts of the **polis**, require only the kind of goodness which fits them to be ruled, since this is their natural and permanent role.

All the moral standards applied to woman, therefore, are determined by her function as the bearer of new citizens and the guardian of the household. Since she has a different function from that of the slave, so must her goodness be different, just as the slave's differs from that of the artisan. Aristotle asserts:

> They must all share in (moral goodness), but not in the same way--each sharing only to the extent required for the discharge of his or her function. The ruler, accordingly, must possess moral goodness in its full or perfect form because his function . . . demands a master-artificer, and reason is such a master artificer; but all other persons need only possess moral goodness to the extent required of them. It is thus clear that . . . . temperance--and similarly fortitude and justice--are not, as Socrates held, the same in a woman as they are in a man. Fortitude in the one, for example, is shown in connexion with ruling; in the other, it is shown in connexion with serving; and the same is true of the other forms of goodness. . . . . To speak in general terms, and to maintain that goodness consists in "a good condition of the soul," or in "right action," or in anything of the kind, is to be guilty of self-deception. Far better than such general definitions is the method

of simple enumeration of the different forms of goodness. . . .[55]

Accordingly, throughout his works, Aristotle proceeds to apply
distinct moral standards to the two sexes, as well as to different
classes of men. He says, for example, that Sophocles' statement,
"A modest silence is a woman's crown" is "a general truth--but a
truth which does not apply to men."[56] Both the bodily and the
moral excellences of the two sexes are differently defined.
Whereas both require beauty and stature, only the male should have
strength and fitness for athletic contests. Whereas both should
have self-control, in the male this should be supplemented by
courage, but in the female by "industrious habits, free from
servility."[57] For what use is courage to one whose occupation
must be the care of a house and the provision of food and clothes
for her family? Moreover, Aristotle asserts that it is not at all
appropriate for a woman to be "manly or clever," and criticizes
Euripides for creating a female character with these unsuitable
qualities.[58]

The only persons who need to possess a full complement of
reason, Aristotle argues, are those who rule over others. While
practical wisdom is necessary in rulers, only "right opinion is
required in women, slaves, and others who are permanently ruled.[59]
Thus, when he ascribes to the various members of the household
different amounts of reason, we are not surprised to find that
each has just that portion of rationality that is necessary for
the performance of his or her function:

It is true that all these persons possess in common the
different parts of the soul; but they possess them in
different ways. The slave is entirely without the
faculty of deliberation; the female indeed possesses it,
but in a form which remains inconclusive; and if children also possess it, it is only in an immature form.[60]

Why should nature, who makes nothing in vain, have given woman
full rationality, when her function does not require it?

Thus, Aristotle has established the standards of physical,
mental and moral excellence in woman according to the functions
she performs for man. To be the best of women, she must have many
qualities, such as quietness and modesty, that are undesirable in
a man. On the other hand, she must **not** have many qualities, such
as manliness, strength or cleverness, that are required of a good
man. Having prescribed for the two sexes separate and frequently
conflicting standards of excellence, however, Aristotle proceeds
to weigh perfection in woman against perfection in man, and to
conclude that woman, even the best possible woman, falls short.

In the **Eudemian Ethics**, it is asserted that "the state of
human character called human goodness is of two kinds." "Let us
assume," Aristotle continues, "that man is one of the things that
are excellent by nature," and he concludes that man's form of
goodness is "good absolutely," while that of the others who are
not excellent by nature is good only relatively--"only good for
that thing."[61] The two examples chosen to illustrate this are the
goodness of a man as compared with that of a woman, and the goodness of a gifted man as compared with that of a dull one. In each

case, the latter is clearly an inferior kind of goodness. This same point is repeated several times in the other works--for example, in the **Rhetoric**, when we are told that "virtues and actions are nobler, when they proceed from those who are naturally worthier, for instance, from a man rather than from a woman."[62] What has happened is that Aristotle arrives at the conclusion that woman is inferior to man by a completely circular process of reasoning. Because he perceives woman as an instrument, he has assigned her an entirely separate scale of values, and then he measures her against the scale of male values, and finds her inferior. But the functionalist treatment of women is itself founded on the assumption of the Aristotelian hierarchy, in which woman is "naturally" placed in an inferior position.

Aristotle's view of society as rigidly hierarchical, patriarchal, and functional allows him to "prove" things about its various classes by drawing on assumptions that already presuppose the things he claims to prove. If it were not for his initial assumption that the free and leisured male is the highest of mortal beings, there would be no grounds from which to argue that all other members of the human race are naturally defined by their functions in relation to him. Objectively speaking, there is no more evidence for the proposition that women are intended by nature to reproduce men than that men are intended by nature to beget women (as the Amazons may have argued in their version of the **Politics**).

Aristotle determines that woman is inferior by considering the functions she performs and the relevant qualities she manifests in Athenian society. This was a society, however, in which she was thoroughly disadvantaged and oppressed--a society dominated by men, in which her role and all the qualities valued in her were dictated by men. Aristotle is not interested in the qualities of women apart from this context. Thus, in spite of his expressed beliefs in the power of the environment to shape and alter the human character and abilities, he is no more interested in applying these beliefs to women than in applying them to slaves. Except for the free and leisured man, Aristotle is not interested in the potential of any living being, but only in those "natural" and "naturally inferior" characteristics which enable each person to perform his or her proper function in the social system which has his approval and which he sets out to justify.

The fact that Aristotle treats the vast majority of people as instruments, and condemns them to a necessarily less-than-human existence, has been treated in various ways by students of his works. A few, even at this point in time, feel no compulsion to take issue with the way in which he disposes of either women or the majority of men. Harry Jaffa, for example, is content merely to summarize what Aristotle says about women, and actually seeks to justify his argument that there are natural slaves.[63] At the other extreme, John Ferguson, in his recent book on Aristotle, points to "the extraordinary mixture of sound scientific observation and grotesque class prejudice" which resulted in the philosopher's teleological conclusions about all relations within the household. Ferguson realistically suggests, moreover, that "those who reject Aristotle's view of the political inferiority of 'servants' and women must be sure that they do not suffer from residual prejudices and are offering an equality that is practical as well as theoretical."[64]

Ferguson's attitude, however, is exceptional among scholars of Aristotle. A number of them, in more recent years, have indeed felt impelled to dissociate themselves from the arguments for slavery. W. D. Ross, for example, says, "What cannot be commended in Aristotle's view . . . is his cutting of the human race in two with a hatchet."[65] No one, Ross objects, can be legitimately treated as both a tool and a man. He objects, too, to Aristotle's regarding the class of mechanics as merely a means to the exist-ence of the **polis** and the happiness of its privileged class. "Society cannot," he argues, "in fact be split into two parts of which one is merely a means to the welfare of the other. Every human being is capable of a life worth living for itself."[66] In the middle of all this dissent, however, Ross upholds Aristotle's defense of the family against Plato, and points out his recogni-tion of it as "a natural and normal extension of personality, a source of pleasure and an opportunity of good activity."[67] No-where does he recognize that Aristotle's "family" involves the treatment of women as mere means to the welfare of men, or that this "natural and normal extension" of the man's personality entails the obliteration of the woman's. Compared with the oppor-tunities available to Plato's female guardians, the Aristotelian household can hardly be regarded as "a source of pleasure and an opportunity of good activity" for its **female** members. Because of his own prejudices, Ross does not see that this other cutting in half of the human race, according to sex, is just as indefensible as that separating master and slaves.

Similarly, D. J. Allan, though he praises Aristotle for his

"breadth of vision" and his "humanity," does acknowledge that his ideal polis does not appear to be "perfect" from the points of view of either the slave or the artisan.[68] He too, however, completely ignores the fact that Aristotle relegates women to a similar condition. Third, G. E. R. Lloyd also is critical of Aristotle's antiegalitarian ideas about slaves, workers and barbarians. Asserting that Aristotle was, in these areas, hardly if at all in advance of contemporary opinion, he concludes that "the effect of his work was to provide some sort of rational justification for some deep-seated Greek prejudices." He simply summarizes, however, without comment, Aristotle's belief in the natural superiority of males to females.[69]

What may initially seem to be a coincidental lack of perception on the part of these scholars becomes totally intelligible in the light of one very significant fact. A large part of Aristotle's "social teleology"--that is, his functional treatment of most men--is no longer acceptable. Given the development, beginning in the seventeenth and eighteenth centuries, of modern concepts of equality and the rights of man, it is no longer regarded as justifiable to designate some men as by nature the instruments of others, or to set up different moral standards for different classes. Thus, those who wish to redeem Aristotle's political and moral philosophy as a whole are obligated either to go out of their way to argue anew for his treatment of slaves and workers, or else explicitly to dissociate themselves from this part of his thought, in order to free the remainder from its taint.

By contrast, the perception and treatment of women in purely functional terms has remained so prevalent that these intelligent

scholars have not felt the need to argue against Aristotle's disposition of the female sex. In fact, it is fairly clear that they
are unable to see that the injustice of his treatment of slaves,
women and workers is all of a piece. The continuing existence of
a double standard of values, which has replaced Aristotle's multiple one, allows them to regard his treatment of women as far more
rational and defensible than his treatment of the majority of men.
The birth of modern egalitarianism by no means brought with it the
demand for the equal treatment of women. . .

* * * *

Alfred North Whitehead once said that "the safest general
characterization of the European philosophical tradition is that
it consists in a series of footnotes to Plato."[70] We have seen
that as far as the philosophical treatment of women is concerned,
Whitehead's statement is clearly untenable. The legacy of Aristotelian thought, while repudiated in many other areas, has continued in modern times to pervade discussions of the subject of
women, their nature, and their proper position and rights in society. The predominant mode of thought about women has been a functionalist one, based on the assumption of the necessity of the
male-headed nuclear family, and of women's role within it.   Now,
after reviewing the course of the argument so far, we shall see
how the mode of perceiving women that has been so predominant
throughout the history of ideas persists in the writings of
influential thinkers of our own time.

Socrates and Plato, having broken away from the prevailing

Greek multiple standard of values, were predisposed to view women from a different perspective from their predecessors. In the **Republic**, moreover, Plato's abolition of the family necessitated his taking a radically new look at the subject of women and their nature. Since they were no longer to be "private wives", or to be defined by the function of motherhood and housekeeping, he was obliged, despite his generally deprecating attitude toward the female sex, to consider their potential as individual citizens--as persons without a preordained and all-encompassing function in life. Book V of the **Republic** contains a more remarkable discussion of the socially and politically relevant differences between the sexes than was to appear for more than two thousand years thereafter. As a consequence of the conclusions he came to, Plato dispensed, in an extremely hierarchial society, with the usual hierarchy of the sexes. He argued for the total equality, in education and role, of the female guardians.

Having once thought about the potential of women, and concluded that societies which confined them all indiscriminately to domestic seclusion were being extremely wasteful of human resources, Plato found himself in a difficult position when, in the **Laws**, he reinstated the family, together with other forms of private property. Whereas the theoretical argument for the equal potential, and therefore the equal education and employment of the two sexes, was carried further here than in the **Republic**, when it comes to applying these precepts, Plato backed away. Clearly the reason is that private wives could not be permitted to lead the same kind of public lives as the female guardians and philosophers of the ideal city. Consequently, women are relegated to their traditional domestic functions and status. They are conspicuously absent from the activities of citizenship. Moreover, in spite of having argued in the **Republic** that men's and women's natures are the same apart from their respective roles in procreation, Plato asserted in the **Laws** that women must be sedate and pure in their natures, whereas their husbands are to be noble and courageous. Thus the nature of women, no less than their role, is prescribed by the presence or absence of the family.

Plato's treatment of women in the **Republic** is clearly unparalleled in the history of Western thought. The essential difference between his discussion of women in the **Laws**, moreover, and the later philosophical treatment of them, is that Plato was aware of what he was doing to the female sex, whereas subsequent philosophers give no indication of being so aware. Since Plato explicitly held that the innate qualities of women could not be known, so long as the socialization and education of the sexes was so different, the "nature" he gave to women in the **Laws** is unambiguously prescriptive, rather than descriptive. It is the way women must be socialized, in order to perform their prescribed functions within the patriarchal and traditional structure of his proposed society.

What Plato did, consciously, to women and their "nature" in the **Laws**, has been done unconsciously by many of those political philosophers since Plato who have concerned themselves with the subject. To the extent that Plato advanced the rational discussion of women and their potential, Aristotle set it back again, and the history of political thought about women has unfortunately up to the present time consisted predominantly of footnotes to this Aristotelian legacy. In contrast to Plato, philosophers who have regarded the family as beyond question--a natural and indispensable part of the human order--have tended to view women entirely in terms of their sexual and procreative functions. Women's interests are not perceived as discrete, but as subsumed within those of the family; women's purpose is seen to be the reproduction and rearing of men, and their nature is prescriptively defined in terms of the optimal characteristics for the performance of these functions.

In the case of Aristotle himself, the treatment of women is consistent with the entire structure of his political philosophy. Because of his fundamental teleology and functionalist treatment of the world as a whole, he relegated the vast majority of people, both male and female, to the status of means, whose purpose was to enable the few to pursue their truly human ends.

In the case of Rousseau, however, the prescriptive, functionalist treatment of women stands out as a curious anomaly, in the context of a philosophy based on the ideals of human equality and freedom. Ignoring in this instance his own speculations about the original state of nature, Rousseau proceeded on the assumption that the patriarchal family was natural and necessary, and that woman's nature must therefore be defined according to its needs. Setting aside the entire environmentalist account of human development which he applied to men, he argued that women are naturally passive, subservient and chaste. They must be educated in such a way as to reinforce these natural qualities, for only thus can they be happy in a world in which they exist in order to please men. Strongly opposed though he was to Aristotle's conclusion that some men are by nature slaves and intended to serve others, Rousseau failed to perceive the applicability of his objections to his own arguments about the female sex. In spite of his preoccupation with the male individual and his rights and freedom, Rousseau continued to apply Aristotelian arguments about the nature and purpose of women. Her role in the bourgeois family was thereby rationalized: that she should propagate and nurture undisputed heirs to the family property, that she should provide for her husband a pleasant solace from the harsh realities of the competitive world outside, that she should obey him without question, be totally dependent on him and value her chaste reputation as her most prized possession—all these were merely the dictates of nature. While his ultimate prognosis for men is that they can be educated to be either individuals or citizens, but not both, his tragic conclusion for women is that they can be neither.

John Stuart Mill tried to integrate women as persons in their own right into his liberal political philosophy. He came to recognize the absurdity of claiming that the contemporary characteristics of that sex which had always been subordinated to the other, constituted female "nature." No one could presume to know the nature of women until women were free to develop it. Mill's conviction of the importance for human happiness of individual freedom and just treatment became the basis of his case for the emancipation of women. However, to the extent that his vision of the liberated woman falls short of complete equality of opportunity or of power, it bears witness to the thesis that it is the philosophers' attitude to the family, above all else, which has determined their conclusions about the rights and the social role of women.

On the one hand, Mill certainly rejected many of the legal and customary inequalities of the patriarchal family. He did not assume, as have so many others, that the best interests of all the members of the family are included in those of the male head. Thus he concluded that women must have equal civil and political rights, and the same education and opportunities to earn their own livings as men. On the other hand, however, Mill never questioned or objected to the maintenance of traditional sex roles within the family, but expressly considered them to be suitable and desirable. In spite of his explicit recognition of the extent to which domestic preoccupations hamper women's progress in other areas of life, he gave no consideration to even the eventual possibility of the sharing of domestic and child-rearing tasks between the sexes. The assumption that married women should not earn their own livings or pursue careers, except insofar as the onerous obligations of the household leaves them free to do so, means that Mill's feminism is severely constrained. He in effect condoned the continuation of considerable differences in power and in opportunity, for men and married women. Thus, though he argued that women must be admitted to citizenship, there is no way that the realities of the lives he envisaged for them could allow them to be equal citizens. While Mill, exceptionally among political philosophers, tried to treat women as individuals whose happiness and freedom were as important as those of men, his reluctance to question traditional family structure and its intrinsic sex roles prevented him from fully succeeding in his aim.

The importance of the preceding analysis is heightened by the fact that the functionalist mode of thinking about women, their rights and needs and their position in society, is by no means dead. Functionalism as a whole has undergone a considerable revival in recent decades, especially in the fields of social psychology and sociology. Two examples--the works of psychoanalyst Erik Erikson and of sociologist Talcott Parsons--will suffice to demonstrate current lines of argument on the subjects of women and the family that parallel those of Rousseau and Aristotle. It is important to understand how this type of thought, as applied to women and the family, retains such appeal.

Freud posed the curious question "What does a woman want?"[71] A number of well-respected psychologists and psychiatrists have not hesitated to provide answers which support the ancient idea that women and her wants and needs are determined by her sexual and reproductive characteristics.[72] Bruno Bettelheim, for example, addressing the subject of women in the scientific professions, asserts:

> We must start with the realization that, as much as women want to be good scientists or engineers, they want first and foremost to be womanly companions of men and to be mothers.[73]

Some male scholars have felt in no way impelled to disguise the fact that they are defining women functionally in relation to society's needs. Psychiatrist Joseph Rheingold, for example writes:

> Woman is nurturance . . . anatomy decrees the life of a
> woman.... When women grow up without dread of their bi-
> ological functions and without subversion by feminist
> doctrine, and therefore enter upon motherhood with a
> sense of fulfillment and altruistic sentiment, we shall
> attain the goal of a good life and secure world in which
> to live it.[74]

It is only, apparently, when women are successfully socialized
into believing that their anatomy is their destiny, that "we"
(who?) shall be able to live the good life.

None of this, of course, is very far removed from the ideas
about women expressed by Rousseau. However, the modern archetype
of his mode of thought is Erik Erikson. In an attempt to revise
the negative Freudian concept that the development of the female
personality derives largely from the little girl's inevitable
penis envy, Erikson instead structures that development around the
possession of an "inner space" with great potential--the womb.[75]
Woman's capacity to bear and nurse children is therefore not just
one aspect of her nature; her entire identity and the life she
lives must revolve around her "inner space" and its desire to be
filled. Erikson tells us that "emptiness is the female form of
perdition . . . standard experience for all women,"[76] and that
whatever sphere of life a woman enters into, she must take her
peculiarly feminine personality--defined by its "inner space" --
with her. In the political sphere, for example, Erikson says,
"the influence of women will not be fully actualized until it reflects without apology the facts of the 'inner space' and the

potentialities and needs of the feminine psyche."[77] Thus, women will always perform a different type of role in life from men; whatever they do, they can never forget the unique "groundplan" of their bodies. "Since a woman is never not-a-woman," Erikson concludes, "she can see her long-range goals only in those modes of activity which include and integrate her natural dispositions."[78]

Thus Erikson claims, no less positively than Rousseau, that he knows what women are really, and naturally, like. The reasoning he employs on the subject, however is no more conclusive or convincing than Rousseau's. His demonstration that women are essentially conscious of their "inner space" is the outcome of an experiment in which boys and girls in their early teens were asked to construct scenes from a number of given toys.[79] Erikson uses the differences between the scenes created by the two sexes as evidence that their respective personalities are greatly affected by the differences in their genitalia and reproductive organs. Reminiscent of Rousseau's neglect, in his discovery of the "natural" differences between the sexes, of environmental influences up to the age of six, Erikson dismisses "the purely 'social' interpretation" quite peremptorily, on account of the fact that it cannot explain all the differences that were observed. He refuses to consider as significant the influences on the scenes constructed by the girls and boys of either their total play experience in a culture in which many toys and activities are considered strictly sex related, or their identification with the socially conditioned behavior and aspirations of the parent and other adults of their own sex.

Later in the essay, Erikson argues that it is the biological necessities of human life which make child-rearing "woman's unique job," and that it is therefore biology which explains many of the observable differences in a little girl. Not only does she react to things with greater compassion than a little boy, but she "learns to be more easily content within a limited circle of activities and shows less resistance to control and less impulsivity of the kind that later leads boys and men to 'delinquency.'"[80] In the absence of any consideration of the socialization of the two sexes or the expectations placed on them by society, how can we be supposed to believe that such differences are the result of biology? Rousseau's similar conclusions are not founded on much worse evidence.

Altogether, Erikson's essay demonstrates well the extraordinary degree of muddled thinking that continues to impede rational discussion of the differences between the sexes. Just as in Rousseau's treatment of the subject, descriptive and prescriptive statements are confusingly interwoven. Erikson tells us, for example, in a statement that is crucial to his argument, that women have "a biological, psychological, and ethical commitment to take care of human infancy."[81] It is difficult to see what could be meant by "a biological commitment"--a commitment, surely, is something that is undertaken by the person involved. That women have the ability to bear children is indisputable, but to call this, let alone the total care of the infant, her biological commitment, is meaningless. As for women's psychological and ethical commitments to raise children, these are both, at least to a very large extent, culture related, and the first is to an unknown degree the result of sex-role conditioning. Erikson's fusing together of a universal biological fact with culturally prescribed factors is a shrewd way of deriving his unwarranted conclusion that child-rearing is necessarily a task in which "years of specialized **womanhours** of work are involved."[82]

The importance of Erikson's work for the defense of the status quo is that it claims to give the sanction of twentieth century science to an age-old myth. This myth claims that existing sex-role differentiation and the aspiration of girls and boys to very different future roles are due not to environmental influences or social sanctions, but to physical sexual differences. Thus the confinement of the vast majority of women to the home or to low-status positions in the sphere of employment is claimed to be in no way an anomaly in the modern world, or a state of affairs which any normal woman would find cause to challenge. This is, Erikson assures us, because their very biology ensures that women --in contrast to men, who have conquered space and disseminated ideas--"have found their identities in the care suggested in their bodies and in the needs of their issue, and seem to have taken it for granted that the outer world space belongs to the men."[83]

The task embarked on by psychologists is completed in the works of sociologists, particularly those of the "structural-functionalist" school. Talcott Parsons and colleagues, in **Family, Socialization and Interaction Process**, and in a number of articles, undertake to demonstrate that it is the essential functions which the nuclear family performs for society that necessitate the conventional differentiation between male and female sex roles. If Erikson, with respect to his treatment of women, is this century's Rousseau, Talcott Parson's functionalist analysis of the family and woman's role within it reveals him to be the modern Aristotle.

Parsons, unlike Erikson, does not appear to believe that the conventional roles of the sexes are a biologically determined extension of their distinct roles in procreation. Rather, the fact that pregnancy and lactation become the basis of an entirely different role and life style for women has to be explained by the mediating factor of the family. "Indeed," Parsons writes, "we argue that probably the importance of the family and its functions for society constitutes the primary set of reasons why there is a social, as distinguished from purely reproductive, differentiation of sex roles."[84] Thus it is the indispensable functions of the modern nuclear family that necessitate "woman's place."

Parson's work has been criticized by recent feminist sociologists.[85] However, there are several issues that warrant discussion in the present context. First, like Aristotle with regard to the **polis** and the Greek household, Parsons takes American society of the 1940s and 1950s and its conventional nuclear family as the basis of his theory. He takes it as given that the adult members of a "normal" family consist of a man who has a job and a woman who either stays home or if employed tends to have a job which does not compete for status with that of her husband.[86] He defines the status of married women as the status derived from their husbands' levels of employment. On the issue of the status of women as compared with that of men, however, he acknowledges the inequalities due to the "asymmetrical relation of the sexes to the occupational structure."[87]

Parsons is not unaware that there are problems, especially

for women, which result from the sex-role structure of the nuclear family he takes as a given. The rigid modern separation of the outside world of "work" from the household, he says, "deprives the wife of her role as a partner in a common enterprise." She is left with "a set of utilitarian functions in the management of the household which may be considered a kind of 'pseudo'-occupation."[88] He points out that, in spite of American high tolerance for drudgery, middle class women tend to employ domestic servants whenever financially able, to dissociate themselves as persons from the performance of household tasks, and to take on roles in community activity in order to avoid "the stigma of being 'just a housewife.'"[89] He also acknowledges that problems arise from the fact that women's child-rearing role is usually ending just as their husbands are at the height of their careers. The confined nature of women's life in the home and the narrow specialization of man's lives at work are not entirely good for either sex, he admits. But whereas the man is likely to be compensated by the achievement and responsibility of his job, it is for the woman, Parsons acknowledges, that the rigid sex-role differentiation of our society is most damaging. "It is quite clear," he writes, "that in the adult feminine role there is quite sufficient strain and insecurity so that widespread manifestations are to be expected in the form of neurotic behavior."[90]

It is particularly striking, given this perception of some of the effects of the conventional structuring of sex roles, that Parsons refuses to consider the possibilities of change. He asserts without comment that sex roles are becoming more rather than less well defined. (He was writing, of course, before the

54

beginning of the current women's movement.) The general movement
of women into the "masculine" pattern of behavior, he believes,
"would only be possible with profound alterations in the structure
of the family," and he regards the traditional structure of the
family as more essential than ever before in terms of its vital
social functions.[91] The implication is that such profound alter-
ation, whatever its repercussions for the mental health of half of
the population, is not an open issue.

From an analysis which takes the contemporary social structure as given, Parsons slides very easily into the role of predicting, or rather prescribing, the future. His tendency to start
from the basis of the American family of his time, and then to
claim that the conclusions he reaches are not "culture bound" is
extremely reminiscent of Aristotle's sanctifying the status quo by
proving it to be the natural order of things. Having justified
male dominance within the family as a result of the husband's
standing in the occupational realm, Parsons goes on to assert:

> Even if, as seems possible, it should come to pass that
> the average woman had some kind of a job, it seems most
> unlikely that this relative balance would be upset; that
> either the roles would be reversed, or their qualitative
> differentiation in these respects completely erased.[92]

As confirmation of this view, Parsons cites the existing distribution of women in the labor force--the fact that they hold predominantly "expressive" roles, "'supportive' to masculine roles. .
. analogous to the wife-mother role in the family." While he

recognizes, then, that there is a connection between the supportive and subordinate roles that women are assigned both inside and
outside the family, Parsons is not at all disposed to consider
that there may be little rational basis for this role assignment
in either case. The fact that **even** in the world of work women
play nurturing roles supposedly reinforces the conviction that
this is their proper role within the home.

The two basic points in Parson's argument about the importance of sex-role differentiation are that the family, like any
small group, must have an "expressive" leader and an "instrumental" leader, and that the mother must assume the first of these
roles and the father the second. The first claim has been well
criticized by Ann Oakley, who points out that all the subjects of
the experiment that Parsons relies upon were the products of socialization within nuclear families of the type he aims to draw
conclusions about. The small groups they formed, then, were
highly likely to take on the structure of the conventional family,
and Parson's conclusion that the characteristics observed are
those of "small groups everywhere" is unfounded.[93]

However, let us accept for the moment these conclusions about
the leadership roles of the small group, and therefore the family.
Why must the mother be assigned the "expressive" and the father
the "instrumental" leadership of the family? Parsons argues that
the mother's expressive role derives from the two facts of pregnancy and lactation. It is by default that the father, since he
cannot perform these functions, must go out to work and become the
instrumental leader.[94] However, since Parsons denies that the
fetal stage has any relevance for the child's socialization, and

he was writing at a time when bottle feeding was at its height and nursing actively discouraged by the medical profession, there appears to be very little foundation to his assignment of life-long roles based on sex. Parsons seems to have been to some extent aware of this problem. Though in general he writes in terms of the "mother-child relationship" and calls the child-rearer the "mother," during his discussion of the crucial stage of oral dependency he says that what is essential for the development of the child's ego is "'attachment' to one or a class of 'social objects' of which the mother is the prototype." He is careful to note that "'agent of care' is the essential concept and that it need not be confined to one specific person; it is the function which is essential."[95] Each time, however, he immediately reverts to calling his agent of care "mother," giving the reader the misleading general impression that it has been demonstrated to be necessarily a female role.

It is clearly during the oedipal stage that Parsons thinks the clear differentiation of the sex roles of parents is most essential for the child's socialization. The reason it is essential, however, is that it is at this stage that the child, largely through identification with the parent of his or her own sex, must be directed successfully into the appropriate sex role. This is a crucial part of the child's absorption of "the institutionalized patterns of the society."[96] In order for the daughter to become a "willing and 'accommodating' person" and the son to become an "adequate technical performer,"[97] they must be socialized in a nuclear family in which this sex-role differentiation is clearly observed. But surely there is something rather circular about such reasoning. A large part of the explanation for the necessity of sex roles rests on the need to socialize the next generation into sex roles, so that they in turn will be able to socialize their children into sex roles, ad infinitum. Especially since Parsons was aware of some of the unhealthy consequences of conventional sex roles, one wonders why he was so concerned to preserve them.

Parsons, as a sociologist, is perfectly entitled to perform a theoretical analysis of the institutions of a sexist culture. However, he is no more justified than Aristotle in presenting a theory about a particular historical set of institutions as a dictum for human behavior throughout eternity. The supposedly neutral and academic nature of his study belies his reactionary conclusions about the necessity of maintaining strict sex roles in order to preserve a healthily functioning society.

Thus, in recent times, strong sanctions have been given to sexist mythology by scholars influential in the mainstream of their respective disciplines. Rousseauian reasoning about the nature of women presented by such thinkers as are exemplified here by Erik Erikson, and Aristotelian assumptions about the sacred immutability of the existing family structure such as are evident in the Parsonian school of sociology, have reinforced justification of the differential treatment of the sexes. Until the beginning of the women's movement in the late 1960s began to break the monopoly, moveover, both men and women were fed throughout their socialization on the fallout from such views. Through textbooks, advertising, child-rearing manuals, and countless other channels, the prescriptive "nature" which was imposed on women by their reproductive biology, in combination with the assumption of the conventional family structure, was virtually unopposed by any alternative views.

FOOTNOTES

[1] G. W. F. Hegel, **The Philosophy of Right**, trans. T. M. Knox (Oxford: Clarendon Press, 1952), p. 11.

[2] Aristotle, **Nichomachean Ethics**, trans. David Ross (London: Oxford University Press, 1954), VI, 1139b.

[3] **Ibid.**, VII, 1145b.

[4] See Donald James Allan, **The Philosophy of Aristotle**, 2nd ed. (London: Oxford University Press, 1970), p. 124; and G. E. R. Lloyd, **Aristotle: The Growth and Structure of His Thought** (Cambridge: Cambridge University Press, 1968), p. 206.

[5] Aristotle, **Politics**, trans. Ernest Barker (Oxford: Oxford University Press, 1946), I, 1253a.

[6] Aristotle, **De Anima**, trans. Kendon Foster and Silvester Humphries, from the version of William of Moerbecke (New Haven: Yale University Press, 1951), II, 412b.

[7] **Ibid.**

[8] **Ibid.**, I, 407b; cf. II, 415b.

[9] Aristotle, **The Generation of Animals**, trans. A. L. Peck (Cambridge, Mass.: Harvard University Press; London: Heinemann, 1943), V, 789P.

[10] Aristotle, **Politics**, VI, 1333a.

[11] **Ibid.**, I, 1256b; cf. also I, 1253a, for an example of nature's "economy."

[12] Aristotle, **Nichomachean Ethics**, I, 1097b.

[13] **Ibid**, I, 1098a.

[14] Aristotle, **Politics**, I, 1252b.

[15] Aristotle, **Nichomachean Ethics**, X, 1177b.

[16] Aristotle, **Politics**, VII, 1328a.

[17] **Ibid.**, I, 1255a, 1252a, 1255b.

[18] Aristotle, **Nichomachean Ethics**, VIII, 1161a.

[19] **Ibid.**, VIII, 1162a; Aristotle, **Eudemian Ethics**, trans. H. Rockham (Cambridge, Mass.: Harvard University Press; London: Heinemann, 1935), VII, 1238b.

[20] Aristotle, **Politics**, III, 1278b.

[21] Aristotle, **Eudemian Ethics**, VII, 1242b.

[22] Aristotle, **Politics**, III, 1277b. See Jean Bethke Elshtain, "Moral Woman and Immoral Man," **Politics and Society** 4 (1974), 453-456, for a discussion of these aspects of Aristotle's functionalism.

[23] See Chapter 3 of Susan Moller Okin, **Women in Western Political Thought** (Princeton, N.J.: Princeton University Press, 1979).

[24] E.g., Aristotle, **Nichomachean Ethics**, II, 1103a, passim.

[25] E.g., Aristotle, **The "Art" of Rhetoric**, trans. John Henry Freese (Cambridge, Mass.: Harvard University Press; London: Heinemann, 1967), I, 1370a.

[26] Aristotle, **Politics**, I, 1252b.

[27] Ibid., I, 1253b.

[28] Ibid., I, 1254a.

[29] Ibid., I, 1253a.

[30] Ibid., I, 1254b.

[31] Ibid., I, 1252b.

[32] Aristotle, **De Anima**, II, 415a. The reason reproduction is the "most natural" function of living beings is that it is their only means of achieving immortality. As is clear from what follows, however, it is only the male who achieves immortality, since it is he, according to Aristotle, who furnishes the child with its soul.

[33] Aristotle, **Generation of Animals**, II, 732a; cf. I, 727b and II, 738b.

[34] Ibid., IV, 767b, 775a.

[35] Ibid., I, 728a, IV, 766a.

[36] Ibid., I, 729a, 731a.

[37] Aristotle, **Politics**, VII, 1334b-1335b.

[38] See Barker's note 2, **Politics**, p. 327.

[39] Aristotle, **Nichomachean Ethics**, VIII, 1162a; **Politics**, III, 12776.

[40] Ibid., II, 1261 a-b.

[41] Ibid., II, 1264b.

[42] Aristotle, **Nichomachean Ethics**, V, 1134b.

[43] Ibid., V, 1138b.

[44] Ibid., VIII, 1161a.

[45] Ibid., VIII, 1158b.

[46] Aristotle, **Oeconomica** (now considered to be spurious, but written by one of the Aristotelian School), trans. G. C. Armstrong (Cambridge, Mass.: Harvard University Press; London: Heinemann, 1933), III, 141.

[47] Aristotle, **Eudemian Ethics**, VII, 1238b.

[48] A. W. H. Adkins, **Merit and Responsibility: A Study in Greek Values** (Oxford: Clarendon Press, 1960), especially pp. 30-31 and 341-342.

[49] Ibid., p. 342.

[50] Aristotle, **Politics**, V, 1312a, where Aristotle gives, without comment, an example of a monarch who was killed, "from the motive of contempt," by a man who saw him carding wool among women. Oddly enough, it is not so much the actual content of the work done by these subordinate classes of people that Aristotle cites as the reason it is so degrading, but rather the fact that it is done at the behest of other people. See **Politics**, VIII, 1337b.

[51] Aristotle, **Eudemian Ethics**, II, 1218b-1219a.

[52] Aristotle, **Poetics**, trans. W. Hamilton Fyfe (Cambridge, Mass.: Harvard University Press; London: Heinemann 1927), XV, 1454a.

[53] Aristotle, **Politics**, III, 1276b.

[54] Ibid., 1277b.

[55] Ibid., I, 1260a.

[56] Ibid.

[57] Aristotle, **Act of Rhetoric**, I, 1361a.

[58] Aristotle, **Poetics**, XV, 1454a.

[59] Aristotle, **Politics**, III, 1277b.

[60] Ibid., I, 1260a.

[61] Aristotle, **Eudemian Ethics**, VII, 1237a.

[62] Aristotle, **Art of Rhetoric**, I, 1367a.

[63] "Aristotle," in **History of Political Philosophy**, 2nd ed.,

Leo Strauss and Joseph Cropsey, eds., (Chicago: Rand McNally, 1972), pp. 74-76.

[64]John Ferguson, **Moral Values in the Ancient World** (London: Methuen, 1958), pp. 139-140.

[65]W. D. Ross, **Aristotle** (London: Methuen, 1923), p. 242.

[66]Ibid., pp. 243 and 249.

[67]Ibid., pp. 245-246.

[68]Allan, **The Philosophy of Aristotle**, p. 161.

[69]Lloyd, **Aristotle: The Growth and Structure of His Thought,** pp. 264-265, 296.

[70]I have been unable to find the original source of this quotation. It is quoted by A. O. Lovejoy, in **The Great Chain of Being** (Cambridge, Mass.: Harvard University Press, 1936), p. 24, but without reference to its source. Even a search of the **Penguin Dictionary of Modern Quotations** proved fruitless, since it lists the quotation as "attributed" to Whitehead. Perhaps he said it in a lecture.

[71]Ernest Jones, **The Life and Work of Sigmund Freud,** Vol. II (New York: Basic Books, 1961), p. 421.

[72]See Naomi Weisstein, "Psychology Constructs the Female" (Andover, Mass.: Warner Modular Publications Reprint 752, 1973). I am grateful to Weisstein for directing me to the examples that follow.

[73]Bruno Bethelheim, "The Commitment Required of a Woman Entering a Scientific Profession in Present Day American Society," **Woman and the Scientific Professions, The MIT Symposium on American Women in Science and Engineering,** ed. J. Mattfield and C. Van Akin (Cambridge, Mass.: MIT Press, 1965), p. 15.

[74]Joseph Rheingold, **The Fear of Being a Woman** (New York: Grune and Stratton, 1964), p. 714.

[75]Erik H. Erikson, "Inner and Outer Space: Reflections on Womanhood," **Daedalus** 93 (1964): 582-606.

[76]Ibid., 596.

[77]Ibid., 604.

[78]Ibid., 605.

[79]Ibid., 588-593.

[80]Ibid., 598-599.

[81]Ibid., 586.

[82]Ibid., 598 (emphasis added).

[83]Ibid., 593.

[84]Talcott Parsons and Robert F. Bales, **Family, Socialization and Interaction Process** (Glencoe, Ill.: Free Press, 1955), p.22.

[85]See, for example, Ann Oakley, **Woman's Work: The Housewife, Past and Present** (New York: Vintage Books, 1974), pp. 178–185; Juliet Mitchell, **Woman's Estate** (New York: Vintage Books, 1973), pp. 116–117.

[86]Parsons and Bales, **Family, Socialization**, pp. 12–15; Parsons, "Age and Sex in the Social Structure of the United States," **American Sociological Review** 7 (1942): 605, 608–609.

[87]Parsons, "Age and Sex," 605.

[88]Ibid., 609.

[89]Parsons and Bales, **Family, Socialization**, p. 129.

[90]Parsons, "Age and Sex," 613.

[91]Ibid., 610.

[92]Parsons and Bales, **Family, Socialization**, p. 15, and note 13.

[93]Oakley, **Woman's Work**, pp. 181–185.

[94]Parsons and Bales, **Family, Socialization**, p. 23.

[95]Ibid., pp. 43, 63.

[96]Ibid., pp. 35, 80, 94, 98, 387.

[97]Ibid., p. 51, Fig. 4.

CHAPTER 2

"THE DISORDER OF WOMEN": WOMEN,

LOVE, AND THE SENSE OF JUSTICE*

Carole Pateman

In his essay on **Politics and the Arts** Rousseau proclaims that
"never has a people perished from an excess of wine; all perish
from the disorder of women." Rousseau states that drunkenness is
usually the sole failing of otherwise upright, decent men; only
the immoral fear the indiscretion that wine will promote. Drunkenness is not the worst of the vices since it makes men stupid
rather than evil, and wine turns men away from the other vices so
it poses no danger to the polity. In contrast, the "disorder of
women" engenders all the vices and can bring the state to ruin.[1]

Rousseau is not the only social or political theorist to
regard women as a permanently subversive force within the political order.   Freud (to whose arguments I shall also refer) argues
in Chapter 4 of **Civilization and Its Discontents** that women are
"hostile to" and "in opposition to" civilization. In a similar
vein, Hegel writes that the community "creates its enemy for
itself within its own gates" in "womankind in general." Women are
"the everlasting irony in the life of the community," and when
"women hold the helm of government, the state is at once in

jeopardy."[2] These arguments are by no means of only historical interest. Although women have now been granted citizenship in the liberal democracies, it is still widely believed that they are unfitted for political life and that it would be dangerous if the state were in their hands. This belief is very complex. One of its central dimensions, which I shall begin to explore in this paper, is the conviction that women lack, and cannot develop, a sense of justice.

The belief in the essential subversiveness of women[3] is of extremely ancient origin and is deeply embedded in our mythological and religious heritage. However, it is only in the modern world that "the disorder of women" constitutes a general social and political problem. More specifically, it is only with the development of liberal individualism and the arguments of its democratic and socialist critics that beliefs about women become an acute, though not always acknowledged, problem in social and political theory and practice. In premodern conceptions of the world, animal and human life were seen as part of a divinely or "naturally" ordered hierarchy of creation; individuals were conceived as born into a natural order of dominance and subordination. Nature and culture were part of a whole in which the hierarchy of social life was grounded in natural differences such as age, sex, and strength. Rulers were those whose "natural" characteristics fitted them for the task. From about the seventeenth century a new and revolutionary conception of social life developed within which the relationship between "nature" and "society," and between women and society, became inherently problematic.

Individuals began to be seen as rational beings, born free

and equal to each other--or as naturally free and equal--and as individuals who create their social relationships and institutions for themselves. Political institutions, in particular, began to be seen as, properly, based on convention--on contract, consent, and agreement. The conception of a conventionally grounded socio-political order brought with it a complex of problems concerning its relation to nature that, three centuries later, is still unresolved. The nature of the individuals who create and take their place within conventional or "civil" associations is one of these problems. Do all individuals have the requisite nature or natural capacities? Or are there some who lack, or cannot develop, the capacities required for participation in civil life? If these individuals exist, their nature will appear as a threat to social life and there has been wide agreement that women are dangerous for this very reason. Women, by virtue of their natures, are a source of disorder in the state.

"Disorder" can be used in either of two basic senses: first, there is the sociopolitical sense of "civil disorder" as in a rowdy demonstration, a tumultuous assembly, a riot, a breakdown of law and order. Second, "disorder" is also used to refer to an internal malfunction of an individual, as when we speak of a disordered imagination or a disorder of the stomach or intestines. The term thus has application to the constitution of both the individual and the state. In addition, its moral content can also be made explicit when it is used to describe a "disorderly house" in which decency and propriety are cast aside. Women, it is held, are a source of disorder because their being, or their nature, is such that it necessarily leads them to exert a disruptive influence in social and political life. Women have a disorder at their very centers--in their morality--which can bring about the destruction of the state. Women thus exemplify one of the ways in which nature and society stand opposed to each other. Moreover, the threat posed by women is exacerbated because of the place, or social sphere, for which they are fitted by their natures--the family. Another of the problems thrown up by the individualist, conventionalist conception of social life is whether all social relations are conventional in character. The family is seemingly the most natural of all human associations and thus specially suited to women who cannot transcend their natures in the manner demanded by civil forms of life. However, if the family is natural, then it is a form of association that stands in contrast to, and, perhaps, in conflict with (conventional) social and political life. These two aspects of the problem of the disorder of women are revealed in the writings of the social contract theorists and especially in Rousseau's theory.

The social contract theorists set out the individualist and conventionalist conception of social life with particular clarity. Their arguments depend on, and thus illustrate, all the ambigui- ties and complexities inherent in the antimony between nature and "convention." Popular contemporary beliefs about women, no less than seventeenth-century patriarchal arguments, rely on an appeal to nature and also on the fact that what is natural or "ordered according to nature" is widely believed to be good and desirable.[4] The contract theorists appealed both to conceptions of individu- als' natures and to the state of nature which natural individuals inhabited--but exactly in what form they inhabited it, and what kind of relationships existed between them, is one of the key questions in the contract story.

Rousseau's version of contract theory highlights the problems in an acute form. He was the only contract theorist willing to pursue the revolutionary implications inherent in the doctrine, but he also believed that women posed a permanent threat to political order. Rousseau's theory contains some profound sociological insights precisely because he was concerned with the interrelations of different dimensions of social life and with transformations of human consciousness. In the **Discourse on Inequality** he attacks the abstract individualism of the liberal contract theorists who postulated a familiar yet natural condition original to humanity. Rousseau argues that, strictly, a natural state is asocial, inhabited only by animals of various kinds, one species of which has the potential to develop into human individuals. That is to say, Rousseau denies that one can draw political conclusions from assertions about the natural characteristics of isolated individuals or individuals seen severally not collectively. His basic premise is that human life is social life, or sociality is natural to humans. According to Rousseau, and here he agrees with Locke, the social state of nature is inhabited not by (isolated) individuals but by families. He writes that "the oldest of all societies, and the only natural one, is that of the family."[5] This is another way of saying that the family precedes, or can exist in the absence of, wider social institutions or "civil society"; it exists in the natural condition. The family is also grounded in the natural ties of love and affection (which are natural because they are within human capacities as, say, flying is not) and it has its origin in the biological process of procreation, in the natural difference between the sexes. Rousseau argues that the family provides us with a major example of a social institution that follows the order of nature because, in the family, age naturally takes precedence over youth and males are naturally in authority over females. For Rousseau, the family is necessarily patriarchal.

The state of nature stands in contrast to civil society, but the family is common to both forms of existence. The family spans the divide between a condition grounded in nature and the conventional bonds of civil life. Few social and political theorists, with the notable exception of Hobbes,[6] have been willing to present the family as a conventional association. Indeed, in the **Philosophy of Right**, Hegel claims that it is "shameful" to see marriage and the family as merely contractual associations. The family is widely regarded as the natural basis of civil life. Familial, or domestic relations, are based on the natural ties of biology and sentiment, and the family is constituted by the particularistic bonds of an organic unity. However, the status of the family as the foundation of civil society means that the contrast between the different forms of social life in "the state of nature" and "civil society" is carried over into civil life itself. The distinction between and separation of the private and public, or particularistic and universal, spheres of association is a fundamental structural principle of the modern, liberal conception of social life. The natural, particularistic family nestles at the center of the private sphere, and it throws into prominence and stands opposed to the impersonal, universal, "conventional" bonds of public life.

Rawls has recently stated that "justice is the first virtue of social institutions."[7] Similarly, Freud argues that "the first requisite of civilization, . . . is that of justice--that is, the assurance that a law once made will not be broken in favour of an individual."[8] But justice is not the virtue of all social institutions. As the preceding discussion suggests, and as Freud (and Hegel) tell us, it is love, not justice, that is the first virtue of the family. The family is a naturally social not a conventionally social institution, but justice is a public or conventional virtue. In the family, individuals appear as unique and unequal personalities and as members of a differentiated unity grounded in sentiment. In civil life individuals transcend, or leave behind, the particular and ascribed characteristics which distinguish them in the private sphere and appear as unrelated equals. They enter the sphere of individualism--which is also universalism--as bearers of rights (liberties), as owners of property, and as citizens. In a civil association, individuals are bound together and their actions are regulated solely by general or universal rules and laws that apply impartially to all. The rules and laws protect the rights and property of all individuals--providing that all do their share to uphold the rules, that is to say, to maintain justice. Particular or private interests of individuals must be subordinated to the public interest, or to the virtue of justice.

Individuals will more readily uphold the rules of civil association if they develop a sense of justice or a morality of order. Individuals must "internalize" the universal rules of the sociopolitical order, understand that they ought to be observed, and wish to act accordingly. The sense of justice is fundamental to the maintenance of public order. However, if individuals exist who, like women according to Rousseau and Freud, naturally are incapable of developing a sense of justice, the basis of civil association is threatened; it contains within itself a permanent source of disorder. The threat is all the greater because the natural morality, or deficiency in moral capacity, of women fits them only for the "natural society" of domestic life. But the family itself is a threat to civil life. Love and justice are antagonistic virtues; the demands of love and of family bonds are particularistic and so in direct conflict with justice which demands that private interest is subordinated to the public (universal) good. The family is thus simultaneously the foundation of the state and antagonistic to it. Moreover, the presence within it of women who have no sense of justice--and whose natures prevent them from leaving the domestic sphere--can only work against and weaken the sense of justice of their male kin who must uphold justice in civil life. "Womankind," Hegel states, "perverts the universal property of the state into a possession and ornament for the family."9

Rousseau and Freud offer a remarkably similar diagnosis of why women are incapable of developing a sense of justice. Both agree that, for women, anatomy is destiny. The biological (natural) differences between the sexes influence and are reflected in their respective moral characters. Rousseau argues that the source of the disorder of women lies in their boundless sexual passion. Women, he claims, foreshadowing Freud, are unable to subdue and sublimate their sexual desires in the same manner, or to the same extent, as men. Men are the active and aggressive sex and are "controlled by nature"; passive and defensive women have only the control of modesty. There must therefore be a double standard of sexual conduct. If both sexes gave equal rein to their passions "the men,. . . would at last become [the women's] victims, and would be dragged to their death without the least chance of escape."[10] Modesty is natural to women, but it provides a weak and uncertain control of their sexual desires. Moreover, as Rousseau argues in **Politics and the Arts**: "even if it could be denied that a special sentiment of chasteness was natural to women, would it be any the less true that in society . . . they ought to be raised in principles appropriate to it? If the timidity, chasteness, and modesty which are proper to them are social inventions, it is in society's interest that women acquire these qualities. . . ."[11] However, even an education specifically designed to foster modesty is not sufficient guarantee against the disorderliness of women. Rousseau spells out this lesson in graphic fashion in **La Nouvelle Heloise**. Julie desires nothing more than to be virtuous and lead an exemplary life as a wife and mother, but she is unable, despite all her efforts and apparent success in passing through the trials set for her by Wolmar, to overcome her passion for Saint Preux. If the good order of Clarens is not to be fatally disrupted, Julie must take the one course left to her; the only solution to the problem of the disorder of women is her "accidental" death.

Rousseau and Freud argue that this fundamental difference between the sexes has existed since the very beginning of social life and, indeed, has structured it. Both claim that the creation of civil society, or "civilizaton," is the work of men. For Rousseau the sexes are equal only when isolated from each other among the animals in the true (asocial) natural conditon. Social life develops as family life, and while charting its emergence Rousseau suddenly announces that "the first difference was established in the way of life of the two sexes, . . .women. . . grew accustomed to tend the hut and the children."[12] His conjectural history of the development of civil society and the transformation of human nature then continues as a history of male activity and male nature. Freud also presents a conjectural history of the development of civil society (civilization) in **Civilization and Its Discontents.** He argues that once "the need for genital satisfaction no longer made its appearance like a guest who drops in suddenly,"[13] males had a reason for keeping females close at hand and the latter, in their turn, were obliged to comply in order to care for their helpless young. Once the family was established, the development of civilization was the work of men alone because it required the "instinctual sublimations of which women are little capable." Only men are capable of sublimating their passions and thus capable of the justice that civil life demands. Furthermore, men's involvement in public life, and their consequent dependence on other men, means that they have little energy left for their wives and families: "thus the woman finds herself forced into the background by the claims of civilization and she adopts a hostile attitude towards it."[14]

No explanation was available of why women are less able than men to sublimate their passions, or how the "special stamp to the character of females as social beings"[15] came about until Freud formulated his psychoanalytic theory. Rousseau can only tell us that men and women differ in this respect—and he prescribes an education for girls that will reinforce their disorderly natures and indifference to justice. Women are "naturally" made to be "at the mercy of man's judgment" and "to endure even injustice at his hands."[16] (Hegel, it might be noted, was content to leave women in their natural state; women, he ways with resignation, are "educated—who knows how?—as it were by breathing in ideas, by living. . . .")[17] Freud argues that the explanation for women's lack of, or deficiency in, a sense of justice is the differential passage of the two sexes through the Oedipus complex and a consequent difference in the development of their super-egos. The super-ego is the "representative for us of every moral restriction"[18] and, especially, of the restrictions that justice demands.

Civilization is the work of men in the most profound sense, for it is men alone who posses a fully developed super-ego. The emergence of the super-ego is bound up with (the conjectural history of) the "original" momentous move from the family to wider communal life. Freud argues that "originally" the "first" sons killed the "first" father, whom they simultaneously loved and hated. Out of the awful act of hatred, remorse and guilt grew from their love, and their subsequent identification with their dead father led to the emergence of the super-ego. The brothers, Freud argues, imposed on each other the mutual restrictions necessary to prevent a repetition of their dreadful deed. Thus the public virtue of justice, or "the first 'right' or 'law'" necessary for civil life, was established—by men; women had no part in this development.[19] In our own time the different manner in which

little boys and girls pass through the Oedipus complex harks back
to the purely masculine "origin" of justice, political right, and
the super-ego.

Little boys have a dramatic passage through the Oedipus
complex. The threat of castration, the force of which is confirmed when the boy sees the "castrated" female genitals, impels
him to identify with his father, and so the Oedipus complex is
"literally smashed to pieces."[20] The super-ego, which is "heir"
to the Oedipus complex, then begins its development. The little
boy "assimilates" his father's ego to his own and thereby interna-
lizes all the restraints embodied in the paternal agency. Thus
the male infant becomes a moral individual, in due course a "man,"
since the creation of the super-ego initiates him into "all the
processes that are designed to make the individual find a place in
the cultural community."[21] For females, however, the process is
quite different. Females are already "castrated" and when they
make this terrible discovery by comparing themselves to little
boys, their Oedipus complex is created, not destroyed. It is a
long and difficult journey through which the little girl comes to
take her father as her object--in fact, she may never surmount the
Oedipus complex. The result is that women lack or, at best, have
a much weaker super-ego than men. Freud writes that "for women
the level of what is ethically normal is different from what it is
in men. Their super-ego is never so inexorable, so impersonal, so
independent of its emotional origins as we require it to be in
men. . . . They show less sense of justice than men, . . . they
are less ready to submit to the great exigencies of life, ...
they are more often influenced in their judgments by feelings of

affection or hostility. . . ."[22]

Freud argues that the creation and dissolution of the Oedipus complex is a universal feature of human existence. The difference in moral capacity between the sexes must, therefore, be accepted. In Rousseau's terms, it is a social reflection of the order of nature. Freud emphasizes the costs of creating civilization,[23] but he has no suggestions for containing the disorderliness of women. Rousseau, however, concludes that the only way in which the state can be protected from the impact of women is through strict segregation of the sexes in their activities, including, as at Clarens, in domestic life. Sexual separation is necessary because even modest (good) women are a corrupting influence on men. Their disorder leads them always to pull men away from civic virtue and to mock at justice. But segregation is only a preventive measure; it does nothing to cure the disorder of women.

This is shown when the separation of the sexes is taken to its logical limit--the seraglio. The seraglio appears to be a secure "asylum against the onslaughts of vice," and the one place where a woman can "be sure about [herself], where there are no dangers to fear."[24] Nevertheless, as Usbek discovers, disorder can break out even in the seraglio. In **La Nouvelle Heloise**, the presence of Wolmar, who epitomizes the qualities of a wise man with a highly developed sense of justice, is not enough to protect Clarens. Julie states that Wolmar never violates "conjugal solemnity," and that even his passion for her is of a kind in which he "loves only as much as he wishes to and . . .he wishes to only as much as reason permits."[25] Yet Julie's passion triumphs over Wolmar's justice. Neither the seraglio nor Clarens can provide a true asylum or substitute for a weak super-ego and natural lack of capacity for sublimation. In any social context "the life of a good woman is a perpetual struggle against self."[26] Julie says everything when she writes on her death-bed that "I dare pride myself in the past, but who might have been able to answer for my future? One day more, perhaps, and I might be guilty!"[27]

Rousseau presents us with many insights into the problem of the disorder of women. However he is, very surprisingly, far less aware of the problem posed by the family. Rousseau's political theory highlights the conflict between the private interests of sectional associations and the general will (or principles of justice) that governs the political order. However, he fails to see that the family, too, is a sectional association that threatens justice. Rousseau pictures the family, the little commonwealth with the father at its head, as the foundation of the state: "Will the bonds of convention hold firm without some foundation in nature? Can devotion to the state exist apart from the love of those near and dear to us? Can patriotism thrive except in the soil of that miniature fatherland, the home? Is it not the good son, the good husband, the good father, who makes the good citizen?"[28] Perhaps--if the father's sense of justice is strong enough to override his love for his family, his desire to protect its interests, and the baleful influence of his wife. Freud argues that the conflict between love, whether sensual or "aim-inhibited," and public life cannot be avoided: "love comes into opposition to the interests of civilization; ...civilization threatens love with substantial restrictions." The more closely that family members are attached to each other, the harder it is for them to enter into public life.[29] Freud might have added that the more diligently husbands and fathers work for the interests of their families, the more likely it is that they will put those interests before the requirements of justice. There can be no easy reconciliation of the virtues of love and justice.

Paradoxically, because the family is the "foundation" of social life in the sense that it is the point of "procreative origin"[30] of society and because it stands directly at the border with nature, women are seen as the guardians of order and morality as well as inherently subversive. It is women who reproduce and have the major responsibility for educating the next generation; it is the mother who turns asocial, bisexual babies into little "boys" and "girls." Rousseau glorifies women's task as mothers. He was one of the first writers to emphasize the moral implications of breast-feeding, and he is careful to stress, for example, that when Julie constructs her natural garden retreat she does not allow the work to interfere with her duties as a mother. (However, it should be noted that the mother's task is completed in the early years; a male tutor takes over from her.) Women's guardianship of order reaches beyond motherhood. Within the shelter of domestic life women impose an order, a social pattern, and thus give meaning to the natural world of birth and death and other physical processes, of dirt and raw materials, that is integral to domestic life. Women are direct mediators between nature and society. However, because women face nature directly, and because, in giving birth and in their other bodily functions, they appear as part of nature, they exemplify the ambiguous status of the family as both natural and social.[31] Women impose order and foster morality; but they are also in daily contact with dirt and with natural processes only partly under our control. They cannot escape being tainted by this contact or completely transcend the naturalness of their own being. Hence they represent both order and disorder, both morality and boundless passion.

It is worth remarking here that one way in which women (and their male kin and keepers) attempt to hide this contact with nature, their own natural functions, and hence their potential for disorder, is through cleanliness--presented as purity. In the **Persian Letters** the chief eunuch stresses to Usbek that he has always been trained to keep the women in the seraglio "absolutely clean . . . and [to take] an infinite amount of care over it."[32] Rousseau proclaims that "nothing could be more revolting than a dirty woman, and a husband who tires of her is not to blame." Emile will never find this fault in Sophy: "things are never clean enough for her. . . . She has always disliked inspecting the kitchen-garden . . .the soil is dirty,. . .absolute cleanliness . . . has become a habit, till it absorbs one half of her time and controls the other; so that she thinks less of how to do a thing than of how to do it without getting dirty. . . . Sophy is more than clean, she is pure."[33]

The profound insights into the contradictions and antagonisms in the dialectic between individuals and their social relations, and between the family and civil society, to be found in the work of thinkers of the stature of Rousseau and Freud, are sadly neglected (or not even recognized) in most contemporary work on the subject of justice and in much feminist writing. In part, this reflects the consolidation of liberal theory over three centuries as the ideology of the liberal capitalist state, centered on the separation of the political and private spheres. The problems which appear explicitly at the origins of liberal theory in the arguments of the social contract theorists and their critics are now either ignored or regarded as unproblematic. In particular, the tension between nature and convention or love and justice is continually glossed over or suppressed.

Early liberal feminist writers such as Mary Wollstonecraft and John Stuart Mill, for example, who agree that women lack a sense of justice, offer a much more superficial diagnosis of the problem than Rousseau (though that is not to underestimate their achievement). They see it primarily as a matter of extending the liberal principles of freedom, equality, and rationality to women through a process of education. In the **Vindication**, Wollstone-craft appeals for the "rights of men and citizens" to be extended to both sexes; reason has no sex. It appears that the virtues are sexually differentiated because women have been turned into "artificial" creatures. Their education (or, more accurately, lack of it) enforces their dependence on men and makes them mean and selfish, narrowing the range of their concerns to exclude the wider community so that they cannot develop a sense of justice. Similarly in **The Subjection of Women**, Mill argues that we cannot say that women are "naturally" fit only for subordination because we know nothing of what they might become if the principles of freedom and equality, now governing the rest of our social institutions, were extended to sexual relations. Mill argues that individuals develop a sense of justice through participation in as wide a range of public institutions as possible; confined to the family--which the law allows to be a "school of despotism"--women can never learn to weigh the public interest against selfish inclination.

The obvious problem with Mill's and Wollstonecraft's arguments is that although they both advocate a proper education for women and a widening of opportunities to enable them to be economically independent of men, they also assume that the opportunities will be largely irrelevant for the majority of women. Most women will continue working within the home since child-rearing will remain their major responsibility. But this means that, despite legal and educational reforms, men's moral understanding will continue to be more highly developed than women's. Women will not obtain within the family the breadth of social experience and practical education that will develop their sense of justice and allow them, with safety, to participate in political life. The problem of the disorder of women, while mitigated by education, remains unresolved. These feminist arguments assume that the family can become the bedrock on which the liberal state is raised, but they also contain a hint that love and justice can conflict. Mill implies that education is the answer here too; educated persons of both sexes should be able to control and subdue their "lower" passions.[34] Wollstonecraft contrasts love, that is, sexual passion, with friendship and mutual respect between equals, and she argues that the latter is the only true basis for marriage and family life. Rousseau, also, thought it "an error" to see sexual passion as the basis of domestic life (he makes it clear that Saint Preux, Julie's lover, would not make a good husband). He claims that: "people do not marry in order to think exclusively of each other, but in order to fulfill the duties of civil society jointly, to govern the house prudently, to rear their children well. Lovers never see anyone but themselves, they incessantly attend only to themselves, and the only thing they are able to do is love each other."[35]

However, given Rousseau's conception of women's nature and his plan for their education, it is impossible that marriage could be placed on this footing--as he shows clearly enough in his story of Wolmar's virtue and Julie's love. To state that sexual attraction is not the proper foundation for marriage solves nothing if it is also believed that women are naturally creatures governed wholly by their sexual passions. More generally, the liberal feminists' recognition that the relationship between the sexes contradicts basic liberal principles and their proposals for social reforms fail to get to the heart of the problem of the disorder of women. Their argument is undercut by the acceptance of the separation of domestic from civil life, which is also a sexual separation; women and love are irrevocably set in opposition to justice. Liberal theory presupposes the opposition between nature and convention but the opposition can be neither admitted nor its implications pursued. The account of the development of the sense of justice in Rawls's extremely influential **A Theory of Justice** shows how liberal theorists consistently obscure one of the major problems in their arguments.

Rawls states that he has drawn on both Rousseau and Freud, but he gives no indication that he has appreciated the relevance of their insights into sexual relationships for the question of justice. Rawls presents an apparently sexually undifferentiated account, arguing that "our moral understanding increases as we move in the course of life through a sequence of positions."[36] The sense of justice develops in three stages; first, the child learns the "morality of order" from its parents. Then the "morality of association," a morality characterized by the cooperative virtues of justice and impartiality, is developed when the individual occupies a variety of roles in a range of institutions. Finally, we reach the stage of the "morality of principles" in which we understand the fundamental role of justice in the social order and we wish to uphold it; the sense of justice is attained. Now this account, of course, has the same obvious failing as the liberal feminist arguments--only if men **and** women can move "through a sequence of positions" will both sexes develop the sense of justice. Rawls, not surprisingly, rejects cries to "abolish the family," but he has nothing to say about the sexual division of labor or the conviction that domestic life is the proper sphere for women. On the contrary, he remarks that if a publicly recognized concept of justice regulates social life it will "reconcile us to the dispositions of the natural order."[37] And what is more natural, or in accordance, with the order of nature, than the division of social life and its virtues between the sexes: conventional political life and justice belong to men; domestic life and love belong to women?

One reaction from the feminist movement to the problems sketched in this paper has been a call for the last vestiges of nature to be swept away. In the **Dialectics of Sex**, Firestone claims that the problem of women and nature can be solved through artifical reproduction which will allow all relationships, including those between adults and children, to be based on convention or to be freely chosen. However, this is to argue that the whole of social life could be fashioned in the image of a philosophically and sociologically incoherent abstract, possessive individualism. It is a "solution" based on a continuing opposition between nature and society rather than an attempt to recreate this relationship. Another feminist response to claims about the disorder of women has been to argue that, since "justice" is the work of men and an aspect of the domination of women, women should reject it totally and remake their lives on the basis of love, sentiment, and personal relations. But this no more solves the problem than a declaration of war on nature; neither position breaks with liberal conceptions or can take account of the dialectic between individual and social life, between the particular or personal and the universal or political. To attempt technologically to banish nature or to deny that justice has any relevance, is to try to wish away fundamental dimensions of human life. Rather, the extraordinarily difficult and complex task must be undertaken of developing a critique of the liberal and patriarchal conception of the relation between nature and convention that will also provide the foundation for a theory of a democratic, sexually egalitarian practice.

The insights and failings of the theorists discussed in this paper provide one starting point for such a critique. I have concentrated on "love," that is to say, sexual passion. However, one of the most urgent tasks is to provide an alternative to the liberal view of justice, that assumes that "a" sense of justice presently exists, developed through the smooth passage of all individuals through social institutions. This claim rests on the uncritical acceptance that the structure of liberal capitalist institutions allows both men and women, working class and middle class, to develop in the same fashion. It ignores the reality of institutions in which the subordination of women and the "despotic organization of production"[38] are seen as natural. Rousseau's critique of abstract individualism and the liberal theory of the state can assist in building a critical theory, just as his many insights into the relationship between sexual and political life, disentangled from his patriarchalism, are essential to a critical theory of the relation between love and justice. Similarly, Freud's psychoanalytic theory is indispensible, but used carefully as part of an account of the historical development of civil society--which includes a specific form of domestic association and "masculine" and "feminine" sexuality--and not, as Freud presents it, an abstract theory of the "individual" and "civilization."[39] This project may sound daunting, even completely overwhelming. Yet once the problem of the disorder of women begins to be seen as a question of social life, not as a fact that confronts us in nature, the reality of the structure of our personal and political lives is beginning to be revealed within the appearance presented in liberal and patriarchal ideology, and the task has already begun.

FOOTNOTES

[1]J. -J. Rousseau, **Politics** and the **Arts: A Letter to M. d'Alembert on the Theatre**, trans. A. Bloom (Ithaca, N.Y.: Cornell University Press, 1968), p. 109. Rousseau also notes that wine attracts old men because youth have other desires; beliefs about the subversiveness of youth are outside the scope of this paper.

[2]G. W. F. Hegel, **The Phenomenology of Mind**, trans. J. B. Ballie (London: Allen & Unwin, 1949), p. 496; **Philosophy of Right**, trans. T. M. Knox (Oxford: Oxford University Press, 1952), addition to par. 166. N. O. Keohane ("Female Citizenship: 'The Monstrous Regiment of Women'" [paper presented at the annual meeting of the Conference for the Study of Political Thought, New York, April 6-8, 1979]) discusses various aspects of the belief that women should not enter the political sphere, with particular reference to ancient Greece and Bodin's theory.

[3]Women have also been perceived from ancient times as guardians of morality and order. This contradictory view is briefly discussed below, but it should be noted that the two conceptions of women are not straightforwardly opposed to each other. The "morality" and "order" represented by women is not the same as the "order" of the political sphere.

[4]But compare Nietzsche: "You desire to live "according to Nature'? Oh, . . .what fraud of words! Imagine to yourselves a being like Nature, boundlessly extravagant, boundlessly indifferent, without purpose or consideration, without pity or justice, at once fruitful and barren and uncertain: imagine to yourselves indifference as a power--how could you live in accordance with such indifference?" (F. Nietzsche, **The Complete Works**, ed. O. Levy [London: Foulis, 1911], vol. 12, **Beyond Good and Evil**, trans. H. Zimmer, chap. 1, par. 9). The same ambiguities and contradictions inherent in our perception of women also surround "nature." Social life can, for example, be regarded as properly a reflection of the harmony in nature or the "order of nature"; alternatively, nature can be seen as the sphere of the uncontrolled, the arbitrary, the capricious, the indifferent that must be transcended in social life. (A discussion of various meanings attributed to "natural" in relation to women can be found in C. Pierce, "Natural Law Language and Women," in **Women in Sexist Society**, ed. V. Gornick and B. K. Moran [New York: Basic Books, 1971].)

[5]J.-J. Rousseau, **The Social Contract**, trans. M. Cranston (Harmondsworth, Middlesex: Penguin Books, 1968), bk. 1, p. 50.

[6]Hobbes's view of the family is discussed in T. Brennan and C. Pateman, "'Mere Auxilaries to the Commonwealth': Women and the Origins of Liberalism," **Political Studies** 27 (1979): 183-200.

[7]J. Rawls, **A Theory of Justice** (Oxford: Oxford University Press, 1971), p. 3.

[8]S. Freud, "Civilization and Its Discontents," in **The**

Standard Edition of the Complete Psychological Works, trans. J. Strachey (London: Hogarth Press, 1961), 21:95.

[9] Hegel, The Phenomenology of Mind, p. 496.

[10] J.-J. Rousseau, Emile, trans B. Foxley (London: Dent, 1911), p. 322.

[11] Rousseau, Politics and the Arts, p. 87.

[12] J.-J. Rousseau, "Discourse on the Origin and Foundations of Inequality," in The First and Second Discourses, trans. R. D. Masters (New York: St. Martin's Press, 1964), p. 147. The speculations of classic theorists about the "natural condition" and "the origin of society" should be compared with the speculations of scientists studying animal life. See the fascinating discussion by D. Haraway, "Animal Sociology and a Natural Economy of the Body Politics, Part II: The Past Is the Contested Zone: Human Nature and Theories of Production and Reproduction in Primate Behavior Studies," Signs 4 (1978): 37-60.

[13] Freud, "Civilization and Its Discontents," p. 99.

[14] Ibid., pp. 103-104.

[15] S. Freud, "Female Sexuality," in On Sexuality, ed. A. Richards (Harmondsworth, Middlesex: Penguin Freud Library, 1977), 7:377.

[16] Rousseau, Emile, pp. 328, 359.

[17] Hegel, Philosophy of Right, addition to par. 166.

[18] S. Freud, "The Dissection of the Psychical Personality," in New Introductory Lectures on Psychoanalysis, ed. J. Strachey (Harmondsworth, Middlesex: Penguin Library, 1973), 2:98.

[19] Freud, "Civilization and Its Discontents," pp. 101, 131-132.

[20] Freud, "Some Psychical Consequences of the Anatomical Distinction between the Sexes," in Richards, ed., 7:341.

[21] Freud, "Female Sexuality," p. 375.

[22] Freud, "Some Psychical Consequences of the Anatomical Distinction between the Sexes," 7:342.

[23] Cf.:"Society cannot be formed or maintained without our being required to make perpetual and costly sacrifices. Because society surpasses us, it obliges us to surpass ourselves, and to surpass itself, a being must, to some degree, depart from its nature. . ." (E. Durkheim, "The Dualism of Human Nature and Its Social Conditions" in Essays on Sociology and Philosophy, ed K. H. Wolff [New York: Harper & Row, 1964], p.338).

[24]Montesquieu, **Persian Letters**, trans. C. J. Betts (Harmondsworth, Middlesex: Penguin Books, 1973), letter 20, p. 68; letter 26, p. 76.

[25]J.-J. Rousseau, **La Nouvelle Heloise**, trans. J. H. McDowell (University Park: Pennsylvania State University Press, 1968), pt. 2, letter 20, p. 260.

[26]Rousseau, **Emile** (n. 10 above), p. 332.

[27]Rousseau, **La Nouvelle Heloise**, trans. J. H. McDowell (University Park: Pennsylvania State University Press, 1968), pt. 4, letter 12, p. 405.

[28]Rousseau, **Emile**, p. 326. I was first alerted to this point by the excellent discussion of Rousseau in S. Okin, **Women in Western Political Thought** (Princeton, N.J.: Princeton University Press, 1980).

[29]Freud, "Civilization and Its Discontents," pp. 102-103.

[30]I am indebted for the phrase to A. Yeatman's unpublished paper "Gender Ascription and the Conditions of Its Breakdown: The Rationalization of the 'Domestic Sphere' and the Nineteenth-Century 'Cult of Domesticity.'"

[31]On these points see M. Douglas, **Purity and Danger** (Harmondsworth, Middlesex: Penguin Books, 1970), S. B. Ortner, "Is Female to Male as Nature Is to Culture?" in **Women, Culture and Society**, ed. M. Rosaldo and L. Lamphere (Stanford, Calif.: Stanford University Press, 1974); and L. Davidoff, "The Rationalization of Housework," in **Dependence and Exploitation in Work and Marriage**, ed. D. L. Barker and S. Allen (London: Longmans, 1976). (On purity see also Ortner's suggestive sketch "The Virgin and the State," **Feminist Studies** 8 [1978]: 19-36.)

[32]Montesquieu, letter 64, p. 131.

[33]Rousseau, **Emile**, pp. 357-358.

[34]Victorian arguments about women's lack of sexual feeling, while oppressive, could also be used to women's advantage. There is an excellent discussion of this area in N. F. Cott, "Passionlessness: An Interpretation of Victorian Sexual Ideology, 1790-1850" **Signs** 4 (1978): 219-36.

[35]Rousseau, **La Nouvelle Heloise**, pt.3, letter 30, pp. 261-2.

[36]Rawls (n. 7 above), p. 468. The discussion here draws generally on secs. 70-72.

[37]Ibid., p. 512.

[38]The phrase is taken from B. Clark and H. Gintis, "Rawlsian Justice and Economic Systems," **Philosophy and Public Affairs** 4 (1978): 302-325. This essay forms part of the "left" critique of

Rawls which, so far, has largely ignored the sexual (in contrast to the class) dimension of subordination and its relevance for justice.

[39] See M. Poster, **Critical Theory of the Family** (London: Pluto Press, 1978), chap. 1 (though women are relegated to a footnote); and "Freud's Concept of the Family," **Telos** 30 (1976); 93-115.

AUTHOR'S NOTE

I am grateful to Anna Yeatman for discussing the questions raised in this paper.

CHAPTER 3

THE HYSTERICAL WOMAN: SEX ROLES AND ROLE CONFLICT

IN 19th-CENTURY AMERICA*

Carroll Smith-Rosenberg

Hysteria was one of the classic diseases of the nineteenth
century.   It was a protean ailment characterized by such varied
symptoms as paraplegia, aphonia, hemi-anaesthesia, and violent
epileptoid seizures.   Under the broad rubic of hysteria, nineteenth-century physicians gathered cases which might today be
diagnosed as neurasthenia, hypochondriasis, depression, conversion
reaction, and ambulatory schizophrenia.   It fascinated and frustrated some of the century's most eminent clinicians; through its
redefinition Freud rose to international fame, while the towering
reputation of Charcot suffered a comparative eclipse.   Psychoanalysis can historically be called the child of the hysterical
woman.

Not only was hysteria a widespread and--in the intellectual
history of medicine--significant disease, it remains to this day a
frustrating and ever-changing illness.   What was diagnosed as
hysteria in the nineteenth century is not necessarily related to
the hysterical character as defined in the twentieth century, or
again to what the Greeks meant by hysteria when they christened

*Carroll Smith-Rosenberg, "The Hysterical Woman: Sex Roles and
Role Conflict in 19th-Century America," Social Research 39, no. 4
(Winter 1972), pp. 652-678. Copyright (c) 1972 by Social Re-
search. Reprinted by permission of Social Research.

the disease millennia ago. The one constant in this varied history has been the existence in virtually every era of Western culture of some clinical entity called hysteria; an entity which has always been seen as peculiarly relevant to the female experience, and one which has almost always carried with it a pejorative implication.

For the past half century and longer, American culture has defined hysteria in terms of individual psychodynamics. Physicians and psychologists have seen hysteria as a "neurosis" or character disorder, the product of an unresolved Oedipal complex. Hysterical women, fearful of their own sexual impulses--so the argument went--channeled that energy into psychosomatic illness. Characteristically, they proved unable to form satisfying and stable relationships.[1] More recently psychoanalysts such as Elizabeth Zetzel have refined this Freudian hypothesis, tracing the roots of hysteria to a women's excessively ambivalent pre-oedipal relation with her mother and to the resulting complications of oedipal development and resolution.[2] Psychologist David Shapiro has emphasized the hysterical woman's impressionistic thought pattern.[3] All such interpretations focus exclusively on individual psychodynamics and relations within particular families.

Yet hysteria is also a socially recognized behavior pattern and as such exists within the larger world of cultural values and role relationships. For centuries hysteria has been seen as characteristically female--the hysterical woman the embodiment of a perverse or hyper femininity.[4] Why has this been so? Why did large numbers of women "choose" the character traits of hysteria as their particular mode of expressing malaise, discontent, anger or pain?[5] To begin to answer this question, we must explore the female role and role socialization. Clearly not all women were hysterics; yet the parallel between the hysteric's behavior and stereotypic femininity is too close to be explained as mere coincidence. To examine hysteria from this social perspective means necessarily to explore the complex relationships that exist between cultural norms and individual behavior, between behavior defined as disease and behavior considered normal.

Using nineteenth-century America as a case study,[6] I propose to explore hysteria on at least two levels of social interaction. The first involves an examination of hysteria as a social role within the nineteenth-century family. This was a period when, it has been argued, social and structural change had created stress within the family and when, in addition, individual domestic role alternatives were few and rigidly defined. From this perspective hysteria can be seen as an alternate role option for particular women incapable of accepting their life situation. Hysteria thus serves as a valuable indicator both of domestic stress and of the tactics through which some individuals sought to resolve that stress. By analyzing the function of hysteria within the family and the interaction of the hysteric, her family, and the interceding--yet interacting--physician, I also hope to throw light upon the role of women and female-male relationships within the larger world of nineteenth-century America society. Secondly, I will attempt to raise some questions concerning female role socialization, female personality options, and the nature of hysterical behavior.[7]

I

It might be best to begin with a brief discussion of three relatively well known areas: first, the role of women in nineteenth-century American society; second, the symptoms which hysterical women presented and which established the definition of the disease, and lastly, the response of male physicians to their hysterical patients.

The ideal female in nineteenth-century America was expected to be gentle and refined, sensitive and loving. She was the guardian of religion and spokeswoman for morality. Hers was the task of guiding the more worldly and more frequently tempted male past the maelstroms of atheism and uncontrolled sexuality. Her sphere was the hearth and the nursery; within it she was to bestow care and love, peace and joy. The American girl was taught at home, at school, and in the literature of the period, that aggression, independence, self-assertion and curiosity were male traits, inappropriate for the weaker sex and her limited sphere. Dependent throughout her life, she was to reward her male protectors with affection and submission. At no time was she expected to achieve in any area considered important by men and thus highly valued by society. She was, in essence, to remain a child-woman, never developing the strengths and skills of adult autonomy. The stereotype of the middle class woman as emotional, pious, passive and nurturant was to become increasingly rigid throughout the nineteenth century.[8]

There were significant discontinuities and inconsistencies

between such ideals of female socialization and the real world in which the American woman had to live. The first relates to a dichotomy between the ideal woman and ideal mother. The ideal woman was emotional, dependent and gentle--a born follower. The ideal mother, then and now, was expected to be strong, self-reliant, protective, an efficient caretaker in relation to children and home. She was to manage the family's day-to-day finances, prepare foods, make clothes, compound drugs, serve as family nurse--and, in rural areas, as physician as well.[9] Especially in the nineteenth century, with its still primitive obstetrical practices and its high child mortality rates, she was expected to face severe bodily pain, disease and death--and still serve as the emotional support and strength of her family.[10] As S. Weir Mitchell, the eminent Philadelphia neurologist wrote in the 1880's, "We may be sure that our daughters will be more likely to have to face at some time the grim question of pain than the lad who grow up beside them. . . . To most women . . . there comes a time when pain is a grim presence in their lives." Yet, as Mitchell pointed out, it was boys whom society taught from early childhood on to bear pain stoically, while girls were encouraged to respond to pain and stress with tears and the expectation of elaborate sympathy.[11]

Contemporaries noted routinely in the 1870's, 1880's and 1890's that middle-class American girls seemed ill-prepared to assume the responsibilities and trials of marriage, motherhood and maturation. Frequently women, especially married women with children, complained of isolation, loneliness, and depression. Physicians reported a high incidence of nervous disease and hysteria among women who felt overwhelmed by the burdens of frequent pregnancies, the demands of children, the daily exertions of housekeeping and family management.[12] The realities of adult life no longer permitted them to elaborate and exploit the role of fragile, sensitive and dependent child.

Not only was the Victorian woman increasingly ill-prepared for the trails of childbirth and childrearing, but changes were also at work within the larger society which were to make her particular socialization increasingly inappropriate. Reduced birth and mortality rates, growing population concentration in towns, cities and even in rural areas, a new, highly mobile economy, as well as new patterns of middle class aspiration--all reached into the family, altering that institution, affecting domestic relations and increasing the normal quantity of infrafamilial stress.[13] Women lived longer; they married later and less often. They spent less and less time in the primary processing of food, cloth and clothing. Increasingly, both middle and lower class women took jobs outside the home until their marriages--or permanently if unable to secure a husband.[14] By the post-Civil War years, family limitation--with its necessary implication of altered domestic roles and relationships--had become a real option within the decision-making processes of every family.[15]

Despite such basic social, economic and demographic changes, however, the family and gender role socialization remained relatively inflexible. It is quite possible that many women experienced a significant level of anxiety when forced to confront or adapt in one way or another to these changes. Thus hysteria may have served as one option or tactic offering particular women otherwise unable to respond to these changes a chance to redefine or restructure their place within the family.

So far this discussion of role socialization and stress has emphasized primarily the malaise and dissatisfaction of the middle class woman. It is only a covert romanticism, however, which permits us to assume that the lower class or farm woman, because her economic functions within her family were more vital than those of her decorative and economically secure urban sisters, escaped their sense of frustration, conflict or confusion. Normative prescriptions of proper womanly behavior were certainly internalized by many poorer women. The desire to marry and the belief that a woman's social status came not from the exercise of her own talents and efforts but from her ability to attract a competent male protector were as universal among lower class and farm women as among middle and upper class urban women. For some of these women—as for their urban middle class sisters—the traditional female role proved functional, bringing material and psychic rewards. But for some it did not. The discontinuity between the child and adult female roles, along with the failure to develop substantial ego strengths, crossed class and geographic barriers—as did hysteria itself. Physicians connected with almshouses, and later in the century with urban hospitals and dispensaries, often reported hysteria among immigrant and tenement house women.[16] Sex differentiation and class distinctions both play a role in American social history, yet hysteria seems to have followed a psychic fault line corresponding more to distinctions of gender than to those of class.

Against this background of possible role conflict and discontinuity, what were the presenting symptoms of the female hysteric in nineteenth-century America? While physicians agreed that hysteria could afflict persons of both sexes and of all ages and economic classes (the male hysteric was an accepted clinical entity by the late nineteenth century), they reported that hysteria was most frequent among women between the ages of 15 and 40 and of the urban middle and upper middle classes. Symptoms were highly varied. As early as the seventeenth century, indeed, Sydenham had remarked that "the frequency of hysteria is no less remarkable than the multiformity of the shapes it puts on. Few maladies are not imitated by it; whatever part of the body it attacks, it will create the proper symptom of that part."[17] The nineteenth-century physician could only concur. There were complaints of nervousness, depression, the tendency to tears and chronic fatigue, or of disabling pain. Not a few women thus afflicted showed a remarkable willingness to submit to long-term, painful therapy--to electric shock treatment, to blistering, to multiple operations, even to amputations.[18]

The most characteristic and dramatic symptom, however, was the hysterical "fit." Mimicking an epileptic seizure, these fits often occurred with shocking suddenness. At other times they "came on" gradually, announcing their approach with a general feeling of depression, nervousness, crying or lassitude. Such seizures, physicians generally agreed, were precipitated by a sudden or deeply felt emotion--fear, shock a sudden death, marital disappointment--or by physical trauma. It began with pain and tension, most frequently in the "uterine area." The sufferer alternately sobbed and laughed violently, complained of palpitations of the heart, clawed her throat as if strangling and, at times, abruptly lost the power of hearing and speech. A death-like trance might follow, lasting hours, even days. At other times violent convulsions--sometimes accompanied by hallucinations--seized her body.[19] "Let the reader imagine," New York physician E. H. Dixon wrote in the 1840's,

> the patient writhing like a serpent upon the floor, rending her garments to tatters, plucking out handsful of hair, and striking her person with violence--with contorted and swollen countenance and fixed eyes resisting every effort of bystanders to control her . . .[20]

Finally the fit subsided; the patient, exhausted and sore, fell into a restful sleep.

During the first half of the nineteenth century physicians described hysteria principally though not exclusively in terms of such episodes. Symptoms such as paralysis and contracture were believed to be caused by seizures and categorized as infraseizure symptoms. Beginning in mid-century, however, physicians became increasingly flexible in their diagnosis of hysteria and gradually the fit declined in significance as a pathognomonic symptom.[21] Dr. Robert Carter, a widely-read British authority on hysteria, insisted in 1852 that at least one hysterical seizure must have occurred to justify a diagnosis of hysteria. But, he admitted, this seizure might be so minor as to have escaped the notice even of the patient herself; no subsequent seizures were necessary.[22] This was clearly a transitional position. By the last third of the nineteenth century the seizure was no longer the central phenomenon defining hysteria; physicians had categorized hysterical symptoms which included virtually every known human ill. They ranged from loss of sensation in part, half or all of the body, loss of taste, smell, hearing, or vision, numbness of the skin, inability to swallow, nausea, headaches, pain in the breast, knees, hip, spine or neck, as well as contracture or paralysis or virtually any extremity.[23]

Hysterical symptoms were not limited to the physical. An hysterical female character gradually began to emerge in the nineteenth-century medical literature, one based on interpretations of mood and personality rather than on discrete physical symptoms—one which grew closely to resemble twentieth-century definitions of the "hysterical personality." Doctors commonly described hysterical women as highly impressionistic, suggestible, and narcissistic. Highly labile, their moods changed suddenly, dramatically, and for seemingly inconsequential reasons. Doctors complained that the hysterical woman was egocentric in the extreme, her involvement with others consistently superficial and tangential. While the hysterical woman might appear to physicians and relatives as quite sexually aroused or attractive, she was, doctors cautioned, essentially asexual and not uncommonly frigid.[24]

Depression also appears as a common theme. Hysterical symptoms not infrequently followed a death in the family, a miscarriage, some financial setback which forced the patient to become self-supporting; or they were seen by the patient as related to some long-term, unsatisfying life situation—a tired school teacher, a mother unable to cope with the demands of a large family.[25]

Most of these women took to their beds because of pain, paralysis or general weakness. Some remained there for years.

The medical profession's response to the hysterical woman was at best ambivalent. Many doctors--and indeed a significant proportion of society at large--tended to be caustic, if not punitive towards the hysterical woman. This resentment seems rooted in two factors: first, the baffling and elusive nature of hysteria itself, and second, the relation which existed in the physicians' minds between their categorizing of hysteria as a disease and the role women were expected to play in society. These patients did not function as women were expected to function, and, as we shall see, the physician who treated them felt threatened both as a professional and as a rejected male. He was the therapist thwarted, the child untended, the husband denied nurturance and sex.

During the second half of the nineteenth century, the newly established germ theory and discoveries by neurologists and anatomists for the first time made an insistence on disease specificity a **sine qua non** for scientific respectability. Neurology was just becoming accepted as a speciality, and in its search for acceptance it was particularly dependent on the establishment of firm, somatically-based disease entities.[26] If hysteria **was** a disease, and not the imposition of self-pitying women striving to avoid their traditional roles and responsibilities--as was frequently charged, it must be a disease with a specific etiology and a predictable course. In the period 1870 to 1900, especially, it was felt to be a disease rooted in some specific organic malfunction.

Hysteria, of course, lacked all such disease characteristics.

Contracture or paralysis could occur without muscular atrophy or change in skin temperature. The hysteric might mimic tuberculosis, heart attacks, blindness or hip disease, while lungs, heart, eyes and hips remained in perfect health.[27] The physician had only his patient's statement that she could not move or was wracked with pain. If concerned and sympathetic, he faced a puzzling dilemma. As George Preston wrote in his 1897 momograph on hysteria:

> In studying the . . . disturbances of hysteria, a very formidable difficulty presents itself in the fact that the symptoms are purely subjective. . . . There is only the bald statement of the patient. . . . No confirming symptoms present themselves. . . and the appearance of the affected parts stands as contradictory evidence against the patient's word.[28]

Equally frustrating and medically inexplicable were the sudden changes in the hysteric's symptoms. Paralysis or anaesthesia could shift from one side of the body to the other, from one limb to another. Headaches would replace contracture of a limb, loss of voice, the inability to taste. How could a physician prescribe for such ephemeral symptoms? "Few practitioners desire the management of hysterics," one eminent gynecologist, Samuel Ashwell, wrote in 1833. "Its symptoms are so varied and obscure, so contradictory and changeable, and if by chance several of them, or even a single one be relieved, numerous others almost immediately spring into existence."[29] Half a century later, neurologist

Charles K. Mills echoed Ashwell's discouraging evaluation. "Hysteria is pre-eminently a chronic disease," he warned. "Deceptive remissions in hysterical symptoms often mislead the unwary practitioner. Cures are sometimes claimed where simply a change in the character of the phenomena has taken place. It is a disease in which it is unsafe to claim a conquest."[30]

Yet physicians, especially newly established neurologists with urban practices, were besieged by patients who appeared to be sincere, respectable women sorely afflicted with pain, paralysis, or uncontrollable "nervous fits." "Looking at the pain evoked by ideas and beliefs," S. Weir Mitchell, America's leading expert on hysteria wrote in 1885, "we are hardly wise to stamp these pains as non-existent."[31] Despite the tendency of many physicians to contemptuously dismiss the hysterical patient when no organic lesions could be found, neurologists such as Mitchell, George M. Beard, or Charles L. Dana sympathized with these patients and sought to alleviate their symptoms.

Such pioneer specialists were therefore in the position of having defined hysteria as a legitimate disease entity, and the hysterical woman as sick, when they were painfully aware that no organic etiology had yet been found. Cautiously, they sought to formally define hysteria in terms appropriately mechanistic. Some late nineteenth-century physicians, for example, still placing a traditional emphasis on hysteria's uterine origins, argued that hysteria resulted from "the reflex effects of utero-ovarian irritation."[32] Others, reflecting George M. Beard's work on neurasthenia, defined hysteria as a functional disease caused either by "metabolic or nutritional changes in the cellular elements of the

central nervous system." Still others wrote in terms of a malfunction of the cerebral cortex.[33] All such explanations were but
hypothetical gropings for an organic explanation--still a necessity if they were to legitimate hysteria as a disease.[34]

The fear that hysteria might after all be only a functional
or "ideational" disease--to use a nineteenth-century term--and
therefore not really a disease at all, underlies much of the
writing on hysteria as well as the physicians' own attitudes
toward their patients. These hysterical women might after all be
only clever frauds and sensation-seekers--morally delinquent and,
for the physician, professionally embarrassing.

Not surprisingly, a compensatory sense of superiority and
hostility permeated many physicians' discussions of the nature and
etiology of hysteria. Except when called upon to provide a hypothetical organic etiology, physicians saw hysteria as caused
either by the indolent, vapid and unconstructive life of the
fashionable middle and upper class woman, or by the ignorant,
exhausting and sensual life of the lower or working class woman.
Neither were flattering etiologies. Both denied the hysteric the
sympathy granted to sufferers from unquestionably organic ailments.

Any general description of the personal characteristics of
the well-to-do hysteric emphasized her idleness, self-indulgence,
her deceitfulness and "craving for sympathy." Petted and spoiled
by her parents, waited upon hand and foot by servants, she had
never been taught to exercise self-control or to curb her emotions
and desires.[35] Certainly she had not been trained to undertake
the arduous and necessary duties of wife and mother. "Young

persons who have been raised in luxury and too often in idleness,"
one late-nineteenth-century physician lectured, "who have never
been called upon to face the hardships of life, who have never
accustomed themselves to self-denial, who have abundant time and
opportunity to cultivate the emotional and sensuous, to indulge
the sentimental side of life, whose life purpose is too often an
indefinite and self-indulgent idea of pleasure, these are the most
frequent victims of hysteria."[36] Sound education, outside interests such as charity and good works, moral training, systematic
outdoor exercise and removal from an overly sympathetic family
were among the most frequent forms of treatment recommended.
Mothers, consistently enough, were urged to bring up daughters
with a strong sense of self-discipline, devotion to family needs,
and a dread of uncontrolled emotionality.[37]

Emotional indulgence, moral weakness and lack of will power
characterized the hysteric in both lay and medical thought.
Hysteria, S. Weir Mitchell warned, occurred in women who had never
developed habitual restraint and "rational endurance"--who had
early lost their power of "self rule."[38] "The mind and body are
deteriorated by the force of evil habit," Charles Lockwood wrote
in 1895, "morbid thought and morbid impulse run through the poor,
weak, unresisting brain, until all mental control is lost, and the
poor sufferer is . . . at the mercy of . . . evil and unrestrained
passions, appetites and morbid thoughts and impulses."[39]

In an age when will, control, and hard work were fundamental
social values, this hypothetical etiology necessarily implied a
negative evaluation of those who succumbed to hysteria. Such
women were described as weak, capricious and, perhaps most impor-

tant, morbidly suggestible.[40] Their intellectual abilities were meager, their powers of concentration eroded by years of self-indulgence and narcissistic introspection.[41] Hysterical women were, in effect, children, and ill-behaved, difficult children at that. "They have in fact" Robert Carter wrote, "all the instability of childhood, joined to the vices and passions of adult age. . . ."[42]

Many nineteenth-century critics felt that this emotional regression and instability was rooted in woman's very nature. The female nervous system, doctors argued, was physiologically more sensitive and thus more difficult to subject to the will. Some physicians assumed as well that woman's blood was "thinner" than man's, causing nutritional inadequacies in the central nervous system and an inability to store nervous energy--a weakness, Mary Putnam Jacobi stressed, women shared with children. Most commonly, a woman's emotional states generally, and hysteria in particular, were believed to have the closest ties to her reproductive cycle.[43] Hysteria commenced with puberty and ended with menopause, while ailments as varied as menstrual pain and irregularity, prolapsed or tipped uterus, uterine tumor, vaginal infections and discharges, sterility, could all--doctors were certain--cause hysteria. Indeed, the first question routinely asked hysterical woman was "are your courses regular?"[44] Thus a woman's very physiology and anatomy predisposed her to hysteria; it was, as Thomas Laycock put it, "the natural state" in a female, a "morbid state" in the male.[45] In an era when a sexual perspective implied conflict and ambivalence, hysteria was perceived by physician and patient as a disease both peculiarly female and peculiarly sexual.

Hysteria could also result from a secret and less forgivable form of sexuality. Throughout the nineteenth century, physicians believed that masturbation was widespread among America's females and a frequent cause of hysteria and insanity. As early as 1846, E. H. Dixon reported that masturbation caused hysteria "among females even in society where physical and intellectual culture would seem to present the strongest barriers against its incursions. . . ." Other physicians concurred, reporting that harsh public and medical reactions to hysterical women were often based on the belief that masturbation was the cause of their behavior.[46]

Masturbation was only one form of sexual indulgence. A number of doctors saw hysteria among lower class women as originating in the sensuality believed to characterize their class. Such tenement-dwelling females, doctors reported, "gave free reign to . . . 'passions of the baser sort,' not feeling the necessity of self-control because they have to a pitiably small degree any sense of propriety or decency." Hysteria, another physician reported, was found commonly among prostitutes, while virtually all physicians agreed that even within marriage sexual excess could easily lead to hysteria.[47]

Expectedly, conscious anger and hostility marked the response of a good many doctors to their hysterical patients. One New York neurologist called the female hysteric a willful, self-indulgent and narcissistic person who cynically manipulated her symptoms. "To her distorted vision," he complained, "there is but one commanding personage in the universe--herself--in comparison with whom the rest of mankind are nothing." Doctors admitted that they were frequently tempted to use such terms as "willful" and "evil", "angry" and "impatient" when describing the hysteric and her symptoms.[48] Even the concerned and genteel S. Weir Mitchell, confident of his remarkable record in curing hysteria, described hysterical women as "the pests of many households, who constitute the despair of physicians, and who furnish those annoying examples of despotic selfishness, which wreck the constitutions of nurses and devoted relatives, and in unconscious or half-conscious self-indulgence destroy the comfort of everyone about them." He concluded by quoting Oliver Wendell Holmes' acid judgment that "a hysterical girl is a vampire who sucks the blood of the healthy people about her."[49]

Hysteria as a chronic, dramatic and socially accepted sick role could thus provide some alleviation of conflict and tension, but the hysteric purchased her escape from the emotional--and frequently--from the sexual demands of her life only at the cost of pain, disability, and an intensification of woman's traditional passivity and dependence. Indeed a complex interplay existed between the character traits assigned women in Victorian society and the characteristic symptoms of the nineteenth-century hysteric: dependency, fragility, emotionality, narcissism. (Hysteria has, after all, been called in that century and this a stark caricature of femininity.) Not surprisingly the hysteric's peculiar passive aggression and her exploitive dependency often functioned to cue a corresponding hostility in the men who cared for her or lived with her. Whether father, husband, or physician, they reacted with ambivalence and in many cases with hostility to her aggressive and never-ending demands.

II

What inferences concerning woman's role and female-male relationships can be drawn from this description of nineteenth century hysteria and of medical attitudes toward the female patient? What insights does it allow into patterns of stress and resolution within the traditional nuclear family?

Because traditional medical wisdom had defined hysteria as a disease, its victims could expect to be treated as sick and thus to elicit a particular set of responses--the right to be seen and treated by a physician, to stay in bed and thus be relieved of their normal day-to-day responsibilities, to enjoy the special prerogatives, indulgences, and sympathy the sick role entailed. Hysteria thus became one way in which conventional women could express--in most cases unconsciously--dissatisfaction with one or several aspects of their lives.

The effect of hysteria upon the family and traditional sex role differentiation was disruptive in the extreme. The hysterical woman virtually ceased to function within the family. No longer did she devote herself to the needs of others, acting as self-sacrificing wife, mother, or daughter. Through her hysteria she could and in fact did force others to assume those functions. Household activities were reoriented to answer the hysterical woman's importunate needs. Children were hushed, rooms darkened, entertaining suspended, a devoted nurse recruited. Fortunes might be spent on medical bills or for drugs and operations. Worry and concern bowed the husband's shoulders; his home had suddenly become a hospital and he a nurse. Through her illness, the bedridden woman came to dominate her family to an extent that would have been considered inappropriate--indeed shrewish--in a healthy woman. Taking to one's bed, especially when suffering from dramatic and ever-visible symptoms, might also have functioned as a mode of passive aggression, especially in a milieu in which weakness was rewarded and in which women had since childhood been taught not to express overt aggression. Consciously or unconsciously, she had thus opted out of her traditional role.

Women did not accomplish this redefinition of domestic roles without the aid of the men in their family. Doctors commented that the hysteric's husband and family often, and unfortunately, rewarded her symptoms with elaborate sympathy. "The hysteric's credit is usually first established," as one astute mid-century clinician pointed out, "by those who have, at least, the wish to believe them."[50] Husbands and fathers were not alone in their cooperation; the physician often played a complex and in a sense emotionally compromising role in legitimizing the female hysteric's behavior. As an impartial and professionally skilled observer, he was empowered to judge whether or not a particular woman had the right to withdraw from her socially allotted duties. At the same time, these physicians accepted as correct, indeed as biologically inevitable, the structure of the Victorian family and the division of sex roles within it. He excused the woman only in the belief that she was ill and that she would make every effort to get well and resume her accustomed role. It was the transitory and unavoidable nature of the sick role that made it acceptable to family and physician as an alternate mode of female behavior.[51]

The doctor's ambivalence toward the hysterical woman, already rooted as we have seen in professional and sexual uncertainties, may well have been reinforced by his complicitory role within the family. It was for this reason that the disease's erratic pattern, its chronic nature, its lack of a determinable organic etiology, and the patient's seeming failure of will, so angered him. Even if she were not a conscious malingerer, she might well be guilty of self-indulgence and moral delinquency. By diagnosing her as ill, he had in effect created or permitted the hysterical woman to create a bond between himself and her. Within the family configuration he had sided with her against her husband or other male family members--men with whom he would normally have identified.[52]

The quintessential sexual nature of hysteria further complicated the doctor's professional stance. As we have already seen, the hysterical patient in her role as woman may well have mobilized whatever ambivalence towards sex a particular physician felt. In a number of cases, moreover, the physician also played the role of oedipal father figure to the patient's child-woman role, and in such instances his complicity was not only moral and intellectual but sexual as well. These doctors had become part of a domestic triangle--a husband's rival, the fatherly attendant of a daughter. This intra-family role may therefore go far to explain the particularly strident and suspicious tone which characterized much of the clinical discussion of hysteria. The physician had, by his alertness to deception and self-indulgence and by his therapeutic skills, to prevent the hysterical woman from using her disease to avoid her feminine duties--and from making him an unwitting accomplice in her deviant role. While tied to her as physician and thus legitimizer of her sick role, he had also to preserve his independence.

Although much of this interpretation must remain speculative, both the tone and substance of contemporary medical reaction to the female hysteric tends to confirm these inferences. Physicians were concerned with--and condemned--the power which chronic illness such as hysteria gave a woman over her family. Many women, doctors noted with annoyance, enjoyed this power and showed no inclinations to get well: it is hardly coincidental that most late-nineteenth-century authorities agreed that removal from her family was a necessary first step in attempting to cure the hysterical patient.[53]

Not only did the physician condemn the hysteric's power within her family, he was clearly sensitive to her as a threat to his own prestige and authority. It is evident from their writings that many doctors felt themselves to be locked in a power struggle with their hysterical patients. Such women, doctors claimed, used their symptoms as weapons in asserting autonomy in relation to their physician; in continued illness was their victory. Physicians perceived hysterical women as unusually intractable and self-assertive. Although patients and women, they reserved the right to judge and approve their male physician's every action. Indeed, much of the medical literature on hysteria is devoted to providing doctors with the means of winning this war of wills. Physicians felt that they must dominate the hysteric's will; only in this way, they wrote, could they bring about her permanent cure. "Do not flatter yourselves. . . that you will gain an easy victory," Dr. L. C. Grey told a medical school class in 1888:

> On the contrary, you must expect to have your temper,
> your ingenuity, your nerves tested to a degree that can-
> not be surpassed even by the greatest surgical opera-
> tions. I maintain that the man who has the nerve and
> the tact to conquer some of these grave cases of hys-
> teria has the nerve and the tact that will make him
> equal to the great emergencies of life. Your patient
> must be taught day by day . . . by steady resolute,
> iron-willed determination and tact--that combination
> which the French . . . call "the iron hand beneath the
> velvet glove."[54]

"Assume a tone of authority which will of itself almost compel submission," Robert Carter directed. "If a patient . . . interrupts the speaker, she must be told to keep silence and to listen; and must be told, moreover, not only in a voice that betrays no impatience and no anger, but in such a manner as to convey the speaker's full conviction that the command will be immediately obeyed."[55]

Much of the treatment prescribed by physicians for hysteria reflects, in its draconic severity, their need to exert control--and, when thwarted, their impulse to punish. Doctors frequently recommended suffocating hysterical women until their fits stopped, beating them across the face and body with wet towels, ridiculing and exposing them in front of family and friends, showering them with icy water. "The mode adopted to arrest this curious malady," a physician connected with a large mental hospital wrote,

> consists in making some strong and sudden impression on
> the mind through . . . the most potent of all impress-
> ions, fear. . . . Ridicule to a woman of sensitive mind,
> is a powerful weapon. . . but there is no emotion equal
> to fear and the threat of personal chastisement. . .
> They will listen to the voice of authority.[56]

When, on the other hand, the hysterical patient proved tract-
able, gave up her fits or paralyses and accepted the physician as
saviour and moral guide, he no longer had to appear in the posture
of chastising father. He could respond to his hysterical patient
with fondness, sympathy, and praise. No longer was she thwarting
him with "temper, tears, tricks, and tantrums"--as one doctor
chose to title a study of hysteria.[57] Her cure demonstrated that
he had mastered her will and body. The successful father-like
practitioner had restored another wayward woman to her familial
duties. Thomas Addis Emmett, pioneer gynecological specialist,
recalled with ingenuous candor his mode of treating hysterics:

> the patient . . . was a child in my hands. In some
> respects the power gained was not unlike that obtained
> over a wild beast except that in one case the domination
> would be due to fear, while with my patient as a rule,
> it would be the desire to please me and to merit my
> approval from the effort she would make to gain self-
> control. I have at times been depressed with the re-

sponsibility attending the blind influence I have often been able to gain over the nervous women under my influence.[58]

Not surprisingly, S. Weir Mitchell ended one of his treatises on hysteria with the comment that doctors, who knew and understood all women's petty weaknesses, who could govern and forgive them, made the best husbands.[59] Clearly the male physician who treated the hysterical woman was unable to escape the sex role relations that existed within nineteenth-century society generally.

III

The hysterical female thus emerges from the essentially male medical literature of the nineteenth century as a "child-woman," highly impressionable, labile, superficially sexual, exhibitionistic, given to dramatic body language and grand gestures, with strong dependency needs and decided ego weaknesses. She resembled in many ways the personality type referred to by Guze in 1967 as a "hysterical personality," or by Kernberg in 1968 as an "infantile personality."[60] But in a very literal sense these characteristics of the hysteric were merely hypertrophied versions of traits and behavior commonly reinforced in female children and adolescents. At a time when American society accepted egalitarian democracy and free will as transcendent social values, women, as we have seen, were nevertheless routinely socialized to fill a weak, dependent and severely limited social role. They were sharply discouraged from expressing competition or mastery in such "masculine" areas

as physical skill, strength and courage, or in academic or com-
mercial pursuits, while at the same time they were encouraged to
be coquettish, entertaining, non-threatening and nurturant. Overt
anger and violence were forbidden as unfeminine and vulgar. The
effect of this socialization was to teach women to have a low
evaluation of themselves, to significantly restrict their ego
functions to low prestige areas, to depend on others and to al-
truistically wish not for their own worldly success, but for that
of their male supporters.

In essence, then, many nineteenth-century women reached
maturity with major ego weaknesses and with narrowly limited compensatory ego strengths, all of which implies, I think, a generic
relationship between this pattern of socialization and the adop-
tion of hysterical behavior by particular individuals. It seems
plausible to suggest that a certain percentage of nineteenth-century women faced with stress developing out of their own peculiar
personality needs or because of situational anxieties might well
have defended themselves against such stress by regressing towards
the childish hyper-femininity of the hysteric. The discontinuity
between the roles of courted woman and pain-bearing, self-sacrificing wife and mother, the realities of an unhappy marriage, the
loneliness and chagrin of spinsterhood may all have made the
petulant infantilism and narcissistic self-assertion of the hysteric a necessary alternative to women who felt unfairly deprived
of their promised social role and who had few strengths with which
to adapt to a more trying one. Society had indeed structured this
regression by consistently reinforcing those very emotional traits
characterized in the stereotype of the female--and caricatured in

the symptomatology of the hysteric. At the same time, the nineteenth-century female hysteric also exhibited a significant level of hostility and aggression—rage—which may have led in turn to her depression and to her self-punishing psychosomatic illness. In all these ways, then, the hysterical woman can be seen as both product and indictment of her culture.

I must conclude with a caution. The reasons why individuals displayed that pattern of behavior called by nineteenth-century physicians "hysteria" must in individual cases remain moot. What this paper has sought to do is to suggest why certain symptoms were available and why women, in particular, tended to resort to them. It has sought as well to use the reactions of contemporaries to illuminate female-male and intrafamilial role realities. As such it has dealt with hysteria as a social role produced by and functional within a specific set of social circumstances.

FOOTNOTES

[1] For a review of the recent psychiatric literature on hysteria see Aaron Lazare, "The Hysterical Character in Psychoanalytic Theory: Evolution and Confusion," **Archives of General Psychiatry,** XXV (August, 1971), pp. 131-137; Barbara Ruth Easser and S. R. Lesser, "Hysterical Personality: A Reevaluation," **Psychoanalytic Quarterly,** XXXIV (1965), pp. 390-405, and Marc H. Hollander, "Hysterical Personality." **Comments on Contemporary Psychiatry, I** (1971), pp. 17-24.

[2] Elizabeth Zetzel, **The Capacity for Emotional Growth, Theoretical and Clinical Contributions to Psychoanalysis, 1943-1969** (London: Hogarth Press, 1970), Chap. 1-f, "The So-Called Good Hysteric."

[3] David Shapiro, **Neurotic Styles,** (New York: Basic Books, 1965).

[4] The argument can be made that hysteria exists among men and therefore is not exclusively related to the female experience; the question is a complex one, and I am presently at work on a parallel study of male hysteria. There are, however, four brief points concerning male hysteria that I would like to make. First, to this day hysteria is still believed to be principally a female "disease" or behavior pattern. Second, the male hysteric is usually seen by physicians as somehow different. Today it is a truism that hysteria in males is found most frequently among homosexuals; in the nineteenth century men diagnosed as hysterics came almost exclusively from a lower socio-economic status than their physicians--immigrants, especially "new immigrants," miners, railroad workers, blacks. Third, since it was defined by society as a female disease, one may hypothesize that there was some degree of female identification among the men who assumed a hysterical role. Lastly, we must recall that a most common form of male hysteria was battle fatigue and shell shock. I should like to thank Erving Goffman for the suggestion that the soldier is in an analogous position to women regarding autonomy and power.

[5] The word choose, even in quotes, is value-laden. I do not mean to imply that hysterical women consciously chose their behavior. I feel that three complex factors interacted to make hysteria a real behavioral option for American women: first, the various experiences that caused a woman to arrive at adulthood with significant ego weaknesses; second, certain socialization patterns and cultural values which made hysteria a readily available alternate behavior pattern for women, and third, the secondary gains conferred by the hysterical role in terms of enhanced power within the family. Individual cases presumably each represented their own peculiar balance of these factors, all of which will be discussed in this paper.

[6] Nineteenth-century hysteria has attracted a good number of students: two of the most important are Henri F. Ellenberger, **The Discovery of the Unconscious** (New York: Basic Books, 1970), and

Ilza Veith, **Hysteria: The History of a Disease** (Chicago: University of Chicago Press, 1965). Ellenberger and Veith approach hysteria largely from the framework of intellectual history. For a review of Veith see Charles E. Rosenberg, "Historical Sociology of Medical Thought," **Science,** CL (October 15, 1965), p. 330. For two studies which view nineteenth-century hysteria from a more sociological perspective see Esther Fischer-Homberger, "Hysterie und Misogynie: Ein Aspekt des Hysteriegeschichte," **Gesnerus,** XXVI (1969), pp. 117-127, and Marc H. Hollander, "Conversion Hysteria: A Post-Freudian Reinterpretation of Nineteenth-Century Psychosocial Data," **Archives of General Psychiatry,** XXVI (1972), pp. 311-314.

[7]I would like to thank Renee Fox, Cornelia Friedman, Erving Goffman, Charles E. Rosenberg and Paul Rosenkrantz for having read and criticized this paper. I would also like to thank my clinical colleagues Phillip Mechanick, Henry Bachrach, Ellen Berman, and Carol Wolman of the Psychiatry Department of the University of Pennsylvania for similiar assistance. Versions of this paper were presented to the Institute of the Pennsylvania Hospital, the Berkshire Historical Society, and initially, in October 1971, at the Psychiatry Department of Hannehmann Medical College, Philadelphia.

[8]This summary of woman's role and role socialization is drawn from a larger study of male and female gender roles and gender role socialization in the United States from 1785 to 1895 on which I am presently engaged. This research has been supported by both the Grant Foundation, New York City and the National Institute of Child Health and Human Development, N.I.H. It is difficult to refer succinctly to the wide range of sources on which this paragraph is based. Such a role model appears in virtually every nineteenth-century woman's magazine, in countless guides to young women and young wives and in etiquette books. For a basic secondary source see Barbara Welter, "The Cult of True Womanhood," **American Quarterly,** XVIII (1966), pp. 151-174. For an excellent over-all history of women in America see Eleanor Flexner, **Century of Struggle,** (Cambridge, Massachusetts: Harvard University Press, 1959).

[9]For the daily activities of a nineteenth-century American housewife see, for example, **The Maternal Physican: By an American Matron** (New York: Isaac Riley, 1811. Reprinted New York: Arno Press, 1972); Hugh Smith, **Letters to Married Ladies** (New York: Bliss, White and G. & C. Carvill, 1827); John S. C. Abbott, **The Mother at Home** (Boston: Crocker and Brewster, 1833); Lydia H. Sigourney, **Letters to Mothers** (New York: Harper & Brothers, 1841); Mrs. C. A. Hopkinson, **Hints for the Nursery or the Young Mother's Guide** (Boston: Little, Brown & Company, 1836); Catherine Beecher and Harriet Beecher Stowe, **The American Woman's Home** (New York: J. B. Ford & Company, 1869). For an excellent secondary account of the southern woman's domestic life see Anne Firor Scott, **The Southern Lady** (Chicago: Unversity of Chicago Press, 1970).

[10]Nineteenth-century domestic medicine books, gynecological

textbooks, and monographs on the diseases of women provide a detailed picture of women's diseases and health expectations.

[11]S. Weir Mitchell, **Doctor and Patient** (Philadelphia: J. B. Lippincott Company, 1877), pp.84, 92.

[12]See among others Edward H. Dixon, **Woman and Her Diseases** (New York: Charles H. Ring, 1846), pp. 135-136; Alice Stockham, **Tokology: A Book for Every Woman** (Chicago: Sanitary Publishers, 1887), p. 83; Sarah A. Stevenson, **Physiology of Women**, 2nd edn. (Chicago: Cushing, Thomas & Co., 1881), p. 91; Henry Pye Chavasse, **Advice to a Wife and Counsel to a Mother** (Philadelphia: J. B. Lippincott, 1891), p. 97. A Missouri physican reported the case of a twenty-eight year old middle class woman with two children. Shortly after the birth of her second child, she miseed her period, believed herself to be pregnant for the third time and succumbed to hysterical symptoms: depression, headaches, vomiting and seizures. Her doctor concluded that she had uterine disease, exacerbated by pregnancy. He aborted her and reported a full recovery the following day. George J. Engelmann, "A Hystero-Psychosis Epilepsy Dependent upon Erosions of the Cervix Uteri," **St. Louis Clinic Record** (1878), pp. 321-324. For similar cases, see A. B. Arnold, "Hystero-Hypochondriasis," **Pacific Medical Journal**, XXXIII (1890), pp. 321-324, and George J. Engelmann, "Hystero-neurosis," **Transactions of the American Gynecological Association**, II (1877),pp.513-518.

[13]For a study of declining nineteenth-century American birth rates see Yasukichi Yasuba, **Birth Rates of the White Population in the United States, 1800-1860** (Baltimore: Johns Hopkins University Press, 1962) and J. Potter, "American Population in the Early National Period," in **Proceedings of Section V of the Fourth Congress of the International Economic History Association**, Paul Deprez, ed., (Winnipeg, 1970), pp. 55-69.

[14]For a useful general discussion of women's changing roles see Eleanor Flexner, **op. cit.**

[15]For a discussion of birth control and its effect on domestic relations see Carroll Smith-Rosenberg and Charles E. Rosenberg, "The New Woman and the Troubled Man: Medical and Biological Views of Women in Nineteenth-century America," **Journal of American History** (in press).

[16]William A. Hammond, **On Certain Conditions of Nervous Derangement** (New York: G. P. Putnam's Sons, 1881), p. 42; S. Weir Mitchell, **Lectures on the Diseases of the Nervous System, Especially in Women**, 2nd edn. (Philadelphia, Lea Brothers & Co., 1885), pp. 114, 110; Charles K. Mills, "Hysteria," in **A System of Practical Medicine by American Authors**, William Pepper, ed., assisted by Louis Starr, vol. V. "Disease of the Nervous System" (Philadelphia: Lea Brothers & Co., 1883), p. 213; Charles E. Lockwood, "A Study of Hysteria and Hypochondriasis," **Transactions of the New York State Medical Association**, XII (1895), pp. 340-351. E. H. Van Deusen, Superintendent of the Michigan Asylum for the Insane reported that nervousness, hysteria and neurasthenia were common

among farm women and resulted, he felt, from the social and intellectual deprivation of their isolated lives. Van Deusen, "Observations on a Form of Nervous Prostration," **American Journal of Insanity**, XXV (1869), p. 447. Significantly most English and American authorities on hysteria were members of a medical elite who saw the wealthy in their private practices and the very poor in their hospital and dispensary work. Thus the observation that hysteria occurred in different social classes was often made by the very same clinicians.

[17]Thomas Sydenham, "Epistolary Dissertation," in **The Works of Thomas Sydenham, M.D. . . . with a Life of the Author**, R. G. Latham, ed., 2 vols. (London: New Sydenham Society, 1850), II, p. 85.

[18]Some women diagnosed as hysterics displayed quite bizarre behaviour—including self-mutilation and hallucinations. Clearly a certain percentage of these women would be diagnosed today as schizophrenic. The majority of the women diagnosed as hysterical, however, did not display such symptoms, but rather appear from clinical descriptions to have had a personality similar to that considered hysterical by mid-twentieth-century psychiatrists.

[19]For three typical descriptions of such seizures, see Buel Eastman, **Practical Treatise on Diseases Peculiar to Women and Girls** (Cincinnati: C. Cropper & Son, 1848), p. 40; Samuel Ashwell, **A Practical Treatise on the Diseases Peculiar to Women** (London: Samuel Highley, 1844), pp. 210-212; William Campbell, **Introduction to the Study and Practice of Midwifery and the Diseases of Children** (London: Longman, Rees, Orme, Brown, Green & Longman, 1833), pp. 440-442.

[20]E. H. Dixon, **op. cit.**, p. 133.

[21]For examples of mid-nineteenth-century hysterical symptoms see Colombat de L'Isere, **A Treatise on the Diseases and Special Hygiene of Females**, trans. with additions by Charles D. Meigs, (Philadelphia: Lea and Blanchard, 1845), pp. 522, 527-530; Gunning S. Bedford, **Clinical Lectures on the Diseases of Women and Children** (New York: Samuel S. & W. Wood, 1855), p. 373.

[22]Robert B. Carter, **On the Pathology and Treatment of Hysteria** (London: John Churchill, 1853), p. 3.

[23]See, for example, F. C. Skey, **Hysteria** (New York: A. Simpson, 1867), pp. 66, 71, 86; Mary Putnam Jacobi, "Hysterical Fever," **Journal of Nervous and Mental Disease**, XV (1890), pp. 373-388; Landon Carter Grey, "Neurasthenia: Its Differentiation and Treatment," **New York Medical Journal**, XLVIII (1888), p. 421

[24]See, for example, George Preston, **Hysteria and Certain Allied Conditons**, (Philadelphia: P. Blakiston, Son & Co., 1897), pp. 31, 53; Charles E. Lockwood, **op. cit.** p. 346; Buel Eastman, **op. cit.**, p. 39; Thomas More Madden, **Clinical Gynecology**, (Philadelphia: J. B. Lippincott, 1895), p. 472.

[25]See W. Symington Brown, **A Clinical Handbook on the Diseases**

of Women, (New York: William Wood & Company, 1882); Charles L. Dana, "A Study of the Anaesthesias of Hysteria," **American Journal of the Medical Sciences** (October, 1890), p. 1; William S. Playfair, **The Systematic Treatment of Nerve Prostration and Hysteria**, (Philadelphia: Henry C. Lea's Son & Co., 1883). p. 29.

[26]For a discussion of the importance of creating such organic etiologies in the legitimization of an increasingly large number of such "functional" ills, see Charles E. Rosenberg, "The Place of George M. Beard in Nineteenth-Century Psychiatry," **Bulletin of the History of Medicine**, XXXVI (1962), pp. 245-259. See also Owsei Temkin's discussion in his classic history of epilepsy, **The Falling Sickness**, 2nd edn., rev. (Baltimore: Johns Hopkins University Press, 1971), of the importance placed by neurologists in the late nineteenth century upon the differentiation of epilepsy and hysteria.

[27]William Campbell, **op. cit.**, pp. 440-441; Walter Channing, **Bed Case: Its History and Treatment** (Boston: Ticknor and Fields, 1860), pp. 41-42, 49. Charles L. Mix, "Hysteria: Its Nature and Etiology," **New York Medical Journal**, LXXII (August, 1900), pp. 183-189.

[28]George Preston, **op. cit.**, pp. 96-97.

[29]Samuel Ashwell, **op. cit.**, p. 226.

[30]Charles K. Mills, **op. cit.**, p. 258.

[31]S. Weir Mitchell, **Lectures on the Diseases of the Nervous System, op. cit.**, p. 66.

[32]Thomas More Madden, **op. cit.**, p. 474. The uterine origin of hysteria was by far the most commonly held opinion throughout the eighteenth and nineteenth centuries. Some believed it to be the exclusive cause, others to be among the most important causes. For three typical examples see: Alexander Hamilton, **A Treatise on the Management of Female Complaints and of Children in Early Infancy** (Edinburgh: Peter Hill, 1792), pp. 51-53. George J. Engelmann, "Hystero-Neurosis," **op. cit.**, note 12; Augustus P. Clarke, "Relations of Hysteria to Structural Changes in the Uterus and its Adnexa," **American Journal of Obstetrics**, XXXIII (1894), pp. 477-483. The uterine theory came under increasing attack during the late nineteenth century. See Hugh J. Patrick, "Hysteria; Neurasthenia," **International Clinics**, III (1898), pp. 183-184; F. C. Skey, **op. cit.**, p. 68.

[33]Robert Barnes, **Medical and Surgical Diseases of Women**, (Philadelphia: H. C. Lea, 1874), p. 101; S. D. Hopkins, "A Case of Hysteria Simulating Organic Disease of the Brain," **Medical Fortnightly**, XI (July 1897), p. 327; C. K. Mills, **op. cit.**, p. 218; J. Leonard Corning, **A Treatise on Hysteria and Epilepsy** (Detroit: George S. Davis, 1888), p. 2; August A. Eshner, "Hysteria in Early Life," read before the Philadelphia County Medical Society, June 23, 1897.

[34]For examples of such concern and complexity, see A. A. King, "Hysteria," **The American Journal of Obstetrics**, XXIV (May, 1891) pp. 513-515; Marshall Hall, **Commentaries Principally on the Diseases of Females** (London: Sherwood, Gilbert and Piper, 1830), p. 118; C. L'Iâre, op. cit., p. 530.

[35]Robert B. Carter, op. cit., p. 140; J. L. Corning, op. cit., p. 70; Mills, op. cit., p. 218.

[36]Preston, op. cit., p. 36.

[37]See, for example: Mitchell, **Lectures on the Diseases of the Nervous System**, p. 170; Rebecca B. Gleason, M.D., of Elmira, New York, quoted by M L. Holbrook, **Hygiene of the Brain and Nerves and the Cure of Nervousness** (New York: M. L. Holbrook & Company, 1878), pp. 270-271.

[38]S. Weir Mitchell, **Fat and Blood** (Philadelphia: J. B. Lippincott, 1881), pp. 30-31.

[39]Lockwood, op. cit., pp. 342-343; virtually every authority on hysteria echoed these sentiments.

[40]Alexander Hamilton, op. cit., p. 52; Dixon, op. cit., pp. 142-143; Ashwell, op. cit., p. 217; Mills, op.cit., p. 230.

[41]Walter Channing, op. cit., p. 28.

[42]Robert B. Carter, op. cit., p. 113.

[43]Mary P. Jacobi, op. cit., pp. 384-388; M. E. Dirix, **Woman's Complete Guide to Health** (New York: W. A. Townsend & Adams, 1869), p. 24; E. B. Foote, **Medical Common Sense** (New York: Published by the author, 1864), p. 167.

[44]Reuben Ludlum, **Lectures, Clinical and Didactic, on the Diseases of Women** (Chicago: C. S. Halsey, 1872), p. 87; Robert Barnes, op. cit., p. 247. In 1847, the well-known Philadelphia gynecologist, Charles D. Meigs, had asked his medical school class the rhetorical question: "What is her erotic state? What the protean manifestations of the life force developed by a reproductive irritation which you call hysteria." Meigs, **Lectures on the Distinctive Characteristics of the Female**, delivered before the Class of Jefferson Medical College, January 5, 1847 (Philadelphia: T. K. & P. G. Collins, 1847), p. 20.

[45]Thomas Laycock, **Essay on Hysteria**, pp. 76, 103, 105. See also Graham J. Barker-Benfield, "The Horrors of the Half-Known Life" (unpublished Ph.D. thesis, University of California at Los Angeles, 1969) and Ann Douglas Wood, "The Fashionable Diseases: Women's Complaints and Their Treatment in Nineteenth Century America," **Journal of Interdisciplinary History** (in press) for a speculative psychoanalytic approach to gynecological practice in nineteenth-century America.

[46]Dixon, op. cit., p. 134: J. Leonard Corning, op. cit., p.

70; William Murray, **A Treatise on Emotional Disorders of the Sympathetic System of the Nerves**, (London: John Churchill, 1866). An extensive nineteenth-century masturbation literature exists. See, for example, Samuel Gregory, **Facts and Important Information for Young Women on the Self-Indulgence of the Sexual Appetite** (Boston: George Gregory, 1857), and Calvin Cutter, **The Female Guide: Containing Facts and Information upon the Effects of Masturbation** (West Brookfield, Mass.: Charles A. Mirick, 1844). Most general treatises on masturbation refer to its occurrence in females.

[47]Preston, **op. cit.**, p. 37; Carter, **op. cit.**, pp. 46, 90. Nineteenth-century physicians maintained a delicate balance in their view of the sexual etiology of hysteria. Any deviation from moderation could cause hysteria or insanity: habitual masturbation, extended virginity, over-indulgence, prostitution, or sterility.

[48]Skey, **op. cit.**, p. 63.

[49]Mitchell, **Lectures on the Diseases of the Nervous System**, p. 266; S. Weir Mitchell, **Fat and Blood, op. cit.**, p. 37.

[50]Carter, **op. cit.**, p. 58.

[51]For an exposition of this argument see Erving Goffman, "Insanity of Place," **Psychiatry**, XXXII (1969), pp. 357-388.

[52]Such complaints are commonplace in the medical literature. See Mitchell, **Lectures**, p. 67; Mitchell, **Doctor and Patient, op. cit.**, p. 117; Robert Thornton, **The Hysterical Women: Trails, Tears, Tricks and Tantrums**, (Chicago: Donohue & Henneberry, 1893), pp. 97-78; Channing, **op. cit.**, pp. 35-37; L'Iêre, **op. cit.**, p. 534.

[53]The fact that the physician was at the same time employed and paid by the woman or her family--in a period when the profession was far more competitive and economically insecure than it is in mid-twentieth century--implied another level of stress and ambiguity.

[54]Channing, **op. cit.**, p. 22; Thomas A. Emmett, **Principles and Practices of Gynecology** (Philadelphia: H. C. Lea, 1879), p. 107; L. C. Grey, "Clinical Lecture," p. 132.

[55]Carter, **op. cit.**, p. 119; Ashwell, **op. cit.**, p. 227.

[56]Skey, **op. cit.**, p. 60.

[57]Robert Thornton, **op. cit.**

[58]Thomas A. Emmett, **Incidents of My Life**, (New York: G. P. Putnam's Sons, 1911), p. 210. These are Emmett's recollections at the end of a long life. It is interesting that decades earlier Emmett, in discussing treating hysterical women, had confessed in hostile frustration that "in fact the physician is helpless

. . . ." Emmett, **Principles and Practices, op. cit.,** p. 107.

[59]Mitchell, **Doctor and Patient,** pp. 99-100.

[60]Samuel Guze, "The Diagnosis of Hysteria: What are We Trying to Do," **American Journal of Psychiatry,** CXXIV (1967), pp. 494-498; Otto Kernberg, "Borderline Personality Organization," **Journal of the American Psychoanalytical Association,** XV (1967), pp. 641-685. For a critical discussion of the entire problem of diagnosis, see Henry Bachrach, "In Defense of Diagnosis," **Psychiatry** (in press).

AUTHOR'S NOTE

This project was supported in part by grant No. 7 F02 HD48800-01Al from the National Institutes of Health and by a grant from the Grant Foundation, New York.

CHAPTER 4

FREUD, ADLER, AND WOMEN: POWERS OF THE "WEAK" AND "STRONG"*

Joseph L. DeVitis

With his special gifts [the artist] molds his fantasies
into a new kind of reality, and men concede them a
justification as valuable reflections of actual life.
Thus by a certain path he actually becomes the hero,
king, creator, favorite, he desires to be, without
pursuing the circuitous path of creating real alternatives in the outer world.

--Freud, "Formulations Regarding the Two

Principles in Mental Functioning"[1]

This essay discusses Freud's original psychoanalytic notions
on women and morality and their influence on constructions of
personality, power, culture, and socioeducational change.   It
contends that the traditional Freudian model views women from a
disjointed perspective, i.e., from (a) an avowedly genetic/biolog-
ical base which posits an internal, intrapsychic frame of reference; and (b) one which erroneously extrapolates from that base to
build claims, presumably from universal necessity, which are
actually expressions of mutable sociohistorical vicissitudes. The

general upshot of such claims has been to assign women to subordinancy and oppression. Freudian critics such as Alfred Adler employ
a larger external lens to focus women's lives in a wider context
of "social interest" and social relationship--one which foreshad-
ows Carol Gilligan's recent work in psychological theory and
women's moral development.[2] In her pioneering research, Gilligan
studies Freud at length but never mentions Adler. It will be
shown that an acquaintance with Adler's analysis would actually
complement and amplify her own argument. Such a reconceptualiza-
tion provides another way of looking at who is "weak" and
"strong"; indeed, it casts power and personality theory in an
altogether new light. In this different context, Freud's view,
which is characterized as essentially one of "enlightened self-
interest," can be seen to be antithetical to a broader development
toward interpersonal synthesis and social reality. (For the sake
of internal consistency and contextual argument, the paper will
analyze psychoanalytic language more or less on its own terms. In
a sense, it will temporarily "suspend belief" about certain Freudian and Adlerian assumptions--many of which appear to be more
prescriptive than descriptive.)

FREUDIAN MAN: FRUSTRATED, "HEROIC" INDIVIDUALISM

Freud's most classic statement of his theoretical and therapeutic mission is contained in this oft-repeated passage from his
New Introductory Lectures on Psychoanalysis: "[My] intention is,
indeed, to strengthen the ego [rationality and reality principle],
to make it more independent of the superego [ego-ideal and

conscience], to widen its field of perception and enlarge its
organization, so that it can appropriate fresh portions of the id
[sexual instincts]. Where id was, there ego shall be."[3] Similarly, in **The Future of an Illusion,** Freud points to an optimal
realization of self-control through an almost stoical exertion of
rationality.[4] Freud invokes such individual self-control because
he contends that a substantial measure of repression is necessary
to balance man's psychic apparatus, especially id impulses, with
the demands of culture. He employs repression to explicate an
irreconcilable conflict between individual autonomy and cultural
restraint. Thus Freud calls upon man to sublimate what he assumes
to be primary aggressive instincts with what is necessary to
constitute civilization: "Civilization thus obtains mastery over
the dangerous love of aggression in individuals by enfeebling and
disarming it, and setting up an institution [super-ego] within
their minds to keep watch over it, like a garrison in a conquered
city."[5] The demands of civilized life require man to struggle
with repression, i.e., to practice a sort of frustrated, "heroic"
individualism. To do otherwise would imperil cultural cohesion,
which would, in turn, endanger individual man. This scenario
summarizes Freud's version of enlightened self-interest--one which
does not bring wholly glad tidings. As therapist and social
analyst, Freud may appear to make men "wiser," but never fully
"happy" or "good":

> The aim of Freudian psychiatry is. . .the reconciliation
> of instinct and intelligence. The intellect is set to
> helping the instincts develop, tolerantly, like a

prudent teacher. Conscience, however, directs us to repress the instincts. The conscience-stricken thus do not appear by Freudian standards to be very intelligent. By viewing conscience as in opposition to intelligence, Freud exhibits a prejudice against virtue fairly common among secular intellectuals---the idea that the merely good person is not likely to be either very clever or very strong.[6]

Though Freudian theory and therapy may provide a modicum of self-insight, their very foundational principle, i.e., the analysis and treatment of the individual, tends to separate thought and practice from wider social and historical contexts. Borrowing one of Freud's own terms, this separation amounts to a curious kind of **displacement**, whereby an internal, intrapsychic paradigm sets man apart from larger social reality. Freud insists that "throughout the life of the individual there is a constant replacement of the external compulsion by the internal."[7] **Ipso facto**, Freud's theoretical base becomes almost solipsistic. Moreover, in practice, it largely compels patients to "blame" themselves, rather than any external social constraints, for anything they cannot "overcome."[8] In this sense, Freud's model of individualism asks man to be a tragic "heroic" figure on a stage without substantial social props. As such, man is doomed to perpetual frustration, if not always abject failure.

Even when it comes time to consider group psychology, Freud insists that "individual psychology is simultaneously social psychology."[9] Indeed, recent critics, including some psychoanalysts,

have argued that he reduces human relations to the level and
pattern of the psyche within the substructure of the nuclear
family.[10] As Freud himself puts it: "The relations of an individual to his parents and to his brothers and sisters, to the
object of his love, and to his physician [a transference figure
for individual family members]--in fact all the relations which
have hitherto been the chief subject of psychoanalytic research--
may claim to be considered as social phenomena."[11] This is not to
deny that family relations are social relations (fundamentally an
Adlerian argument) but to underline Freud's reductionism. In
essence, his major hypothesis about all social action is that it
recapitulates the emotional psyche of the family. He universalizes certain internalized family matrices, failing to weigh the
impact of dominant external social structures of particular times
and places (in his case, patriarchal Victorian society):

> The hero [Freudian man] is able to attain to "individual
> psychology" only because he internalizes his father at a
> deep enough level; he creates an "ego-ideal" in himself.
> Hence the mechanism for reproducing individuals--those
> who are free, who can think, who can restrain their emo-
> tions, who can be distinctive--is the key to history...
> [and] the mechanism for this degree of individualization
> is the patriarchal nuclear family.[12]

FREUDIAN WOMAN: EVE WITHOUT THE EMPEROR'S CULTURAL ARMOR

Freud's paradigm of the internalized patriarchal family and

his neglect of sociohistoric context make life a doubly dubious battle for Freudian woman, particularly as he casts much of the basis for morality in his own conjectural dramaturgy, i.e., the primal horde and Oedipus mythology. According to Freud, it is a psychological impossibility for girls to achieve a strong sense of morality because of what he assumes to be weaker superego development in females. Unlike boys, who presumably fear castration and thus internalize and identify with the father figure, girls are already "castrated" and thus cannot experience the same fears and threat of loss.[13] Consequently, Freudian woman is often reconciled to frustration, with fewer opportunities for heroism. In fact, her part in Freud's unfolding drama is more invidious: she is the temptress and scorner of civilization, the Eve-like character who squanders men's attempts to sublimate their energy to "higher" cultural tasks:

> The girl remains in the Oedipus situation for an indefinite period; she only abandons it late in life and then incompletely. The formation of the Super-Ego must suffer in these circumstances; it cannot attain the strength and independence which gives it cultural importance, and feminists are not pleased if one points to the way in which this factor affects the development of average feminine character.[14]

The next discord is caused by women, who soon become antithetical to cultural trends, and spread around them their conservative influence--the women who at the

beginning laid the foundation of culture by the appeal
of their love. Women represent the interests of the
family and the sexual life; the work of civilization has
become more and more men's business; it confronts them
with even harder tasks, compels them to sublimations of
instinct which women are not easily able to achieve.
Since man has not an unlimited amount of mental energy
at his disposal, he must accomplish his tasks by distributing his libido to the best advantage. What he
employs for cultural purposes he withdraws to a great
extent from women and his sexual life.[15]

These quotations are cited at length because they expose a number
of troublesome features in Freudian thought: (1) its superimposition of a Newtonian (energy) model of physics onto psychic
life; (2) its bifurcation of the instincts and rationality in the
classic Western formulation of "lower" and "higher" functions; (3)
the resultant frustration Freud posits for both men and women, the
locus of that frustration resting on the roles assigned to the
players; and (4) Freud's own almost imperceptible admission that
those roles may be more or less changeable, after all (if Freud
could only concede their sociohistoric underpinnings), i.e., his
Freudian slip to the effect that "civilization has become more and
more men's business."[16]

Undaunted in his Oedipal logic, Freud assigns the male the
role of cultural architect: "It seems that the male sex has taken
the lead in developing all these moral acquisitions; and that they
have been transmitted to the woman by cross-inheritance."[17] Like

Rousseau's Emile and his solicitous Sophie, Freud relegates woman to the hearth and home, presumably to fulfill her own psychological well-being. In Freud's scheme, childbearing and attendant household duties will partially compensate woman for her frustrating lack of a penis.[18] However, woman is unable to wear the Emperor's clothes or enjoy his status as "moral" and "cultural" leader. This is the case so long as the dominant culture views things through Freud's eyes; and dominant groups and institutions, male or otherwise, are slow to remove blinders which bestow certain prerogatives of definitional power. Likewise, other inhabitants of civilization, seeking after solutions for social cohesion and personal solace, mirror and accept interpretations of such cultural teachings as if they were "universal" and "objective" guides to heart and mind for generations to come:

The requirements of art, patriotism, morality in general and social ideals in particular, correctness in practical judgment and objectivity in theoretical knowledge, the energy and the profundity of life--all these are categories which belong as it were in their form and their claims to humanity in general, but in their actual historical configuration they are masculine throughout. Supposing that we describe these things, viewed as absolute ideas, by the single word "objective," we then find that in the history of our race the equation objective = masculine is a valid one.[19]

At this point it is appropriate to enlist some distinctions

made by one of Freud's major recent revisionists, Herbert Marcuse. Though he does not specifically treat the issue of women and morality in his **Eros and Civilization: A Philosophical Inquiry into Freud,** Marcuse's concepts of "basic" versus "surplus" repression shed light on the problem in question. Extrapolating on Freud's cultural paradigm, Marcuse defines "basic" repression as that modification of the "instincts necessary for the perpetuation of the human race in civilization," e.g., provision of food and shelter and combating of disease. By contrast, "surplus" repression refers to those "restrictions necessitated by social domination," i.e., additive forms of constraint over and above that which is vital to civilized life. Surplus-repression has been a result of sociohistory, not one of necessity; as such, it is amenable to social change.[20]

In his characterization of female physiology, Freud appears to extend a **prima facie** case of biological determination and differentiation (which he couches in "descriptive" terms of "unwelcome knowledge" of presumed feminine "deficiency") into an extra-layered case of surplus-repression. As Elizabeth Janeway points out:

Freud himself occasionally warned [in his essay on "Femininity"]. . .against the "superimposition" of unjustified significance on the facts of physical differences between the sexes. But these differences are just what he cites to account for the social roles of men and women, even though anyone reading him today can follow his arguments perfectly well (indeed better) by taking these differences as **symbolic** of assigned gender roles. . .of the socialization process of learning and accepting norms of behavior and expression.[21]

In this new light, "castration" anxiety itself becomes an additive cultural introjection (surplus-repression), not an inevitability (basic repression).

ADLER'S RESPONSE:

POWERS OF "SOCIAL INTEREST" AND "MASCULINE PROTEST"

It is difficult to conceptualize Adler's treatment of women and morality without first introducing his theory of "power." This is so because the notion of power is perhaps the most misconstrued concept in his psychology and because it is crucial to his discussion of human behavior. Initially, Adler borrowed Nietzsche's term "will to power," an adaptation which has plagued him and his followers to this day. Adler did not have in mind a striving for power over others when he used that phrase. Indeed, he viewed such behavior as "neurotic," in contrast to his explicit axiology, which was one of cooperation. The essence of the term "will to power" derives from his claim that man, from an original position of inferiority, should "strive toward overcoming" a feeling of powerlessness.[22] Later, Adler would make this distinction in his axiology clearer: "[The task of life is] to show the way in the reduction of the striving for personal power and in the education toward the community. . .and the development of social interest."[23] Thus, the terms "power" and "inferiority" are integral to Adler's most overarching principle, "social interest," which he characterizes as "compensation for all the natural weaknesses of individual human beings."[24] Social interest encompasses communal feeling, interpersonality, and empathy for others. Furthermore, it is a hypothesis of man which, if equally speculative, is nonetheless at counterpoint to Freud's more competitive, aggressive portrait.

Adler conceives of "social interest" as both inborn and capable of nurture and development. His "iron-clad law of social living" actually requires such growth if mankind is to survive and thrive: "The very concept of 'human being' includes our entire understanding of social feeling. . .[We have] always lived in groups, unless separated from one another artifically or through insanity. . .In the deepest sense, the feeling for the logic of human living together is social feeling."[25] Tied to his notion of "social interest" is the evolutionary unfolding of equality. As social interest increases, equality in all aspects of life becomes a necessity--one which rises out of the will to overcome, to withstand subordinate/superordinate relationships. According to Adler, such unequal relationships injure **both** parties. It is in this sense that he advocates the "equal worth of the sexes": "Women have to suffer because in our culture it is much easier for man to play the leading role. But the man also suffers because by his fictitious [spurious] superiority he loses touch with the underlying values."[26]

Adler also replaced the notion of "aggressive drives" (another **intrapsychic** Freudian concept) with his own more dialectical social dynamics because he wanted to avoid Freud's biological

reductionism. The term "masculine protest" became Adler's conceptual vehicle for expressing interpersonal interaction in social
contexts of inferiority/superiority. It signified a present, but
mutable, condition of "feminine" traits, primarily a feeling of
inferiority due to the social circumstances of male domination.
For Adler, the future antithesis to this situation is couched in
strivings for superiority in the sense of wanting to overcome
social conditions of subordinancy and oppression.[27] Freud de-
nounced Adler's theory of masculine protest by reducing it once
again to an example of the universal castration anxiety and aggressive propensities which he saw in mankind.[28]

In Marcusean terms, Adler recognized the difference between
basic and surplus-repression in ways which Freud did not. Adler
formulated "masculine protest" not in reference to physiological
sex differentiation, but in terms of culturally preferred criteria
favorable to males. Consequently, he viewed sexual inequality as
an unnecessary condition resulting more from social than biological determination:

> In our society, an exaggerated importance is attached to
> masculinity, and the inferiority of the female sex is
> assumed as a generally established principle. Even if
> sexual equality is admitted theoretically [social]
> actions. . .usually speak the contrary. . . From the
> earliest days the child is led to believe that the male
> is the more valuable sex.[29]

Accordingly, Adler renounced the attendant strife and competition which social and cultural circumstances bred between men and women. Seeing them as changeable conditions, he sought to modify circumstances through social reform. Whereas Freud's pessimism about change forestalled his considering reform, Adler established child guidance clinics (**Erziehungsberatungsstellen**) and experimental schools throughout Austria.[30] Modern developments show that Freudian psychiatry, despite its reliance on the theoretical paradigm of the family, has been rather reticent about the prac-tice of family **therapy**. This curious irony is largely due to the fact that its analytic focus of treatment remains essentially individualistic.[31]

Therapeutically, Adler's emphasis on social relationships is also distinct from Freudian practice. For Adler, the therapist is not a distant authoritative interpreter, but rather one who at-tempts to kindle social interest in tune with the client's own "private logic" and intentions. But self-insight (Freud's end of therapy) is insufficient, sometimes unnecessary, in Adlerian coun-seling; its aim is to **activate** the client in the **social** arena. As Adler sees it, to do otherwise is to risk mental illness. This seems to be a risk which Freud's internal, intrapsychic perspec-tive does not quite fathom. Indeed, one might argue that excess-ive self-analysis, even as self-insight, could conceivably foster a flight into various forms of pathology (e.g., narcissism and paranoia).

IMPLICATIONS FOR FUTURE MORAL AND SOCIAL DEVELOPMENT

In the years before the war,. . .I [Freud] made it a

rule never to take for treatment anyone who was not **sui juis**, independent of others in all the essential re-lations of life.[32]

This psychoanalytic parameter nicely encapsulates the main misgiving about Freudian thought and practice which runs through-out this paper. It is a misgiving that has apparently escaped many major paradigms of psychology since Freud, including Kohl-berg's present-day model of moral development. By focusing on **internal**, **individual**, and **differential** measures of man, such models appear to lapse into a certain kind of "theoretical ego-centrism."[33] In relying on such constructs as "genetic defic-iencies," "weak superegos," and "pre/post/conventional personal-ities," a certain set of preconceptions about the nature of human beings, their morality, and the possibilities for socioeducational change begins to emerge. A given belief system, or ideology, begins to mask and submerge other ways of looking at the nature of things and ideas. Other **possible** perspectives, e.g., those of **collective** and **external** reference, are thus seen as tangential to descriptive and explanatory reality.[34] Adler's view of women and morality would seem to reacquaint psychology with this now more subterranean but still important perspective. In David Bakan's more recent terminology, it points to possibilities for **communal** as well as "agentic" development.[35]

This is a development which is also postulated as a **possibil-ity** in Gilligan's research. While still speculative, somewhat intuitive, and therefore inconclusive, her counterparadigm to Kohlberg juxtaposes **particular social context** against his more hierarchical, invariant pattern of moral growth. Both Freud and Kohlberg (who studies primarily men) attempt to fit mankind into assumed universal thought structures undergirded by internal, **individualistic** frames of reference, (Fittingly, Kohlberg sees himself as a successor to Freud in the broad tradition of psychology.)[36] For example, Kohlberg's model of justice tends to concentrate on those rights, liberties, and duties (particularly protection of one's property) which are cornerstones of **liberal individualism.**[37] Similarly, Betty Sichel has argued that the rather "warm reception" given to Kohlberg's paradigm may be explained, in part, by its tendency to reinforce "current dominant views about pluralistic democracy and justice as fairness."[38]

On the other hand, Adler's response would seem to reinforce the basic thrust of Gilligan's findings for a language of care, responsibility, and not wanting to hurt others, i.e., that strain of morality which considers "sympathy, compassion, and human concern" as paramount.[39] If anything, Adler might actually serve to **extend** Gilligan's argument in that the latter speaks only in terms of **private** social relationships (e.g., family members, friends, and colleagues) rather than a larger social community.

In his emphasis on interpersonal social relationships, Adler, like Gilligan, does not fully account for larger, more amorphous power structures and sociopolitical constraints. Nor does he envision the deep-seated possibilities for conflict which are integral to Freud. For instance, Adler does not adequately distinguish the boundaries between social "cooperation" and social "constraint" or "conformity."[40] Though his social analysis lacks rigor and precision, it does allow for and encourage **collective**

public action in a manner unknown to Freud (and apparently many of
his successors). Freud took collective action to be largely
"regressive" and antithetical to intelligent self-restraint.[41]
Adler advocates the power of public, social solidarity as a cata-
lyst for change. This is because, unlike Freud, he does not posit
dialectical synthesis within a more or less self-contained individualistic ideal.[42] Indeed, the Adlerian perspective has much to
offer that minority wing of academic psychology and education
which is now attempting to combat "theoretical egocentrism" and
the more popular "cults of narcissism."

Significantly, Adlerian psychology has the added virtue of
relying on actual behavior as well as abstract thought in its
theory and practice. While the dominant Kohlbergian model of
moral development is grounded in hypothetical, imaginary constructions (what Mannheim termed a "contemplative" universe of
discourse), Adlerian agendas attend primarily to human action. As
Adler's principal disciple, Rudolf Dreikurs, once put it:
"Thoughts, desires, and emotions [fail] to give sufficient. .
.consideration [to] our actions--to what we do."[43] By contrast,
contemporary cognitive-structural models (constructed on attitud-
inal feedback) offer no conclusive proof that what subjects in
experiments say will be what they do.[44] Finally, there is a
considerable body of empirical evidence to show that engagement in
actual social interaction (coincidentally, interactions of relative equality) may, in fact, be the most effective way to develop
a morality of tolerance.[45] This is a moral pattern which Adler
pointed to for both men and women.

POSTSCRIPT

There were two groups in society whom Freud admitted he understood least. One was the artists (see prefatory note to this essay). The other, naturally enough, was women--that "dark continent" of his psychology which was "veiled in impenetrable obscurity."[46] For Freud, women played a certain subversive role in Victorian culture: that of the "hysteric."[47] Depending on how one interprets woman's role in society and how one measures personal intentions and cultural consequences, such a role may have been adaptive and necessary for feminine well-being and survival. Definitions of mental health, forces of strength and weakness, become problematical once one considers the context of thought and action. This is especially relevant when artistic "heroes," following Freud, define well-being and "mold fantasies" so that "real alternatives in the outer world" are never fully visualized and thus never seriously entertained as projects for social change.

One final irony: Josef Breuer and Freud's original example of a "hysteric" patient, Anna O., eventually became a prominent social reformer in Germany, working in the cause of women's emancipation. This occurred some years after she had left analysis, so we cannot be sure whether it had anything to do with her rebellion against Victorian sex roles. In 1922, Anna wrote: "If there is any justice in the next life women will make the laws there and men will bear the children."[48] One thing is sure: in this life, Freud himself never rebelled so completely.

FOOTNOTES

[1] Sigmund Freud, "Formulations Regarding the Two Principles in Mental Functioning," in **The Standard Edition of the Complete Psychological Works of Sigmund Freud**, vol. 12, ed. James Strachey (London: Hogarth Press, 1953-1966), p. 224.

[2] Carol Gilligan, **In a Different Voice: Psychological Theory and Women's Development** (Cambridge, Mass.: Harvard University Press, 1982).

[3] Sigmund Freud, "New Introductory Lectures on Psycho-analysis," in **Standard Edition**, vol. 12, p. 80.

[4] See generally Sigmund Freud, **The Future of an Illusion**, trans. W. D. Robson-Scott (Garden City, N.Y.: Doubleday, 1964). Freud fails to recognize fully that it is extremely difficult to exercise "rational" powers unless material and social circumstances are favorable to such exertion. For an argument on this theme, see Ernest Nagel, **Sovereign Reason: And Other Studies in the Philosophy of Science** (Glencoe, Ill.: Free Press, 1954), pp. 267, 274-75.

[5] Sigmund Freud, **Civilization and Its Discontents**, trans. J. Strachey (New York: W. W. Norton, 1961), p. 105.

[6] Philip Rieff, **Freud: The Mind of the Moralist** (Garden City, N.Y.: Doubleday, 1959), p. 305-6. Kurt Vonnegut pictures the Freudian dilemma more comically--and, of course, tragically: "[In] the suppression of an overactive conscience by the rest of the mind. . .the leader most prompt to appear. . .[is] Enlightened Self-Interest. . .It is essentially the black and white Jolly Roger, with these words written beneath the skull and crossbar, 'The hell with you, Jack, I've got mine!' [Thus]. . .a normal person, functioning well on the upper levels of a prosperous, industrialized society, can hardly hear his conscience at all." Given this sad state of affairs, Vonnegut finds only a rare few individuals, usually branded as fools, "who reach biological maturity still loving and wanting to help their fellow men." Vonnegut, **God Bless You, Mr. Rosewater: Or Pearls Before Swine** (New York: Dell, 1965), pp. 42-43.

[7] Sigmund Freud, "Thoughts for the Times on War and Death," in his **Civilization, War, and Death: Selections from Three Works by Sigmund Freud**, ed. John Rickman (London: Hogarth Press and the Institute of Psycho-Analysis, 1939), p. 9.

[8] William Ryan explores the enormous ramifications in public policy generated by internal, intrapsychic paradigms in his **Blaming the Victim** (New York: Pantheon, 1976). Ryan argues that such theoretical models, translated into policy, have been most injurious to those least prepared to cope within the social system, i.e., the poor. Cf. also Kenneth D. Benne, "The Process of Re-Education: An Assessment of Kurt Lewin's Views," **Groups and Organizational Studies** 1 (1976): 33, "Counseling and therapy have traditionally sought to facilitate change in persons with little

or no assumption of responsibility for facilitating changes in the cultural environment in which people function outside the counseling or therapeutic setting. This tends to place the entire burden of behavior [change] upon the individual."

[9]Sigmund Freud, **Group Psychology and the Analysis of the Ego**, trans. J. Strachey (New York: W. W. Norton, 1965), p. 3. Cf. Sigmund Freud, **New Introductory Lectures**, trans. J. Strachey (New York: W. W. Norton, 1964, p. 179: "For sociology, too, dealing as it does with the behavior of people in society, cannot be anything but applied psychology. Strictly speaking, there are only two sciences: psychology, pure and applied, and natural science."

[10]See W. R. Bion, **Experience in Groups** (New York: Ballantine, 1974).

[11]Freud, **Group Psychology**, p. 3.

[12]Mark Poster, **Critical Theory of the Family** (New York: Seabury, 1980), pp. 34-35.

[13]Freud, **New Introductory Lectures**, p. 166.

[14]Ibid. As Poster sees it, "The problem here is not a biological one: it is rather that Freud is blind to the power relationships of the family, seeing them as natural. Thus he assumes that the problem is the material lack of the penis, when it is already the valuation placed on the penis and on males in general by parents in Victorian society. It is also the limitations imposed on the mother in male-dominated society, limitations that are both sociological and psychological." Poster, **Critical Theory of the Family**, p. 209.

[15]Freud, **Civilization and Its Discontents**, p. 73.

[16]See also Freud, **The Future of an Illusion**, p. 10, where he comes to this same seemingly unwitting conclusion: "[Cultural] difficulties are not inherent in the nature of culture itself, but are conditioned by the imperfections of the cultural forms that have so far been developed." Freud's claims for weak superego structure in women exhibit a circular form of reasoning about culture: How is it possible for women to develop fully a "superego" (ego-ideal and conscience) without their being fully represented in a culture which supposedly forges superego development? Jean Baker Miller makes this point in her **Toward a New Psychology of Women** (Boston: Beacon Press, 1976), pp. 71-72.

[17]Sigmund Freud, **The Ego and the Id**, trans. Joan Riviere (New York: W. W. Norton, 1960), p. 50.

[18]Ibid.: "For the great majority of women the 'deprivation' sense is resolved, at least tolerably, through the specially feminine functions, directly by childbearing, more indirectly by childtending, by home-making or some kindred activity. In this way she becomes equal to man and is vindicated."

[19] Georg Simmel, **Philosophische Kultur**, as quoted in Karen Horney, "The Flight from Womanhood: The Masculinity-Complex in Woman as Viewed by Men and by Women," in her **Feminine Psychology**, ed. Harold Kelman (New York: W. W. Norton, 1967), pp. 55-56.

[20] Herbert Marcuse, **Eros and Civilization: A Philosophical Inquiry into Freud** (New York: Vintage Books, 1962), pp. 32-34. According to Marcuse, these distinctions eluded Freud due to his lack of a thoroughgoing critique of dominant socioeconomic systems within civilization. Though critical of this neglect, Marcuse is also apologetic to Freud to the extent that he sees psychoanalytic theory as potentially liberating, i.e., if it extrapolates from its analysis and transfigures those additive forms of "surplus-repression." Unfortunately, Marcuse does not analyze Freudian therapy on the gound that it is separable from its theory. However, divorce of theory and therapy was never Freud's intention; moreover, such a tack whould obviously obviate much of Marcuse's apology--if one agrees, with Freud, that his therapy was meant to cure the individual. In addition, Marcuse largely affirms Freud's reliance on patriarchal family structure as a testing ground for the reality principle, i.e., he views matriarchy as an insufficient, more "Idealistic" preparation for the tasks of life.

[21] Elizabeth Janeway, **Cross Sections: From a Decade of Change** (New York: William Morrow, 1982), pp. 78-79. See also Sigmund Freud, **Three Essays on the Theory of Sexuality**, trans. J. Strachey (1905; New York: Basic Books, 1962).

[22] Alfred Adler, **Co-operation Between the Sexes: Writings on Women and Men, Love and Marriage, and Sexuality**, ed. Heinz L. and Rowena R. Ansbacher (New York: W. W. Norton, 1978), pp. 49, 147-48, 168-69.

[23] Alfred Adler, **The Nervous Character: Fundamentals of a Comparative Individual Psychology and Psychotherapy**, 4th ed. (Munich: Bergmann, 1928, pp. iv-vi.

[24] Alfred Adler, **Problems of Neurosis** (London: Kegan Paul, 1929), p. 31.

[25] Adler, **Co-operation Between the Sexes**, p. 107. Freud was unable to appreciate any "oceanic" feeling or "sensation of 'eternity'" (what Adler termed the **sub specie aeternitatis** of "social interest") in his own theory. This feeling of social unity was rejected as illusory by Freud on the ground that "from my own experience I could not convince myself of the primary nature of such a feeling" and because "it fits in so badly with the fabric of our psychology." However, Freud did acknowledge that "this gives me no right to deny that [such feeling] does not in fact occur in other people." Yet he adds: "The only question is whether it is being correctly interpreted." Freud, **Civilization and Its Discontents**, 64 ff.

[26] Alfred Adler, **The Education of Children** (New York: Greenberg, 1930), p. 222. Adler's major disciple, Rudolf Dreikurs,

has extended this theme in his **Social Equality: The Challenge of Today** (Chicago: Regnery, 1971). For another submerged Victorian voice who bemoaned the "sultanlike" sense of superiority which subverted individual men and women, see John Stuart Mill, "On the Subjection of Women" (1869), in **The Feminist Papers: From Adams to de Beauvoir**, ed. Alice Rossi (New York: Columbia University press, 1973).

[27]Ansbacher, in Adler, **Co-operation Between the Sexes**, pp. 155-56, 162-64.

[28]Sigmund Freud, "Analysis Terminable and Interminable," in **The Collected Papers of Sigmund Freud**, vol. 5, ed. J. Strachey (London: Hogarth Press, 1950), p. 357a: "We must not be misled by the term 'masculine protest' into supposing that what the man repudiates is the attitute of passivity, or, as we may say, the social aspect of feminity....What they reject is not passivity in general but passivity in relation to **men**. That is to say, the 'masculine protest' is in fact nothing other than fear of castration."

[29]Lewis Way, **Adler's Place in Psychology: An Exposition of Individual Psychology** (New York: Collier Books, 1962), p. 34. Cf. also Ansbacher, in Adler, **Co-operation Between the Sexes**, p. 143. In **Feminine Psychology**, pp. 221-24, Horney treats the historical relationship between man and woman in similar, but starker, terms analogous to the master/slave theme.

[30]See Rudolf Dreikurs, "Early Experiments in Social Psychiatry," **International Journal of Social Psychiatry**, 7 (1961): 141-47; and Ernest Papanek, **The Austrian School Reform** (New York: Frederick Fell, 1962).

[31]A notable exception to this rule is the family analyst Nathan W. Ackerman. See his critique of Freud in part 1 of **The Psychodynamics of Family Life: Diagnosis and Treatment of Family Relationships** (New York: Basic Books, 1958).

[32]Sigmund Freud, **Introductory Lectures on Psycho-Analysis** (New York: W. W. Norton, 1929), pp. 385-86. Before World War I, **sexual** instincts were crucial in Freud's psychology; thereafter, aggression and the death instinct (Thanatos) seemed to become as critical. In either case, man was still viewed from an **internal** psychic lens, i.e., his motivations, unconscious or not, appeared to lurk within the individual.

[33]Robert Hogan, "Theoretical Egocentrism and the Problem of Compliance," **American Psychologist** 30 (1975): 533-40.

[34]William Ryan, **Equality** (New York: Pantheon, 1981), elucidates these individual/internal versus collective/external distinctions in clear, commonsense fashion.

[35]David Bakan, **The Duality of Human Existence** (Chicago: Rand McNally, 1966). As its title implies, Bakan's work moves within dualisms rather than synthesis in human reality. However, it does

highlight the submerged **communal** side of that duality. Similarly, Karen Horney's principle of security needs--e.g., moving "toward," "away from," or "against" people--presages a break, in part, from self-contained psychoanalysis. See her **The Neurotic Personality of Our Time** (New York: W. W. Norton, 1937); and **Our Inner Conflicts: A Constructive Theory of Neurosis** (New York: W. W. Norton, 1945), esp. chaps. 3, 4, and 5.

[36]Lawrence Kohlberg, **The Philosophy of Moral Development** (San Francisco: Harper and Row, 1981).

[37]Carole Pateman makes much the same assessment of Rousseau and Freud in her "'The Disorder of Women': Women, Love, and the Sense of Justice," **Ethics** 91 (October 1980): 20-34.

[38]Betty A. Sichel, "Moral Development and Education: Men's Language of Rights and Women's Language of Responsibility," **Contemporary Education Review** 2 (Spring 1983): 33-42. The author is indebted to Sichel for pointing out Gillgan's tendency toward privatism (see footnote 39).

[39]Lawrence A. Blum, **Friendship, Altruism and Morality** (London: Routledge & Kegan Paul, 1980). Cf. also Gilligan, **In a Different Voice.**

[40]See my "Cooperation and Social Equality in Childhood: Adlerian and Piagetian Lessons," **Journal of Research and Development in Education** 17 (Winter 1984): 21-25.

[41]Poster, **Critical Theory of the Family**, pp. 37-38. Cf. Harold Lasswell's political adaptation of the Freudian model in his "Psychopathology and Politics," in **The Political Writings of Harold D. Lasswell** (Glencoe, Ill.: Free Press, 1951), pp. 194, 202: "The permanent removal of the tensions of the personality may depend upon the reconstruction of the individual's view of the world, and not upon belligerent crusades to change the world."

[42]For a more complete treatment and critique of this ideal in American psychology and social policy, see Edward E. Sampson, "Psychology and the American Ideal," **Journal of Personality and Social Psychology** 35 (1977): 767-82.

[43]Rudolf Dreikurs, "On Knowing Oneself," **International Journal of Individual Psychology** 3 (1937): 18.

[44]For a larger view of the entire "attitude/behavior" question, see Irwin Deutscher, **What We Say/What We Do** (Glenview, Ill.: Scott, Foresman, 1973).

[45]See Robert C. Serow, **Schooling for Social Diversity: An Analysis of Policy and Practice** (New York: Teachers College Press, 1983), esp. chaps. 2 and 3, for a perceptive review of this research literature.

[46]See David Stafford-Clark, **What Freud Really Said** (New York:

Schocken Books, 1965), p. 195.

[47]For an interesting historical account which describes psychoanalysis as the "child of the hysterical woman," see Carroll Smith-Rosenberg, "The Hysterical Woman: Sex Roles and Role Conflict in Nineteenth-Century America," **Social Research** 39 (Winter 1972): 652-78. Cf., more generally, Thomas S. Szasz, **The Myth of Mental Illness** (New York: Hoeber-Harper, 1961), for an intriguing analysis of the role-playing of "hysterics" in psychiatric circles. In the ironic words of Ehrenreich and English: "Freud's cure eliminated the confounding question of whether or not the woman was faking [or malingering]: in either case it was a mental disorder." Barbara Ehrenreich and Deirdre English, "The Sexual Politics of Illness," in **The Sociology of Health and Illness: Critical Perspectives**, eds. Peter Conrad and Rochelle Kerr (New York: St. Martin's Press, 1981) p. 347.

[48]Ernest Jones, **The Life and Work of Sigmund Freud**, vol. 1 (New York: Basic Books, 1953), p. 224.

CHAPTER 5

CRITIQUE OF EMPATHIC SCIENCE:

SEXISM AND THE HIDDEN SOCIETY*

Edward Jones

Kohut's work on narcissism represents one of the most cele-
brated developments of modern psychoanalytic theory. What does it
have to say to the social problem of sexism and feminine development? Nothing. And, since this work is increasingly cited in
social theory which attempts to describe the psychological reality
of the modern family, does it offer useful insights in this
sphere? No, because it has from the start severed the family from
its social context and offered us an ideological picture rather
than an accurate analysis.

. . . The central problem of psychoanalysis [is] its indi-
vidualism--the tendency to treat the psychological aspects of
phenomena which can only be understood if both their psychological
and sociological dimensions are considered together. Such an
analysis would be a truly dialectical analysis.

In this paper, I will take up two issues fundamental to a
dialectical analysis of the self--the social problem of sexism and
the social constellation of the family. I will try to restore the
social dimension of the self which Kohut's work scants by

*Edward Jones, "Critique of Empathic Science II: Sexism and the
Hidden Society", Psychology and Social Theory, no. 3 (1982, pp.
53-68. Copyright (c) 1982 by Psychology and Social Theory.
Reprinted by permission of Psychology and Social Theory.

counterposing to self psychology more socio-logically-informed work by Chodorow on feminine development and by Zaretsky on family life. The beginnings of a dialectical analysis of the self should emerge, as well as a concrete sense of the ideological qualities of Kohut's theory. We find that self psychology replaces any sense of a clash between self and society or of the impact of broad social constraints on the child with the elaboration of developmental phases which naturally unfold and demand certain "optimal" and "phase-appropriate" behaviors from parents.

SEXISM AND THE HIDDEN SOCIETY

The charge of individualism has been raised so often within and without psychoanalysis that one might suspect Kohut has some-how resolved it, especially in his later work. To be sure, he addresses the impact of social factors directly in the "epilogue" to **The Restoration of the Self**.[1] Certain statements there about the relationship between personality patterns and changing social factors appear to contradict such an indictment. However, Kohut's argument clears the way for isolating the parent-child relation-ship to be studied "for itself," while at the same time recogniz-ing that social factors (e.g., size of families, percentage of time spent by children with their parents, with servants, and with peers) can heighten or dampen the effect of the parent's person-ality on the child. He acknowledges the relationship between society and the individual as a legitimate issue, but asserts that whatever connections might be hypothesized, no factor can challenge the priority of the personality of the parent.

Ultimately, self pathology breeds self pathology: self constellations form a circle of explanation. Unempathic mothers
cause the development of defective selves in their children, even
though it can be argued that their negative influence is given
free reign by various social developments. By this logic, then,
one can treat parent and child in unmediated terms as essentially
a biological unit (self/self-object matrix), and the formation of
the self can be treated strictly from the genetic point of view.
Social factors are real and present, but not of immediate consequence. Clearly, Kohut's individualism has been tempered by the
social perspectives of neo-Freudianism.

In opposition to Kohut, I would stress that our nuclear
ambitions and ideals emerge within a family that is significantly
shaped by society: our narcissistic needs are fundamentally
social needs. It is not enough to suggest, as Kohut does, that
social factors influence family and self. This much is self-
evident. The decisive resolution is to show how social relations
of power--the inferior social position of women, for example--are
constitutive of family and self. Kohut has an opportunity for
expressing this in his argument on the origins of the self, but he
restricts himself to a three-person psychology. While his earlier
work conveys the impression that the child possesses certain
innate narcissistic needs, he later dispels such a notion by
stating that the empathic parental environment

not only anticipates the later self-awareness of the
child, but already, by the very form and content of its
expectations, begins to channel it into specific

directions.

> ... the self-objects emphatically respond to certain
> potentialities of the child (aspects of the grandiose
> self he exhibits, aspects of the idealized image he
> admires, different innate talents he employs to mediate
> creatively between ambitions and ideals), but not to
> others. This is the most important way by which the
> child's innate potentialities are selectively nourished
> or thwarted. (RS: 100)

Kohut astutely recognizes here that parents do not simply respond to the child's grandiose displays, but help constitute the very character of the grandiosity which is expressed. However, he treats this in an imploded fashion, rather than focusing on social mediations.

According to Kohut, depth psychology need not examine the manner in which society is a formative matrix for the self/self-object matrix. The depth psychologist is not necessarily disinterested in such questions, but Kohut assumes that the results of sociohistorical investigation will in some way correspond with or complement a psychology of the individual. Such a division of labor may seem appealing until we must provide adequate answers to some basic questions. For example, at a lecture in 1974, Kohut was asked "why so few women have been idealized figures in society" (SS: 776). His answer is remarkable for its scant reference to the social subordination and devaluation of women in society.

Kohut stresses that we cannot overestimate the importance of the empathy shown by parents. If they admire "a little girl as a

little girl, in her sweetness, in the future bearing of her children, in whatever potentials of femininity she displays," she will
grow up to be a secure idealizable adult. A boy's development
depends on these same empathic conditions. Kohut admits to puzzlement about why, given identical requirements for growth in
self-esteem and idealizability, women should be so rarely idealized. He suggests that perhaps parents have historically valued
boys more highly for certain potential contributions such as being
a "warrior" or a "tiller of the soil." It is quite disappointing
for an esteemed theorist to be so tepid in asserting that women
have been devalued and abused throughout history, but there is a
more serious failure in his statement. All he expects from a
socio-historical inquiry into the devaluation of women is an
identification of the reasons why parents have not appropriately
admired their little girl's femininity. He never recognizes that
admiring a girl for proud display of femininity might lead to non-
idealizability because femininity itself is a category of inferiority. He fails to note that feminine roles are experienced as
forms of violence by women (Gornick and Moran, 1971). In short,
Kohut's individualistic perspective does not complement, but
rather, conflicts with, or more pointedly, obscures the social
understanding.

Returning to Kohut's earlier statement on the parental
shaping of narcissistic needs, we must ask: is the selective
encouragement of certain potentialities by a parent strictly a
private or personal determination, or even more, can the parent's
nuclear ambitions and ideals be comprehended apart from the context of such realities as sexism? For purposes of therapy it

might be beneficial to restrict one's focus to the parent's empathic responsiveness or capacity for being idealized, but carrying this restriction over to theory produces the ideology of
parent-blaming, which is usually mother-blaming. Such a perspective ignores the extent to which parents and children participate
in an historically-specific family structure which determines, for
instance, who is the primary empathic caretaker, what the realms
of power are for each family member, and what ambitions and ideals
are appropriate for each sex.

It is important to see the perspective from which Kohut
approaches his subject. He looks primarily to the form in which
the self appears--firm, weak, vulnerable, fragmented, etc.--and
much less to the specific ambitious or idealistic contents of this
presumed structure. In his view people suffer because they lack a
firm cohesive self, not because they hold damaging ideals or
ambitions. A sense of enduring identity derives ultimately not
from the content of the nuclear self, but from the nature of the
relationship between the constituents of the self (RS: 182).
Based on this, it is reasonable to propose that the primary factors in development are empathy and idealization, regardless of
what ambitions or ideals are established in the process. The
quality of response holds priority over which talents, aspirations, and the like receive that response.

This is an appealing position since communication between
people at an emotional, qualitative level is clearly important.
Yet, this emphasis alone distorts a theory of psychic development.
Kohut consistently sidesteps the question of whether certain
ambitions and ideals--such as the suppression of emotionality in

boys and the feminine ideal of always pleasing others--can be damaging to the experience of children, even though the quality of the parent-child relationship may be irreproachable. Avoiding such complex questions lends an undeserved aura of clarity to Kohut's work. But even more importantly, refusing to confront this obviously value-laden area serves only to legitimize existing social values and ideals. Kohut restricts his theoretical focus to the formal aspect of such things as ideal formation. Specific ideals and ambitions promoted in the contemporary family are not critically examined and so given wholesale legitimation.[2] One might say that all family structures, all "sex/gender systems" (Rubin, 1975) are acceptable to Kohut so long as a cohesive self can develop. Ideals and ambitions are treated as neutral facts in the world: the same ideal or ambition may be constitutive of a firm cohesive self in one person and of a fragmented self in another. From Kohut's point of view, nothing more need be said. His theory portrays the social system as an elaborate means to serve private ends.[3]

We must reject the excessive generality of Kohut's theory-- the self is portrayed as a formal structure without any social content. Psychic structures are related in extrinsic fashion to family and societal structures. Furthermore, while Kohut does not explicitly contend that the self is a universal psychological structure, his entire approach is to highlight what is universal in the development of self-esteem, a sense of continuity, and so on. Clinical illustrations demonstrate these general processes, and otherwise there is scarcely a hint of historical or social detail. In a lecture to historians, for example, one of Kohut's main points is that

> In the setting of history, thwarted narcissistic aspira-
> tions, hurts to one's pride, injuries to one's prestige
> needs, interferences with conscious, preconscious, or
> unconscious fantasies concerning one's greatness, power,
> and specialness, or concerning the greatness, power, and
> specialness of the group that one identifies with are
> important motivations for group behavior. (SS: 773)

Kohut's words are well-chosen here--history certainly does seem to
him a "setting," a mere backdrop for the play of these universal
narcissistic themes. His theory is a collection of general,
abstract propositions, which are presumably meant to be filled in
with historically specific contents. Drivenness to amass wealth
is replaced by drivenness to express oneself creatively or artis-
tically--the specifics change (perhaps because social changes have
created new adaptational tasks, R.S: 279) while the basic form of
the grandiose self remains the same.[4]

Kohut reasons that people universally encounter narcissistic
issues (e.g., empathic mirroring in early childhood) which vary in
their specifics for each individual according to personal, family,
and social idiosyncrasies. However, the socio-historical does not
simply influence psychic development, as he assumes, but rather
constitutes it fundamentally. For instance, while men and women
alike grapple with issues of self-esteem, to simply say that the
particular contents of self-esteem (particular ambitions, aspirations, talents, and the like) tend to differ according to sex

misses the point. Such a position simplifies "the way gender
identity and expectations about sex roles and gender consistency
are so deeply central to a person's consistent sense of self"
(Chodorow, 1975:43). Social forces, such as sexism, produce a
different order of expectations and limitations for each sex, and
this reality is an integral part of our narcissistic experiences.
There is a tension between the general and the particular: the
general situation of women is lived in particular ways. The dichotomy implied in Kohut's work, however—universal versus socio-
historical—is a poor substitute for this social dialectic. It is
ultimately an impossible dichotomy since opposing terms exist at
widely different levels of abstraction (McDonough and Harrison,
1978: 24-25). Kohut's supposed universals are highly abstract,
referring to general patterns or formal consistencies, while the
historical refers to the actual or existent phenomena. In short,
he postulates abstract and concrete levels of analysis which can
never be suitably integrated.

KOHUT'S PSYCHOLOGY OF WOMEN

The feminist movement has highlighted the socio-political
aspect of women's psychological issues, and as a result, analysts
such as Kohut have been sensitized to past errors of psychoanalysis. Kohut explicitly criticizes certain of Freud's arguments and
offers a theory of gender development which discards Freud's
problematic notion of compensation for innate inferiority. One
becomes suspicious, however, upon reading that Freud's basic error
lay not in sexist assumptions, but in failing to gather all the

available data--specifically, in missing the data of self-development (SS: 228-229). Kohut would have us believe the issue is strictly empirical, value-free, and only indirectly related to social factors. In short, while Kohut's theory appears shorn of sexism and Freudian ideology, a closer analysis shows it to be little more than the reintrenchment of psychoanalysis in conservative sexual politics.

A brief outline of Kohut's views on the psychology of women will be offered before undertaking a critical analysis. He argues (SS: 738-792) that men and women have equal chances of developing healthy self-esteem because the crucial determinant is the same for both--empathic mirroring by a parent in early childhood. While the mother is generally the empathic self-object, Kohut notes that "not infrequently" for girls the mother serves both functions (RS: 185). Kohut argues that Freud over-estimated the significance to the young girl of not having a penis because he never recognized the importance of the early development of the self. Kohut does not question Freud's position that this discovery constitutes an "injury to body narcissism" in all cases. He does question whether this is an important formative experience by itself.

> If there is empathic mirroring acceptance of the little girl's self, if she can merge with the idealized admired parental imago, then the recognition of the sexual difference will cause no permanent harm, will not lead to a lasting disturbance of the narcissistic equilibrium. (SS: 791)

On the other hand, if a girl has suffered narcissistic deprivation as an infant (been deprived of empathic acceptance), then the injury to self which accompanies recognition of her lack of a penis "will lead to a significant (depressive) lowering of self-esteem, and in turn, to (paranoid) chronic rage and destructiveness." The impact of penis envy is dependent on prior self-development. Finally, Kohut argues that the woman's wish for a baby is not typically reducible to her wish for a penis, as Freud presumed, but rather is a manifestation, or even more, "the high point" of the development of her most central ambitions and ideals.

Kohut's thoughts on femininity merit further elaboration in this context. Kohut rejects penis envy both as the primary root of self-esteem and as the basis of the girl's gender self-image. Instead, Kohut sees feminine gender identity developing as part of the cohesive self through the parent's admiring responses to "feminine" traits. Kohut's recommendation to admire the girl's display of "feminine potentials" is echoed in a more detailed analysis by devotees of his approach to gender:

If reproductive potential and mothering capacity are treasured and mirrored by the parents, representations of pregnancy and childbearing, or breast symbolism will become highly cathecized core attributes of the primitive mind-body self. If parents respond positively and nontraumatically to the female qualities of the girl, femininity will be reinforced and built into the cohesive self.

> Achievement of pregnancy and motherhood constitutes a
> subsequent pillar of feminine self-esteem, particularly
> when culturally reinforced. (Barglow and Schaefer, 1976:
> 346)

It seems that a significant ingredient in the optimal mirroring of the little girl (and therefore optimal self development) is the empathic fostering of feminine qualities, especially the desire to become a mother. Freud and Kohut might disagree on certain psychological components, but they seem to agree that having a baby completes a woman's development. Freud offered women motherhood as a means to fill an innate deficiency, while Kohut promotes it as the ultimate joyful realization of the self.

Kohut's theory is remarkable in several ways, but most of all perhaps for its restraint. He restrains himself, as Freud did not, from making even the slightest departure from depth psychology--that is, from an empathic approach to his subject. He does not flirt with biological thinking--for example, attribute gender differences ultimately to genital differences, as Freud did--nor does he explore social determinants of gender identity and personality. History might create masculine and feminine roles, but the only history of interest to a depth psychologist is experiential, accessible only from the genetic point of view. Historical phenomena such as gender roles are treated as neutral facts to be incorporated by individuals in one way or another--history serves personal genesis. Kohut rejects Freud's biological enshrinement of gender differences, and so appears on the side of those seeking liberation from rigid social roles. However, his emphasis on our common humanity, our common need for empathic confirmation, then reduces gender roles to incidentals which hardly seem worth any liberating struggle. He sees only a cohesive self which also happens to be masculine or feminine. He might grant that our sense of masculinity or femininity is in large part socially derived, but from his point of view it is not so important what these categories entail as whether a child is warmly admired for displaying typical traits. Perhaps sociologists can evaluate these roles and discuss other social possibilities, but for the depth psychologist they are accomplished facts.

Kohut's position, in effect, endorses the **status quo** as a whole. His writing suggests that he finds little fault with present social arrangements in any case, but his decision to treat masculinity and femininity as neutral facts assures the legitimation of present social norms. It should be noted, however, that his support for women becoming mothers is active and strong, rather than resulting from neglect of the issue. We see here an unexplored conviction that being a mother is a natural part of being female. There is little attempt to distinguish giving birth to child (a biological fact) from being primary caretaker of that child (a social fact). All we need to know is that women have done both through the ages, experiencing these achievements as a "pillar of feminine self-esteem." A depth psychologist such as Kohut does not speculate on the biological versus cultural roots of these phenomena. Instead, two sorts of women receive most of his attention--women who find being a mother the essence of self-realization and women who are bad mothers because self defects prevent proper empathic responsiveness. Such a limited view speaks for itself.

The relation between gender and self must be addressed differently. The sociology of gender must be brought to bear on
Kohut's theory of self to reveal the effects of sexism within the
individual. We must ask why women are primary parents and what
the ramifications of these arrangements are for children of both
sexes. The work of Nancy Chodorow (1971, 1974, 1978, 1979) is
extremely helpful in this regard since she has focused on questions of this sort. Her work allows us to see that Kohut sub-
merges critical differences between women and men with regard to
self development.

CHODOROW'S THEORY OF GENDER

Chodorow approaches the issue of gender personality with the
assumption that it matters a great deal which parent is the primary caretaker. That is to say, an empathic self-object has a sex,
and it is important for an infant whether that primary parent is
the same or the opposite sex. Of course, women have long had
primary responsibility for infants, and this has typically been
taken for granted. Kohut is not unusual then in failing to pursue
how this social fact determines basic personality differences in
men and women. Chodorow argues that women, as mothers, produce
sons and daughters with different capacities, needs, etc., largely
because women relate differently to boy and girl infants, not
simply because they deliberately socialize or train them differently. She proposes, in essence, that from the mother-daughter
relationship grows a girl who defines herself in relation and

connection with other people and so desires to be a mother, while from the mother-son relationship develops a boy who is not prepared for nurturant relationships, but rather for independent activities outside the family. These relationships take on greater meaning when seen in the context of sexism. The relegation of women to the family as wives and mothers has been analyzed (Chodorow, 1979; Rowbotham, 1973; Zaretsky, 1976) as the key element accounting for their secondary status in male-dominated society.

> Women's mothering determines women's primary location in the domestic sphere and creates a basis for the structural differentiation of domestic and public spheres. But these spheres operate hierarchically . . . Culturally and politically, the public sphere dominates the domestic, and hence men dominate women. (Chodorow, 1978: 10)

If the mother-daughter relationship is the key to the "reproduction of mothering," then it is also central to maintaining women in a subordinate social position.

While the mother-child relationship can be examined for the quality of empathy, one can also study the manner in which the mother identifies with the young child. Chodorow stresses that this factor is different for boys and girls at the pre-Oedipal state--the stage of a child's development when parental empathy is most crucial. Klein and Riviere were the first to describe how the experience of being a mother stimulates a "double identification" (Chodorow, 1974: 47) for a woman. She identifies with a mother who once cared for her and experiences once again (though not at a fully conscious level) what it felt like to be the cared-for child. It is reasonable to expect that this experience is heightened when the infant is the same sex as the mother. After all, she was once a girl cared for by a female parent. This would explain a common observation first made by Freud—that the pre-Oedipal mother attachment is longer for girls than for boys. The attachment is also different in nature, since the boy is soon experienced as the male opposite. Mothers tend to push this differentation and establish the basis for the sexually-toned relationship of the Oedipal period which Freud noted (Chodorow, 1974: 48). These suggested differences in maternal behavior do not involve greater warmth or praise for girls than for boys, but instead relate to differences of "nuance, tone, quality" in the relationships.[5] Chodorow's main point, then, is that mothers generally identify more with daughters and experience them as less separate. A basic sense of relation and connection with others is established here for girls, as well as a basic threat of over-closeness and over-dependence. Popular books by Hammer (1975) and Friday (1977) confirm this idea, and Chodorow cites the report of a 1976 panel of psychoanalysts: "There is increasing evidence of a distinction between the mother's basic attitudes and handling of her boy and girl children starting from the earliest days and continuing thereafter" (1978: 99). Admiration for gender-related displays, which Kohut stresses, would seem to be a secondary reinforcement of this relational shaping of needs and capacities.

A different development of the sexes after this early period is widely acknowledged. The relevance of such differences to our argument will become especially clear later when gender differences in psychopathology are examined. The main distinction is that while the girl's establishment of a feminine identity is continuous with her early maternal attachment, the boy must replace his primary tie to the mother with a masculine identification. Furthermore, girls can easily and securely learn what femininity entails by forming a personal identification with the mother, but since the organization of work and family in our society creates a considerable degree of normal "father absence," the boy generally develops a "positional identification" with the masculine role. He generally cannot form the same close personal relationship with father as with mother. Instead, he tends to identify with the cultural role or stereotype, and represses all signs of femininity in his personality as an assurance that he has "achieved" his gender identity. Chodorow cites work by Slater (1961, 1970), Lynn (1959, 1962), Mitscherlich (1970), and Winch (1962) on this issue.

Lastly, Chodorow (1974) notes that the close mother-daughter bond tends to be problematic in Western middle class families, but not necessarily in other cultures. She examines cross-cultural research and specifies certain aspects of a mother's role in our society which account for the mother's tendency to keep "her daughter from differentiation and from lessening her infantile dependence" (1974: 64). She concludes that in a situation where women are primary parents, caring for children with little regular assistance, and having only devalued housework and mothering as potential realms of self-realization, there will be special difficulties for girls developing a sense of independence and self-esteem. It is the mother "cooped up" in the home, the mother subordinated to the male "head of the family" and so unable to claim that home as a sphere of control, who forma a problematic bond with her daughter.[6] This does not necessarily mean that men will have higher self-esteem, but rather that different expectations and limitations define their situation. Masculinity must be continually earned (rather than being "ascribed" as with femininity, Chodorow: 1971), and approval is attendant upon success. Chodorow notes a clear advantage for the boy, since giving up his maternal tie for this elusive masculinity means separating from a gender defined by passivity, regression, dependence, and lack of reality orientation, in order to experience himself as part of a gender defined by activity, progression, independence and reality orientation.[7]

GENDER AND SELF DEVELOPMENT

We can now begin to see the impact of these gender-related issues on self theory. The central point is that theorizing about the self in general terms obscures specific problems men and women confront in establishing their nuclear ambitions and ideals. We will be limited here to summarizing how the sociology of gender must be brought to bear in three areas: the formation of central ambitions for men and women; the development of psychological ambitions which are gender-specific; and, the significance of idealization in male and female development.

Kohut's theory fails to recognize and explore a rather commonly noted fact--men and women are generally driven by different

types of ambitions. Subordination of women is a chief source of
this fact, and furthermore, the preservation of this subordination
is one of its consequences. This is what Chodorow means by the
"reproduction of mothering:" sexist social arrangements (such as
relegating primary caretaking of infants to women) are the basis
of certain psychological needs and aspirations which contribute to
the maintenance or reproduction of these social conditions (e.g.,
little girls grow up wanting to recreate the intense mother-child
relationship). Motherhood is an extremely positive, joyful experience for many women, but it is also a subordinate, relatively
powerless social position. It is surely a double-edged ambition,
and one with psychological ramifications which cannot be ignored.

It has been argued that women tend to maintain close, affectionate ties longer, and feel sense of sameness more intensely with
daughters than with sons. This particular "matrix of empathy"
tends to produce girls whose central ambition is to be involved in
mothering type relationships, or in different terms, "preoccupied
with those very relational issues that go into mothering" (Chodorow, 1978: 110). For instance, the jobs traditionally held by
women outside the home involve these relational capacities--school
teaching, nursing, social work, and so on. "The wants and needs
which lead women to become mothers put them in situations where
their mothering capacities can be expressed" (1978: 205).[8] A girl
does not simply identify with and try to be like her mother in
specific ways, but rather "mother and daughter maintain elements
of their primary relationship which means they will feel alike in
fundamental ways" (1978:110). Little girls grow up to want intense primary relationships--that is, they grow up to possess

maternal potential which Kohut takes for granted.

Male infants, on the other hand, are treated by mothers less like the self and more as an opposite or "other." From this matrix of empathy grows men who define themselves less in relational terms, being driven instead by central ambitions related to personal accomplishment and success. Again, this masculine orientation toward achievement is a double-edged ambition. The widely discussed difficulties men have with intimacy and in expressing emotions are often a counterpart of this drivenness to achieve (Pleck and Sawyer, 1974). As Chodorow (1978: 196) notes, the repression of affective relational needs is part of the training for masculinity.

It would be reasonable to assume that because women mother and form different relationships with sons and daughters, there would be some consistent differences between men and women in forms of psychopathology. Chodorow notes some general differences which a number of clinical cases report--extreme individual problems for daughters and various consequences for boys of a sexually-toned male-role relation with the mother. Ideally, one would hope to find a type of sexual disturbance which is much more common in one sex than in the other. It happens that sexual perversion (fetishism, exhibitionism, pedophilia, etc.) is such a problem since it is found most often in males (Stoller, 1975). Fortunately, Kohut has also written on this subject. His thoughts can be compared directly with work by Robert Stoller (1975), a theorist who focuses specifically on male versus female development.

Kohut's thoughts on sexual perversion are largely framed as

an attack on the significance of libido theory. He argues that from the beginning drive experiences are subordinated to the child's experience of relation between self and self-object. In the case of perversion, a damaged self sexualizes its frustrated need for the self-object to respond empathically or to serve as an idealized extension of self. Stoller similarly notes the presence of a wish for merger, but he examines this from the perspective of gender development.[9] He would not find Kohut's gender-blind explanations adequate. For example, Kohut overlooks crucial aspects of psychological experience and development when he argues in a case of fetishism that a "specific traumatic absence of maternal empathy for the healthy grandiosity and the healthy exhibitionism of his forming independent self" caused the man's fixation. Such an explanation will never grasp why more men than women engage in fetishistic activities.

Stoller emphasizes the significance of the boy's dis-identification with his mother, to end his "security-giving closeness" with her. He stresses that the mother is a "female with a feminine gender identity" and that we might expect in every male "at least a trace" of the earliest merging with the mother's "femaleness and femininity" (1974: 137). In the case of boys who develop perversions, Stoller notes difficulty in counteracting the primitive yearning for oneness with the mother. This constitutes a threat to masculinity, given that the suppression of such desires forms the basis of masculine identity. Consequently, we can see the fetishistic cross-dresser, for instance, merging with or undoing separation from the mother through certain rituals. at the same time, those rituals promote separation and preserve masculinity since the boy actively controls a fantasy in which women's clothes and the appearance of femininity are used to attain erection and orgasm: proof of maleness. "They have at least some masculinity, to be preserved at any cost" (1975: 152). One might argue that the "self" is being preserved, but this is a vague statement which, far from being the bedrock of analysis, misses the crucial struggle over masculinity. In such cases there is usually a history of attempted femininization of the boy by the mother--this is the trauma which the boy replays in act and fantasy. Stroller demonstrates how these cases are extreme instances of normal male development. Kohut can see only how they are instances of abnormal self development, which doesn't begin to address the specificity of the problem. It is largely a male problem because women are primary parents from whom boys must separate in certain prescribed ways, if a stable masculine identity, and thereby a stable self-image, are to be achieved.

Implicit in the foregoing discussion is the idea that a longing for merger does not threaten women in the same manner that it does men--to an extent it helps sustain female identity. Of course, it has already been noted that the mother-daughter bond can be so intense and prolonged (because of "faulty empathy," as Kohut would have it) that the daughter fails to individuate adequately. It is at this point--threat of engulfment by mother--when an idealized father may become important to a girl.

Fathers serve in part to break a daughter's primary
unity with and dependence on her mother. For this and a
number of other reasons, fathers and men are idealized.

A girl's father provides a last-ditch escape from maternal omnipotence, so a girl cannot risk driving him away.
(Chodorow, 1978: 195).

It appears that idealization means different things for male and
female children.

Kohut (RS: 11) states that turning to an idealized father "is
a very typical psychological move" when a child has experienced
"faulty" maternal empathy. He does not elaborate on typical male
and female issues in this move, and we cannot derive even a vague
sense of difference from his case studies since only four female
patients are briefly discussed in comparison to eighteen males.
It must be noted that parental failures in empathy or idealization
are usually not total rejections of the child, but failed
attempts. The parent is perhaps not attuned to the child's developing needs or is in subtle ways not open to idealization, but
there is an investment in the relationship nonetheless. Simply, a
mother-child relationship might be both close and disappointing.
A girl is likely to emerge from such a relationship with the
relational needs and capacities previously discussed, but maternal
conflict and disappointment will render these relational needs and
capacities previously discussed, but maternal conflict and disappointment will render these relational, affective needs problematic. A psychological move to the father may compensate for
these problems to some degree, but a fundamental contradiction is
her sense of femininity and relatedness remains. A boy who moves
from such a damaging maternal relationship to the father has the
possibility of moving toward a strong, nonconflictual masculine

identity. The "escape" from the mother does not hold the same promise for boys and girls. Kohut obscures this by saying that everyone has "two chances" in development and that "a failure experienced at the first way station can be remedied by a success at the second one" (RS: 186).

While Kohut observes that many, if not most, girls turn to the father as an idealized self-object, he never surmises that for such a girl "idealization of the father may be at the expense of her positive sense of feminine self" (Chodorow, 1974: 65). A girl who turns away from her mother to seek self-esteem and independence through her father rejects a part of herself in a more fundamental sense than does a boy.[10] Furthermore, if we examine the other possibility--a girl's idealization of her mother--a psychological bind becomes apparent. Idealization is interrupted at an interpersonal level because of sheer familiarity of the mother. "Coming in at intervals from the outside world in contrast to the intense mother-child relationship, he is a figure idealized early and may avoid the ambivalence caused by daily familiarity (Barglow and Schaefer, 1976: 343).[11]

In addition to this interpersonal level, the idealization of women has never been allowed to exist as a general social phenomenon, given that ours is a male-dominated society where masculinity is defined largely through the non-existence or suppression of feminine traits and tendencies. One should not mistake the various ideologies of motherhood throughout history--the "moral mother" (Chodorow, 1979: 92) and the "cult of true womanhood" (Welter, 1978), for instance--for the idealization of women. These are essentially rationales for enforcing the maternal role, which is simultaneously the reinforcing of male dominance. The same has been said of post-Freudian psychologies which emphasize the crucial importance of the mother for the child's development (Chodorow, 1979: 94), along with the special narcissistic gratifications of motherhood. Mitchell (1973) comments on how the emphasis on motherhood as an "honorable, but different role" (compared with the role of men in economic production) is similar to racist "separate-but-equal" ideology--they both conceal social subordination.

The main point is not that motherhood is inherently dishonorable or unworthy of idealism, but rather that it cannot be understood apart from its constitutive social context. Implicit in the idealization of motherhood by post-Freudian analysts is the idea that we can ignore the real powerlessness of the mother and treat motherhood as "an apparently constant atemporal phenomenon---part of biology rather than history" (Mitchell, 1973: 107). The little girl who idealizes her mother as a strong, admirable figure in times of distress, need, and fatigue (Barglow and Schaefer, 1976: 343), and thereby follows a similar course in life, soon discovers, if she had not by the age of five, that she has "bought" a bittersweet package, at best. Her route to developing a "cohesive self" has placed her in a position of subordination. Realities, not excessive sensitivity or vulnerability, will pose a threat to self-esteem.

Kohut addresses an area of psychology--the development of ambitions and ideals--in which one can discriminate the psychological effects of social position, but he produces a theory which is nonspecific and noncritical. When examined in relation to different social groups, or more specifically in relation to the oppression of women, ambitions and ideals appear to bear the stamp of power. A critical theory of these psychological phenomena specifies how repressive social arrangements impose different "psychological tasks" on men and women. Kohut's general theory of development, on the other hand, misunderstands the struggles of specific social groups and passively (or at times actively) legitimates the social arrangements which mold these struggles. Minority groups have long understood the transformation of their ambitions and ideals as an important psychological component of their liberation; Kohut's thought obscures their predicament.

Empathy is a limited tool incapable of grasping the objective social conditions which structure our lives. Chodorow has explored the objective state of women's oppression and empathically-understood experience, so producing a feminist theory of the "reproduction of mothering." Other feminists (Lorber, Coser, Rossi and Chodorow, 1981) have raised serious objections to her thought, but these have not been treated here because they would divert attention from the main problem—differentiating critical from neopositivist thinking about a specific issue. Empathic science is a neopositivism which obscures mediations and produces theory supportive of the **status quo**.

THE HIDDEN SOCIETY

When we treat social groups or social realities as if they do not exist, we do not thereby prevent them from affecting us. The disregarded can have profound effects. So it is with the hidden social realities of Kohut's psychological theory. Despite his steadfast vigilance, certain social forces thrive in his thought, asserting themselves behind his back.

Kohut believes the modern world is forcing us to turn to inner satisfaction, to the "elaboration and expansion of man's inner life" (ss: 540). He assumes that personal fulfillment or self-realization is possible without major transformations in a society which threatens the "survival of the human race." He joins humanistic psychologists in proposing that while a hostile environment might damage the self, the problem can still be addressed at a personal level and resolved through a personal solution. It might seem that the determination to expand "man's inner life" is a timeless pursuit, since we know, for instance, that the ancient Greeks aspired to the ideal: "Know Thyself." However, this is a general truth which appears relatively trivial once historical detail is provided. Contemporary concern with an inner life largely derives from social developments pertinent to the family. Kohut's humanistic concept of self-realization appears similarly trivial and superficial when analyzed against historical realities.

An attempt to reflect Kohut's theory against society, or in other terms, to undertake an ideology-critique (Jones, 1981a; Krueger and Silvert, 1981) of his work, demands an adequate social theory. Zaretsky's (1976) social theory of the family will be presented not only because it treats the segment of society most closely tied to the striving for self-realization, but also because it recognizes that family life must be understood through its connection with the public sphere of work. Industrial society has transformed the family into a protected sphere of "personal life," a sphere for the pursuit of inner, personal satisfactions apart from society. Of course, the family is still a place of work for women, and this cultivation of a personal realm has long been a characteristically middle-class pursuit. Nonetheless, there has been a general change in the function of the family with the rise of industrialization, and our advanced industrial society has witnessed an increasing concern with inner fulfillment by people from all classes.

I will sketch a socio-historical picture of the family and inner life to begin my critique, and then ask whether Kohut's theory speaks to the significant forces affecting people's lives or instead simply mirrors the prevailing expectations of family and personal life. I contend that Kohut's call to inwardness dismisses social forces threatening self-realization and thereby confirms these forces. That is to say, because he fails to analyze critically how social forces shape the family and personal life, he creates a theory of personal life which can itself be understood as a product of those forces.

THE HISTORY OF THE FAMILY AND PERSONAL LIFE

The contemporary concepts of family life and childhood originated during the eighteenth century. As Philippe Aries argued:

Until the end of the seventeenth century, nobody was ever left alone. The density of social life made isolation virtually impossible . . . . This sociability

had for a long time hindered the formation of the
concept of the family, because of the lack of privacy .
. . In the eighteenth century, the family began to hold
society at a distance, to push it back beyond a steadily
expanding zone of private life (excerpted in Skolnick
and Skolnick, 1971: 99).

Beginning in the eighteenth century, then, we can identify certain
enduring characteristics of the "modern family." It

cuts itself off from the world and opposes to society
the isolated group of parents and children. All the
energy of the group is expanded on helping the children
to rise in the world, individually and without any
collective ambition: the children rather than the
family (Aries: 104).

The "triumph of the modern family," as Aries calls it, must not be
misunderstood. It is a transformation of the prevailing conception or expectation of family life. The family was from this time
on regarded as private and child-centered. In order to understand
this conceptual transformation we need to examine broad socio-
-economic realities in addition to factors such as the "density of
social life." Specifically, changes in the role of economic
production should be explored in reciprocity with changes in the
family; and, the family should be investigated in relation to
specific social classes. The problem of class is not treated here
for brevity's sake, and in any case an accent on the middle-class

is appropriate since this is the family which psychoanalysis has investigated.

The decline of feudalism in the fourteenth century brought the family to the force as the basic or lowest social unit in place of the feudal manor. The so-called "patriarchal family" emerged in England in the sixteenth and seventeenth centuries as a self-contained productive unit headed by a "paterfamilias" who worked in cooperation with his wife, children, and employees (Zaretsky, 1976: 39). We witness during this period the beginnings of capitalism--that is, the advancement of private productive property and the familial economic unit over the manor or village economy with feudal kinship ties. While it is taken for granted today that the family exists outside or apart from the economy, during this period family labor had Protestant blessings as the basis of the economy (Zaretsky, 1976: 41). The family of this period was "workshop, church, reformatory, school, and asylum" (Hareven, 1976: 198).

All of this changed with industrialization and the rise of the factory system. The workplace was gradually removed from the home; the master replaced the father as the supervisor of production. The family unit was not transformed immediately, however, as early forms of factory organization demonstrate. Families often worked as a unit in the mills and manufacturing shops of the early eighteenth century (Hareven, 1976: 199; Zaretsky, 1976: 46), even though the decisive change had taken place--each worker now earned a wage for his or her labor. As the transfer of its productive functions to other institutions proceeded, the family assumed a new social role.

The family became a specialized unit, its tasks limited
primarily to procreation, consumption, and child rearing. With a shift of focus to the emotional contents of
relations, the family turned inward and assumed domesticity, intimacy, and privacy as major characteristics
(Hareven, 1976: 198).

This is the modern family of which Aries speaks. It is rooted in
the division between work and family life which accompanies capitalist industrialization.

Zaretsky (1976: 30) argues that just as work and family were
separated, so too was a sphere of personal life divorced or separated from the public realm of work. The family become the center
of this sphere of personal fulfillment, and as Zaretsky notes,
this has been an important element in the family's persistence
despite the decline of many of its earlier functions. The impersonal, often brutal public realm, where long hours of labor earned
a barely adequate wage, drove individuals at the beginning of the
nineteenth century to the family as a refuge from industrial
society, a "haven in a heartless world" (Lasch, 1977). The ideal
of the family which emerged in nineteenth century Victorian
society (an ideal based on the middle-class family, but pervading
the life of industrial working-class families as well) is clearly
depicted in the writings of John Ruskin:

it is the place of peace; the shelter, not only from all
injury, but from all terror, doubt, and division. . . So

far as the anxieties of the outer life penetrate into it
. . . it ceases to be a home; it is then only a part of
the outer world which you have roofed over and lighted
fire in (cited in Zaretsky, 1976: 51).

It is within this enclave that individualism, self-consciousness,
a new attention to domestic relations, and an inner world of
personal feeling begin to flourish. Of course, men and women held
very different roles in this family.

Ruskin's depiction of the family betrays a male perspective.
With industrialization the man became a wage-laborer under the
control of the new capitalist, and he sought in his personal life
a sense of uniqueness and self-determination. Women, on the other
hand, continued their traditional tasks of housewife and mother
and were given responsibility for maintaining the new "emotional
and psychological realm of personal relations" (Zaretsky, 1976:
31). This emotional support given by wives can be seen as an
"important siphon" for the discontents of wage-labor in capitalist
society (Chodorow, 1979: 96). The integration of women into the
labor force in the second half of the twentieth century should not
be overlooked, yet the most significant aspects of this phenomenon
are that women have generally been given the lowest-level jobs and
held responsible for their families first and foremost. Consequently, women have escaped neither their material oppression nor
their identification with emotional life (Easton, 1979; Rowbotham,
1973: 82-83).[12]

An examination of housework and childrearing can reveal a
great deal not only about the situation of women, but also about

the common notion that the economy and the family are fundamentally separate realms. Quite simply, these activities are absolutely necessary to maintaining life in any society and so must be
considered part of the economy (Rowbotham, 1973; Zaretsky, 1976:
25). However, with industrialization, labor has been valued in
accord with the wage it commands, and since housewives and mothers
are unpaid, their work has been considered both non-economic and
secondary in importance to economic (commodity) production. While
it is true that the family and personal life have been formed in
opposition to economic production, this fact is an integral part
of the overall social structure. In other words, the tension
between personal and public spheres indicates not an absence of
relationship, but a specific form of relationship. The appearance
of disjunction should not mislead the theorist to think that
family and personal life can be understood in isolation, without
regard for the realities of economic production. Similarly, the
theorist should not fail to note that women's work is part of the
economy, even though wages are not paid.

The conflict between individual and society, which theorists
such as Freud and Weber mistakenly portrayed as the "human
condition," must be understood in the context of the society which
was emerging in the nineteenth century. An isolated individual
faced an antagonistic society at this point in history because
"work" and "life," public and private spheres, had been formed in
opposition by capitalist industrialization. Throughout the nineteenth century, we can see a series of romantic figures standing
apart from the society: the hero, the virtuoso, the mystic, the
world traveler, the wandering Jew, the genius, the dandy

(Zaretsky, 1976: 58059). This exaltation of the individual against society found an institutional base in the family. The romantic tradition of individualism with its emphasis on the emotions, love, beauty, innocence, and childhood converged with the Victorian ideal of the family. By the twentieth century, the family was clearly regarded as the primary institution in which personal happiness, love, and fulfillment could be sought. For the great mass of people employed as wage-laborers: "One's individual identity could no longer be realized through work or through the ownership of property: individuals now began to develop the need to be valued 'for themselves" ' (Zaretsky, 1976: 61). It is in such a world that psychoanalysis developed. As one might expect, a theory addressing the emotional life of the family could not develop until the family became a specialized realm of emotional and personal development.

The creation of a sphere of "personal life" for the great mass of working people in twentieth century America is rooted in the immense productivity of the capitalist system. Productivity increased in the nineteenth and twentieth centuries because of mechanization and also as a result of the "division of labor in production"--the process in which a given type of work is broken down into its constituent elements and each detail assigned to different workers (Braverman, 1974: 70-83)). By the 1920's, many firms in the U.S. had given in to the strongest labor demand of the nineteenth century--a shorter work day. High productivity and increasing American dominance in the world market made this possible (Zaretsky, 1976: 67). The emergence of free time or "leisure time" marks the rise of personal life, with its attendant promises and expectations, for people of all social classes. The American "ethic of consumerism" spread as industries promoted new leisure goods and encouraged people to "live well, consume pleasurably, and enjoy the fruits of one's labor" (Zaretsky, 1976: 69). While the family was a sphere of production in pre-industrial society, it was now more a sphere of consumption, at least for male members uninvolved in childrearing and housekeeping. Work in industrial society might be experienced as routine and unfulfilling, but one could expect to compensate for this lack of freedom in personal life. At the end of a work day, one could attend to needs for trust, intimacy, creative expression, self-knowledge, and a full emotional and sexual life.

The twentieth century family might appear different from the nineteenth century family in various ways, yet fundamentally both have been spheres for personal life. Present differences can be partly attributed to the resurgence in the late 1960's of a feminism opposed to inequality within the family. In addition, new dimensions (and a new, desperate, driven quality) have been added to the twentieth century conception of personal life with such developments as the liberation of sexuality (Zaretsky, 1976: 111, 113). Most interesting in this, perhaps, is the fact that liberated sexuality has significantly failed to enhance the individual's freedom. This can be seen as a powerful illustration of the central dilemma of personal life. Sexuality has been commercialized and integrated into such things as media and advertising, while at the same time, a "good sex life" is pursued as the consummate pleasures of personal life, compensating for the nonerotic routines of work life. Sexual repression has been greatly eased, but the lifting of social restraint has been contained within bounds which ensure that this heightened sense of liberty does not tap the discontents from the public arena; there is "repressive desublimation," in Marcuse's (1964) phrase. Increasingly, the pursuit of personal freedom becomes a futile passion. Attempts to find personal meaning and fulfillment outside work expand into ever new domains--sexuality, creative hobbies, experimental lifestyles, new psychotherapies--and as expectations remain unmet, new realms are sought.

In general, then, we cannot say that the development of personal life has meant an increase in human freedom. Free time brought the promise of freedom, but it must be recognized that the only way to realize this promise is to abolish the "forced separation and isolation" of personal life (Zaretsky, 1976: 141). The needs and aspirations which have developed in the "new historical space" of personal life are certainly positive, but the idea that we can satisfy these needs apart from the "system" or the "mass society" is illusory. The major problem is that this sphere cannot bear the burden of being the sole haven from the pressures of industrial society. We need only witness the suffering and the violence in the family, the institutional realm of personal life (Walker, 1979; Zaretsky, 1976: 141). We are faced with "false freedoms," then, not simply in the sense that personal choices are often more limited to one's type of "life-style," but more profoundly because the joys of personal life are compartmentalized and greatly taxed by social forces.

The dialectic of personal life must be grasped. A majority of people today aspire to lead a life which is not dominated by

the rigors of production. This is surely a progressive development of great potential. But, the pursuit of such self-realization in isolation from society, without the simultaneous rebuilding
of society to better serve people, can mean only the frustration
of those ambitions and the promotion of ideological thought.
Individuals need specific retreats from society.[13]

THE IDEOLOGICAL SELF

It is from this historical orientation that we must examine
psychoanalysis, especially the contribution of Kohut. The psychoanalytic tradition clearly reflects the widespread search in our
society for fulfillment in personal life, but this is not a criticism in itself. To be sure, the needs addressed by pyschoan-
alysis, such as intimacy and self-understanding, have gained
ascendance historically, but this only specifies a concrete social
base for psychological concerns. The problem is that psychoanalysis generally misrepresents historically-specific family and
personal constellations as natural, ahistorical phenomena (Poster,
1978a). In other words, the family and personal life are accepted
at face value as existing apart from other social realities in
some isolated sphere of intimacy. This encourages the idea that
our "human needs" can be met apart from any transformation of the
society.

I am not criticizing psychoanalysis for its therapeutic focus
on helping individuals overcome problems of emotional life.
Rather, its implicit theory of society is at question, along with
its agenda for individual happiness and fulfillment. Freud

elaborated a pessimistic view: society was repressive and the individual might best aspire to lucid, realistic adaptation.

> If civilization imposes such great sacrifices not only
> on man's sexuality but his aggressivity, we can under-
> stand better why it is hard for him to be happy in that
> civilization. In fact, primitive man was better off in
> knowing no restrictions of instinct. To counterbalance
> this, his prospects of enjoying this happiness for any
> length of time were very slender. Civilized man has
> exchanged a portion of his possibilities of happiness
> for a portion of security (1962: 62).

While Freud revealed the emotional and sexual underside of the Victorian ideal of family, he failed to locate these phenomena clearly within the society, within the scope of social change (Poster, 1978a: 1-41). Kohut similarly falls into individualism and ahistoricism, but is can be argued that he propounds an ideology more deeply mystifying than Freud's. His optimism that self psychology will develop the means to "scientifically" elaborate and intensify the "inner life" serves to reinforce and deepen the social contradiction between work and life. He naively suggests that we can achieve self-realization in spite of this social split. Freud, on the other hand, at least recognized limitations to personal fulfillment, even though he universalizes and mythologizes (Eros-Thanatos) basic social conflicts.

Both Freud and Kohut fail to understand the sociohistorical basis for the separation of production and family, public activity

and inner life, but Kohut is more sanguine about pursuing a "whole
universe of experiences . . . which is hardly related to the
realities of our everyday existence" (SS: 543). If the foregoing
historical analysis of the family and personal life is accurate,
we must conclude that such promise of fulfillment reinforces the
very social arrangements which prevent the fulfillment of that
promise. So long as self-fulfillment is a private affair, se-
cluded from the ever-encroaching pressures of society, it will be
a flimsy haven, an escape, but not a true realm of freedom and
autonomy. Kohut does not comprehend how the family and personal
life form an important part of socio-economic structure, and
consequently, he abstracts an impersonal "mass society" or "everyday existence" at one pole of analysis and an inner self at the
other. This enables him to discuss the realization of self apart
from all considerations of society. He reasons that as society
becomes more opaque, anonymous, and overwhelming, the task for the
individual is to achieve a deeper subjectivity, an intensification
of the inner life. He fails to see that this recommendation is
precisely what society has imposed on the individual for centu-
ries--the pursuit of freedom outside the public realm. He also
does not recognize that such inner pursuits have been frustrated
because of their "forced separation and isolation," not for lack
of an empathic approach.

Kohut is hardly alone in his belief: "Most psychologists today are committed to a viewpoint which sees self-actualization as
totally dependent on the individual" (Beit-Hallahmi, 1974: 128).
A concrete sociohistorical analysis seems to be the most appropriate way to combat the idea in Kohut's work that ours is the era of

"Tragic Man," the era in which man has "fallen from grace more definitely than previous generations" (SS: 925). Even though Kohut believes our fragmentation can potentially spur great future achievements as we attempt to recapture the lost wholeness of the self (SS: 926), there is an undertone to these world-historical speculations which glorifies the past in certain ways. This is most clearly seen in his discussion of the family.

Kohut argues that in today's family children are often under-stimulated and lonely because of the emotional distance or re-moteness of parents (RS: 271). He does not cite any positive features of the contemporary family. In the era of "Guilty Man," on the other hand, while there was a threat of overcloseness be-tween parents and children, he identifies certain "wholesome social factors" such as "firmness of the family unit, a social life concentrated in the home and its immediate vicinity, and a clearcut definition of the roles of father and mother" (RS: 269). In other words, he finds the nineteenth century idea of the family as a haven, a protected sphere in which to raise children, to be "wholesome."

Yet it must be stressed that the middle-class family during Freud's time was not a haven for women, in spite of how comforta-ble it might have seemed to men. Feminist demands to gain equal rights in the public arena began in this period, and in our time women have more strongly rejected their confinement to a purely maternal role within the family (Easton, 1979). In his conserva-tive defense of the nuclear family, Christopher Lasch (1977) writes that feminists must "acknowledge the deterioration of care for the young." He glorifies the "intense emotional involvement" of the nineteenth century family, and longs for the time when the family was supposedly a "haven in a heartless world".[14] Both he and Kohut not only tend to submerge the problems of the woman's role in this family, but also celebrate the (male) individual produced in such a family as highly cohesive and autonomous. One might easily forget that the cohesiveness of the nineteenth century individual often included such qualities as an impoverishment, if not fear of emotional life, intellectual rigidity, sexual repression, a strong inhibition by internalized parental standards, and an aversion toward cooperative and collective action (Gadlin, 1976; Poster, 1978b). Even if Kohut is correct about the passing of such an individual, we should hardly look upon it with a sense of nostalgia. Likewise, women will probably not be overwhelmed by the wholesomeness of having "clear-cut" parental roles on the nineteenth century model. Kohut does not explicitly advocate a return to these things, of course, but there is a strong undercurrent in his work inclined toward the family and the individual of an earlier era.

The twentieth century has surely been marked by tragedy, but a major source of turmoil has been the crystallization and expansion of nineteenth century trends, not the abandonment of an earlier innocence. A separate private life has increasingly absorbed the energies and the discontents of people, and the stresses of this situation have begun to show. The family is still the main institution entrusted with the job of providing an outlet for frustrations, a ground for self-expression, a protected area for intimacy and sexual life. It simply cannot meet all these demands, and it would seem that increasingly we must seek "the enhancement of personal life through the enhancement of social life" (Zaretsky, 1976: 141). Furthermore, women are increasingly unwilling to bear the responsibilities assigned them by men: "No group experienced the subjective isolation of personal life so deeply as women, trapped as they were within the family, blamed for its egregious faults, or forced to negotiate the limbo between it and the world of wage-labor" (Zaretsky, 1976: 113).

Kohut is able to see effects, but not causes. He witnesses the turmoil within the contemporary family, but can do little more than blame parents. He fails to realize that this era is no more tragic than any other--fundamental divisions remain the same as in Freud's time. Self-realization has long been something pursued in private, on-off hours, and it has just as long been a false promise. Kohut theorizes about the inner life as though it were invisible, as if social barriers related to sex, class, race, and so on did not stand in the way of self-development. One of the more commonplace tragedies of our time is the insistence by respected scholars that the self is an autonomous realm apart from society. Such ideological conceptions secure a place for Kohut's self psychology with the ranks of the "culture industry" (Horkheimer and Adorno, 1972) along with current forms of popular psychology. It is the final, embarrassing spectacle of a psychology which refuses to embrace social theory as a necessary component in its investigations.

EMPATHIC VS. DIALECTICAL THOUGHT

Kohut celebrates empathy as the most significant component

in the creation of an adequate psychological theory. I would insist that a more potent form of thought exists. It has been termed "critical analysis" here, but this type of thought has also been described as the "sociological imagination" (Mills, 1959) or the "dialectical imagination" (Jay, 1973). The differences between dialectical thought and empathic thought are considerable.

The empathic theorist describes the inner life of the individual and creates concepts which express the general vicissitudes of this life. One moves conceptually from immediate experience to general formulations about that experience, and at no point is attention devoted to society or to the social dimension of experience. Dialectical thought, on the other hand, always advances psychological theory from an understanding of specific social problems. Historically-bound truths are sought, rather than an illusory pure knowledge of the inner life.

Empathic thought is lacking in two important ways. Since the general social situations (class, gender, race, etc.) which significantly constitute experience are treated as peripheral and non-essential, empathic theory cannot accurately depict the psychological struggles of specific social groups. For example, general stages of self development are proposed which conceal critical differences between male and female development. In addition, empathic (neopositivist) explanations of human behavior are finally unsatisfying because the phenomena at hand are viewed in isolation, rather than in interconnection with other realities. The empathic theorist might relate present to past experience, but experience is not related to objective social conditions. Presumably, the oppressed situation of minorities, the degraded

nature of work, and the repressively desublimated state of sexuality, to mention a few pertinent realities, merely add specific
content to the universal, human nature of experience. Yet, to the
dialectical theorist who understands the essence of a phenomenon
as existing in its underlying connection, its mediated relation to
the whole, this restriction to general patterns of individual experience is fatal for theory.

Empathic and dialectical thought not only differ with regard
to what is, but also in relation to what ought to be. The two are
intimately connected. When a general theory of the self is rejected for its failure to distinguish how men and women actually
struggle for self-esteem, that theory is also being rejected for
its acceptance of the social situation which forms these struggles. Social problems must be analyzed critically, first as
elements of a complexly-mediated society, and also as they translate into the psyche of individuals. That is to say, we must
criticize sexism, racism, and the like in all their dimensions.
Social science should ideally help construct a society which is
more humane, more rational. The theorist who refuses to evaluate
social phenomena critically helps only to reinforce the status
quo. This is the case with the empathic theorist who abandons
responsibility for evaluation by resting on a "value-free" description of the individual's inner life. Critical analysis rests
on a theory of society which transcends the view of empathically-
understood individuals. It moves beyond "facts" about the individual in an effort to conceptualize how society and individual
exist in reciprocity. Empathy is only a limited tool in this
effort.

The foregoing critique of empathic science operates at a
fundamental level. However, it would be a misunderstanding of
critical analysis to think that empathic data, or more broadly,
neopositivist sciences, are to be eliminated, and that something
else is to replace them. There is no need to substitute anything
for empathically understood experience. Rather, the imperative is
to integrate different levels of analysis, to examine how experience is interconnected with social conditions and institutions.
Empathy is accordingly limited for the theorist, just as research
methods producing "harder" data are limited. The shortcoming
cannot be rectified by introducing other empirical tools to replace or complement existing ones. Moreover, the challenge is not
to present new areas for research. Psychologists have many appropriate concerns, but the usual manner in which phenomena are
conceptualized is inadequate. One's empirical method is typically
the predominant consideration, and questions resistant to this
method of data gathering are slighted. The general theories proposed (on the basis of "value-free" facts) commonly fail to dis-
close the significant mediations which relate a given phenomenon
to others in society. The self is thereby conceptualized as complete in itself; the potentialities of personal life are explored
apart from the realities of work life.

While conceptual integration is emphasized within the dialectical tradition, a formal synthesis is not sought. Dialectical
thought should not be confused with those integrative approaches-
-such as functionalism, systems theory, or various psycho-social
schemes--which are concerned with the theoretical elaboration of
harmoniously integrated systems. For instance, systems theorists

stress that "things are interrelated and should not be analyzed in isolation," yet this is simply a warmed-over version of "an older 'organic' image of society, which sees social institutions as knit together in a manner analogous to the organs of the body" (Lilienfeld, 1975: 647, 656). The phenomena themselves resist such formal unity. Any integration of psychology and sociology must recognize that individuals tend to encounter an antagonistic society and not some conceptual balance of social components, not some smooth ordering of particular and general interests (Adorno, 1967). At a slightly more abstract level, it should be understood that while the theoretical and empirical must be integrated, empirical studies lend accuracy to one's theories on certain points, but they are not equal partners which merge along an imagined continuum of fact and theory. We can document our theories at key points with more detailed information, but the advancement of social science rests with the growth of disciplined thought, of a sociological imagination.

> For that imagination is the capacity to shift from one perspective to another--from the political to the psychological; from the examination of a single family to comparative assessment of the national budgets of the world; from the theological school to the military establishment; from considerations of an oil industry to studies of contemporary poetry. It is the capacity to range from the most impersonal and remote transformations to the most intimate features of the human self-- and to see the relations between the two. Back of its

use there is always the urge to know the social and historical meaning of the individual in the society and in
the period in which he has his quality and his being
(Mills, 1959: 7).

At present such an imagination is achieved at great effort.
Kohut's work is one prominent example of how neopositivist approaches control current thinking in psychology, and how theory is
commonly subordinated to therapy. Critical thought can require
argument at different analytic levels and competence in diverse
academic disciplines. Such work is demanding, yet these analytic
difficulties are perhaps no greater than those obstacles presented
by the minority status of the critical approach. Like any developing approach in social science critical of the dominant approach, it meets with opposition. When that approach is also
critical of society, lines of opposition tend to stiffen. This
situation is not surprising: social science is a socio-political
enterprise. Problems are solved in historical struggle, not in a
realm of disembodied ideas.

FOOTNOTES

[1]Kohut's works are abbreviated: AS, The Analysis of the Self; RS, The Restoration of the Self; SS, The Search for the Self.

[2]See a similar argument by Poster (1978a) regarding Erikson's theory.

[3]This is one feature of individualist theory which Avinieri (1968) has noted.

[4]It is interesting to note Kohut's attempt to bootleg values into his analysis. Several of his patients turned to creative pursuits through analysis and Kohut often notes (SS: 543, 681, 775) how the more private and inward pleasures of the creative artist will be increasingly important as the mass society approaches. This is as close as he gets to evaluating social values and ideals, but he presents it as a statement about which pursuits are more adaptable. The problem here is not simply that the evaluative component is masked, but that adaptability is embraced as a yardstick.

[5]This would explain why the experimental literature measuring observable behaviors does not verify such differences. Maccoby and Jacklin (1974) surveyed this area and found no consistent gender differences.

[6]We might note here that the traditional female forms of control have therefore become "subtle manipulation and invoking of guilt" (Bart, 1971: 116).

[7]Barglow and Schaefer (1976: 339) claim that it is "extremely difficult to demonstrate that there is a gender-linked difference in the self-esteem of men and women," but offer as proof of this contention only the Maccoby and Jacklin survey and the failure of Freud's approach to the question. Equal scores for self-esteem on standardized tests cannot begin to address the issue here, and Freud's failures indicate simply that Freud's genital theory was wrong. Barglow and Schaefer focus only on the quantitative issue of higher or lower self-esteem, ignoring the problem of gender-related avenues to self-esteem. Their primary goal seems to be to affirm that "women's position in a male chauvinistic culture" does not have any bearing on psychic development.

[8]One should not take this to mean that traditional women's jobs were created primarily because women wanted or needed them psychologically. The primary social reality is that women were (and to a great extent continue to be) limited to such jobs. The psychological characteristics noted here must be seen as one element in the reproduction of such a job structure, just as psychology functions in the "reproduction of mothering."

[9]It should be stressed that "merger" is discussed here only with respect to dependence in a specific psychological area. That

is to say, the issue is one of "focal symbiosis," in Greenacre's terms. An individual tends to remain functionally dependent in such an area without being disposed to experience the total, primitive merger of self and other (Stoller, 1975: 142n).

[10]It is worth noting the real, external roadblocks to the woman who idealizes her father and on this basis pursues a career outside the home.

The norms of our society are such that a woman is not

expected to "fulfill" herself through an occupation, but

rather through the traditional roles of wife and mother.

More than this, she is not allowed to do so. The great

discrimination against "uppity women"--women profession-

als--the cruel humor, not being taken seriously, the

lower pay scale, the invisibility (literally and meta-

phorically), make it suicidal for a woman to attempt to

give meaning to her life through work (Bart, 1971: 116).

Of course, more and more women are successfully demanding and achieving such fulfillment, but the internal and external conflicts which must be surmounted separate such an experience from that of the successful male who is led by nuclear ideals of achievement.

[11]One must wonder to what extent the importance of idealization in development is attributable to present social arrangements. Kohut presents it as a natural fact--the infant preserves the original narcissistic perfection through two mechanisms: "I am perfect:" "You are perfect, but I am part of you." However, if idealization usually or optimally requires an intense relationship with a primary parent along with a less familiar, dominant parent who is open to such idealization, then our sexist society is the perfect foundation. We might postulate that idealization would have a much different role and significance in psychological development in a society where families were structured around shared parenting.

[12]It is interesting to note in regard to this last point what Lillian Rubin (1979: 55) found in her interviews with middle-aged women: "Most striking was the fact that, although half the women I talked to hold paid jobs outside the home, not one--including those who work at high-level professional jobs--described herself in relation to her work." Meanwhile, not one of the thirty-five men with whom she talked failed to define himself in relation to his work.

[13] It is important to distinguish the argument made here from critiques of the nuclear family by Slater (1970), the Skolnicks (1971), and others. They too criticize the isolation of the family, but their argument is based on a celebration of the need for "human interdependence" or "social solidarity" or "community." The Skolnicks, for example, "hope to recreate the kind of social solidarity that exists in the extended family, or the medieval village described by Aries" (1971: 30). It is quite valid to argue that the isolation of mother and children in the home is negative for all involved, but proposing to reshape the nuclear family into a more extended or communal form does not respond to the fundamental social dynamic of industry-family, work-personal life. Reforming the family does not change the fact that in our society mechanization and routine have degraded work to the extent that it is generally not considered gratifying in itself, but rather only for what it enables us to purchase and consume in personal life. So long as the family and personal life bear the burden of providing fulfillment and gratification, any family type will be pressured to the breaking point.

[14] It might be noted in passing how Lasch uses the work-life dichotomy. He recognizes that in the nineteenth century "deprivations experienced in the public world had to be compensated in the realm of privacy" (1977: 7). He then bemoans how since 1920 social scientists, policy makers, and other experts have spearheaded a broad social attack on this realm of privacy. In other words, his argument is essentially a defense of the retreat to family and personal life. He believes it is a positive phenomenon which we should try to strengthen today.

REFERENCES

Adorno, T. W. 1967.
"Sociology and Psychology," **New Left Review,** 6, 67-80.

Aries, P. 1971.
"From the Medieval to the Modern Family," in **Family in Trans-ition,** ed. A. Skolnick and J. Skolnick.
Boston: Little, Brown.

Avinieri, S. 1968.
The Social and Political Thought of Karl Marx.
Cambridge: Cambridge University Press.

Barglow, P. and Schaefer, M. 1976.
"A New Female Psychology?" **Journal of the American Psycho-analytic Association,** 24: 5, 305-350.

Bart, P. 1971
"Depression in Middle-Aged Women," in **Women in Sexist Soci-ety,** ed. V. Gornick and B. Moran.
New York: Basic Books.

Beit-Hallahmi, B. 1974.
"Salvation and Its Vicissitudes," **American Psychologist,** February, 124-129.

Braverman, H. 1974.
Labor and Monopoly Capital.
New York: Monthly Review Press.

Chodorow, N. 1971.
"Being and Doing: A Cross-Cultural Examination of the So-cialization of Males and Females," in **Woman in Sexist Society,** ed. V. Gornick and B. Moran.
New York: Basic Books.

Chodorow, N. 1974.
"Family Structure and Feminine Personality," in **Women, Cul-ture, and Society,** ed. M. Rosaldo and L. Lampere.
Stanford: Stanford University Press.

Chodorow, N. 1978.
The Reproduction of Mothering: Psychoanalysis and the Soci-ology of Gender.
Berkeley: University of California Press.

Chodorow, N. 1979.
"Mothering, Male Dominance, and Capitalism," in **Capitalist Patriarchy and the Case for Socialist Feminism,** ed. Z. Eisen-stein.
New York: Monthly Review Press.

Easton, B. 1979.
"Feminism and the Contemporary Family," in **A Heritage of Her**

Own, ed. N. Cott and E. Pleck.
New York: Simon and Schuster.

Freud, S. 1962.
Civilization and Its Discontents.
New York: Norton.

Friday, N. 1977.
My Mother/My Self.
New York: Dell.

Gadlin, H. 1976.
"The Return to Freud?" **New German Critique**, 7, 122-135.

Gornick, V. and Moran, B. 1971.
Woman in Sexist Society.
New York: Basic Books.

Hammer, S. 1975.
Daughters and Mothers: Mothers and Daughters.
New York: Quadrangle.

Hareven, T. 1976.
"Modernization and Family History: Perspectives on Social
Change," **Signs**, 2: 1, 190-206.

Horkheimer, M. and Adorno, T. 1972.
Dialectical Imagination.
Boston: Little, Brown.

Jones, E. 1981a.
"Technocratic or Critical Analysis," **Psychology and Social
Theory**, 1, 26-39.

Jones, E. 1981b.
"Critique of Empathic Science: On Kohut and Narcissism,"
Psychology and Social Theory, 2, 29-43.

Kohut, H. 1971.
The Analysis of the Self.
New York: International Universities Press.

Kohut, H. 1977.
The Restoration of the Self.
New York: International Universities Press.

Kohut, H. 1978.
The Search for the Self: Selected Writings of Heinz Kohut,
1950-1978 (1 and 2), ed. P. Ornstein.
New York: International Universities Press.

Krueger, M. and Silvert, F. 1981.
"Toward an Ideologiekritik of Psychological Explanations of
Student Protest," **Psychology and Social Theory**, 1, 40-51.

Lasch, C. 1977.

Haven in a Heartless World.
New York: Basic Books.

Lilienfield, R. 1975.
"Systems Theory as an Ideology," Social Research, 42: 4, 637-660.

Lorber, J., Coser, R. L., Rossi, A. S., and Chodorow, N. 1981.
"On Reproduction of Mothering: A Method Debate," **Signs**, 6: 3, 482-514.

Lynn, D. 1959.
"A Note on Sex Differences in the Development of Masculine and Feminine Identification," **Psychological Review**, 66, 126-135.

Lynn, D. 1962.
"Sex Role and Parent Identification," **Child Development**, 33, 555-564.

Maccoby, E. and Jacklin, C. 1974.
The Psychology of Sex Differences.
Stanford: Stanford University Press.

Marcuse, H. 1964.
One-Dimensional Man.
Boston: Beacon Press.

McDonough, R. and Harrison, R. 1978.
"Patriarchy and Relations of Production," in **Feminism and Materialism**, ed. A. Kuhn and A. M. Wolpe.
Boston: Routledge and Kegan Paul.

Mills, C. W. 1959.
The Sociological Imagination.
London: Oxford University Press.

Mitchell, J. 1973.
Woman's Estate.
New York: Random House.

Mitscherlich, A. 1970.
Society Without the Father: A Contribution to Social Psychology.
New York: Schocken Books.

Ornstein, P. (ed.). 1978.
The Search for the Self: Selected Writing of Heinz Kohut 1950-1978.
New York: International Universities Press.

Pleck, J. and Sawyer, J. (eds). 1974.
Men and Masculinity.
Englewood Cliffs, New Jersey: Prentice-Hall.

Poster, M. 1978a.

Critical Theory of the Family.
New York: Seabury.

Poster, M. 1978b.
    "Review of Haven in a Heartless World," by Christopher
    Lasch," Telos, 35, 226-230.

Rogers, C. 1977.
    On Personal Power.
    New York: Dell.

Rowbotham, S. 1973.
    Woman's Consciousness, Man's World.
    Baltimore: Penguin.

Rubin, G. 1975.
    "The Traffic in Women: Notes on the 'Political Economy' of
    Sex," in Toward an Anthropology of Women, ed. R. Reiter.
    New York: Monthly Review Press.

Rubin, L. 1979.
    Women of a Certain Age.
    New York: Harper and Row.

Sartre, J. P. 1968.
    Search for a Method.
    New York: Random House.

Schafer, R. 1976.
    A New Language for Psychoanalysis.
    New Haven: Yale University Press.

Skolnick, A. and Skolnick, J. 1971.
    Family in Transition.
    Boston: Little, Brown.

Slater, P. 1961.
    "Toward a Dualistic Theory of Identification," Merrill-Palmer
    Quarterly of Behavior and Development, 7: 2, 113-126.

Slater, P. 1970.
    The Pursuit of Loneliness,
    Boston: Beacon Press.

Stoller, R. 1975.
    Perversion: The Erotic Form of Hatred.
    New York: Harper and Row.

Welter, B. 1978.
    "The Cult of True Womanhood: 1820-1860," in The American
    Family in Socio-Historical Perspective, ed. M. Gordon.
    New York: St. Martin's Press.

Winch, R. 1962.
    Identification and Its Familial Determinants.
    New York: Bobbs-Merrill.

Zaretsky, E. 1976.
    Capitalism, the Family, and Personal Life.
    New York: Harper and Row.

CHAPTER 6

MATERNAL THINKING*

Sara Ruddick

We are familiar with Victorian renditions of Ideal Maternal
Love. My own favorite, like so many of these poems, was written
by a son.

> There was a young man loved a maid
> Who taunted him. "Are you afraid,"
> She asked, "to bring me today
> Your mother's head upon a tray?"
>
> He went and slew his mother dead,
> Tore from her breast her heart so red,
> Then towards his lady love he raced,
> But tripped and fell in all his taste.
>
> As the heart rolled on the ground
> It gave forth a plaintive sound.
> And it spoke, in accents mild:
> "Did you hurt yourself, my child?"[1]

*Sara Ruddick, "Maternal Thinking," Feminist Studies 6, no. 2
(Summer 1980), pp. 342-367. Copyright (c) 1980 by Feminist
Studies. Reprinted by permission of Feminist Studies, Inc., c/o
Women's Studies Program, University of Maryland, College Park, Md.
20742.

Many of this story's wishes and fantasies are familiar. Our love for our sons is said to be dangerous to the "maid" who seeks to take him from us. Like the first mother, a mother-in-law is a maid's rival for the sexual possession of a man. We too were maids and lovers before we were mothers; we understand. We understand too that our love may jeopardize our sons' manhood. As "good" mothers we allow our sons contempt for our feelings ("the normal male contempt for women"),[2] if not for our lives, so that they may guiltlessly "separate themselves" from us. There is, however, an unfamiliar twist to the poem. The lady asked for our head, the son brought our heart. She feared and respected our thoughts. He believes only our feelings are powerful. Again we are not surprised. The passions of maternity are so sudden, intense, and confusing, that we ourselves often remain ignorant of the perspective, the **thought** that has developed from our mothering. Lacking pride, we have failed to deepen or to articulate that thought. This is a paper about the head of the mother.

***

Central to our experience of our mothers and our mothering is a poignant conjunction of power and powerlessness. In any society a mother is unavoidably powerless. Nature's indifference--illness, death, and damage to the child or its closest loved ones--can frustrate the best maternal efforts. To unavoidable powerlessness is added avoidable social powerlessness. Almost everywhere the practices of mothering take place in societies in which women of all classes are less able than men of their class to determine the conditions in which their children grow. Throughout history, most women have mothered in conditions of military and social violence, as well as economic deprivation, governed by men whose policies they could neither shape nor control.

Powerless mothers are also powerful. "Most of us first know both love and disappointment, power and tenderness, in the person of a woman."[3] For a child, a mother is the primary, uncontrollable source of the world's goods; a witness and judge whose will must be placated, whose approval must be secured.[4] Some of a mother's power is avoidable if childcare is shared, from infancy on, with other adults and older children. However, a mother has a residual power accruing from her capacity to bear and nurse infants. So long as she is able and chooses to utilize her reproductive body in her own and her children's interest, she will, in the predictable technological future, have power to give or deny children to men as well as to maintain some irreducible power over her children by dint of her unique and extraordinary physical intimacy with them.

In most societies however, women are socially powerless in respect to the very reproductive capacities that might make them powerful. The primary bodily experience of mothers is a poignant reminder that to think of maternal power is immediately to recall maternal powerlessness—and conversely. Freudians and feminists have made us aware of the unfortunate consequences of this lethal conjunction. Children confront and rely upon a powerful maternal presence only to watch her become the powerless woman in front of the father, the teacher, the doctor, the judge, the landlord—the world. A child's rageful disappointment in its powerless mother,

combined with resentment and fear of her powerful will, may account for the matriphobia so widespread in our society as to seem
normal. For whatever reasons, it seems almost impossible for
older children or adults to construct a coherent, let alone a
benign, account of maternal power.[5]

The conjunction of maternal power and powerlessness makes
maternal practices oppressive to mothers and children alike. The
oppression is real; much more could be said about it. However, to
suggest that mothers are principally victims of a kind of crippling work is an egregiously inaccurate account of women's own
experience as mothers and daughters. Although one can sympathize
with the anger that insists upon and emphasizes the oppressive
nature of maternal practices, an account that describes only
exploitation and pain is itself oppressive to women.[6] Mothers,
despite the inevitable trials and social conditions of motherhood,
are often effective in their work.

In articulating those conditions of mothering that allow for
happiness and efficacy, we need to remember some simple facts.
Maternal practices begin in love, a love which for most mothers is
as intense, confusing, ambivalent, and poignantly sweet as any
they will experience. Although economic and social conditions,
such as the poverty that is widespread and the isolation that is
typical in America, may make that love frantic, they do not kill
the love. For whatever reasons, mothers typically find it not
only natural but compelling to protect and foster the growth of
their children. Relatedly, mothers, especially those who have
chosen or come to welcome parenthood, experience a social-bio-
logical pride in the function of their reproductive processes, a

sense of the activation of maternal power.   In addition to a sense of reproductive power, many mothers early develop a sense of maternal competence, a sense that they **are** able to protect and foster the growth of their children.

That maternal love, pleasure in reproductive powers, and a sense of maternal competence survive in a patriarchal society where women are routinely derogated, makes one wonder at the further possibilities for maternal happiness in decent societies. Even in this relatively indecent society, mothers are usually socially rewarded for their work by the shared pleasure and confirmation of other women, by the gratitute and pride of grandparents, and frequently by the intense, appreciative paternal love of their mates. Moreover, mothers who work primarily at home frequently have more control over the details of their working day than is available to other workers.[7]   Many mothers, whatever their work in the public world, feel part of a community of comothers whose warmth and support is rerely equaled in other working relationships.   Loving, competent, and appreciated, a mother need not experience her work as oppressive. When their children flourish, mothers have a sense of well-being.

On the other hand, no children flourish all of the time.   The emotional and physical pains of their children are anguishing for mothers, inducing a sense of helplessness and guilt.   Isolation, restricted options, and social devaluation can make mothering grim even for economically privileged women.   It is difficult when writing about motherhood--or experiencing it--to be balanced about both its grim and its satisfying aspects.

Yet loving, competent well-being is an important element in

our (my) memories of our mothers and mothering. We must bear these memories in mind if we are to understand that neither the world's misogyny nor our own related psychic dramas have totally prevented us from acquiring an image of benign maternal power. Whatever their scientific status, persistent interest in and positive response to myths of matriarchy show how avidly women search for a society in which mothers are powerful. Feminist utopias are apt to assign government to mothers. "You see we are mothers," their authors seem to say, as if in saying that they have said it all.[8] Cultural myths and our own dreams tell of us a connection we would wish to make with a mother who is socially as well as personally powerful, powerful in adult as well as in infants' eyes. The construction of matriarchal pasts and futures signal longing and regret; longing for a powerful mother we remember and wish we could recognize; regret, often resentful and blaming, that she does not come again after the years of childhood.

My mama moved among the days
like a dreamwalker in a field;
seemed like what she touched was hers
seemed like what touched her couldn't hold,
she got us almost through the high grass
then seemed like she turned around and ran
right back in
right back on in.[9]

It is enormously difficult to come by an image of maternal

power that is even coherent, let alone benign: it is easy to come by images of powerlessness and malign power. I consider my attempt to express and respect maternal thought one contribution to an ongoing shared, feminist project: the construction of an image of maternal power which is benign, accurate, sturdy, and sane.

My particular project, the expression of maternal thought, connects to a general question. Do women, who now rightfully claim the instruments fo public power, have cultures, traditions, and inquiries which we should insist upon bringing to the public world? If the "womanly" can be identified, should we respect it or attempt to surpass it? These questions divide feminists. The ideology of womanhood has been invented by men. It confines as it exalts us. On the other hand, the ideology of androgyny is often a disguised ideology of manhood that continues the disrespect for women shared by both sexes.

I am aware of the oppressive uses to which any identification of the "womanly" can be put. Our current gender dichotomies are rigid and damaging. Praising cultures of oppression comes close to praising oppression itself. Often we celebrate our mothers' lives only because we are afraid to confront the damage our past wrecked upon them and us. Despite these doubts, I am increasingly convinced that there are female traditions and practices out of which a distinctive kind of thinking has developed.

Maternal thought does, I believe, exist for all women in a radically different way than for men. It is because we are **daughters** that we early receive maternal love with special attention to its implications for our bodies, our passions, and our ambitions. We are alert to the values and costs of maternal practices whether we are determined to engage in them or to avoid them. Although some men do, and more men should, acquire maternal thinking, their ways of acquisition are necessarily different from ours.[12]

I do not wish to deny any more than I wish to affirm some biological bases of maternal thinking. The "biological body" (in part a cultural artifact) **may** foster certain features of maternal practice, sensibility, and thought. Neither our own ambivalaence to our women's bodies nor the bigoted, repressive uses which many men, colonizers, and racists have made of biology, should blind us to our body's possibilities. In concentrating on what mothers do rather than upon what we are, I postpone biological questions until we have the moral and political perceptions to answer them justly.[13]

Along with biology, I put aside all accounts of gender dif- ference or maternal nature which would claim an essential and ineradicable difference between female and male parents. However, I do believe that there are features of mothering experience which are invariant and nearly unchangeable, and others which, though changeable, are nearly universal.[14] It is therefore possible to identify interests that appear to govern maternal practice throughout the species. However, it is impossible even to begin to specify those interests without importing features specific to the class, ethnic group, and particular sex-gender system in which those interests are realized. I will be drawing upon my knowledge of the institutions of motherhood in middle-class, white, Protes- tant, capitalist, patriarchal America as these have expressed themselves in the heterosexual nuclear family in which I mother and was mothered. Although I have tried to compensate for the limits of my particular social and sexual history, I principally depend upon others to correct my interpretations and to translate across cultures.[15]

I speak about a mother's **thought**--the intellectual capacities she develops, the judgments she makes, the metaphysical attitudes she assumes, the values she affirms. A mother engages in a discipline. That is, she asks certain questions rather than others; establishes criteria for the truth, adequacy, and relevance of proposed answers; and cares about the findings she makes and can act upon. Like any discipline, hers has **characteristic** errors, temptations, and goals. The discipline of maternal thought consists in establishing criteria for determining failure and success, in setting the priorities, and in identifying the virtues and liabilities which the criteria presume. To describe the capacities, judgments, metaphysical attitudes, and values of maternal thought does not presume maternal achievement. It is to describe a **conception** of achievement, the end to which maternal efforts are directed, conceptions and ends quite different from dominant public ones.[16]

In stating my claims about maternal thinking, I use a vocabulary developed in formulating theories about the general nature of thought.[17] According to these theories, all thought arises out of social practice. In their practices, people respond to a reality that appears to them as given, as presenting certain **demands**. The response to demands is shaped by **interests** which are generally interests in preserving, reproducing, directing, and understanding individual and group life. These four intersts are general in the sense that they arise out of the conditions of humans-in-nature and characterize us as a species. However, these interests are always and only expressed as interests of people in particular cultures and classes of their cultures, living in specific geographical, technological, and historical settings. They are always and only responses to some realities--human and nonhuman, natural and supranatural--which present themselves to particular interested people as given. Thinking is governed by the interests of the practice out of which it arises. Thinking names and elaborates the "given" reality to whose demands practice is responding. It expresses, refines, and executes the interests of the practice in a way that is disciplined, directive, and communicable.

Maternal practice responds to the historical reality of a biological child in a particular social world. The agents of maternal practice, acting in response to the demands of their children, acquire a conceptual scheme--a vocabulary and logic of connections--through which they order and express the facts and values of their practice. In judgments and self-reflection, they refine and concretize this scheme. Intellectual activities are distinguishable, but not separable from disciplines of feeling. There is a unity of reflection, judgment, and emotion. It is this unity I call "maternal thinking." Although I will not digress to argue the point here, it is important that maternal thinking is no more interest governed, no more emotional, no more relative to its particular reality (the growing child) than the thinking that arises from scientific, religious, or any other practice.

Children, "demand" that their lives be preserved and their growth be fostered. Their social group "demands" that their growth be shaped in a way acceptable to the next generation.

Maternal practice is governed by (at least) three interests in satisfying these demands for preservation, growth, and acceptability. Preservation is the most invariant and primary of the three. Because a caretaking mother typically bears her own children, preservation begins when conception is recognized and accepted. Although the form of preservation depends upon widely variant beliefs about the fragility and care of the fetus, women have always had a lore in which they recorded their concerns for the baby they "carried." Once born, a child is physically vulnerable for many yars. Even when she lives with the father of her child or other female adults, even when she has money to purchase or finds available supportive health and welfare services, a mother typically considers herself and is considered by others to be responsible for the maintenance of the life of her child.

Interest in fostering the physical, emotional, and intellectual growth of her child soon supplements a mother's interest in its preservation. The human child is typically capable of complicated emotional and intellectual development; the human adult is radically different in kind from the child it once was. A woman who mothers may be aided or assulted by the help and advice of fathers, teachers, doctors, moralists, therapists, and others who have an interest in fostering and shaping the growth of her child. Although rarely given primary credit, a mother typically holds herself and is held by others to be responsible for the **malfunction** of the growth process.

From early on, certainly by the middle years of childhood, a mother is governed by a third interest. She must shape natural growth in such a way that her child becomes the sort of adult that she can appreciate and others can accept. Mothers will vary enormously, individually and socially, in the traits and lives that they will appreciate in their children. However, a mother typically takes as the criterion of her success the production of a young adult acceptable to her group.

These three interests in preservation, growth, and acceptability of the child govern maternal practices in general. However, not all mothers are, as individuals, governed by these interests. Some mothers are incapable of interested participation in the practices of mothering because of emotional, intellectual, or physical disability. Severe poverty may make interested maternal practice and therefore maternal thinking nearly impossible. Then, of course, mothers engage in practices other than and often conflicting with mothering. Some mothers, aware of the derogation and confinement of women in maternal practice, may be disaffected. In short, actual mothers have the same sort of relation to maternal practice as actual scientists have to scientific practice, or actual believers have to religious practices. As mothers, they are governed by the interests of their respective practices. But the style, skill, commitment, integrity, with which they engage in these practices, differ widely from individual to individual.

The interest in preservation, growth, and the acceptability of the child are frequently and unavoidably in conflict. A mother who watches a child eagerly push a friend aside as she or he climbs a tree will be torn between preserving the child from danger, encouraging the child's physical skills and courage, and shaping a child according to moral restraints--which might, for example, inhibit the child's joy in competitive climbing.

Although some mothers will deny or be insensitive to the conflict and others will be clear about which interest should take precedence, mothers typically will know that they cannnot secure each interest, will know that goods conflict, will know that unqualified success in realizing interests is an illusion. This unavoidable conflict of basic interests is one objective basis for the maternal humility which I will shortly describe.

A mother, acting in the interest of preserving and maintaining life, is in a peculiar relation to "nature." As a childbearer, she often takes herself and is taken by others to be an especially "natural" member of her culture. As a childtender, she must respect nature's limits and court its favor with foresightful actions ranging from immunizations; to caps on household poisons; to magical imprecations, warnings, and prayers. "Nature" with its unpredictable varieties of dirt and disease, is her enemy as much as her ally. Her children themselves are natural creatures, often unable to understand or abet her efforts to protect them. Because they frequently find her necessary direction constraining, a mother can experience her children's own liveliness as another enemy of the life she is preserving.

It is no wonder then that as she engages in preservation, a mother is liable to the temptations of fearfulness and excessive control. If she is alone with two or more young children as she tries to carry out her responsibilities, then control of herself, her children, and her physical environment is her only option, however rigid or excessive she looks to outsiders. Though necessarily controlling in their acts, reflecting mothers themselves identify rigid or excessive control as the likely defects of the

very virtues they are required to practice. It is the identification of liability as such, with its implication of the will to
overcome, which characterizes this aspect of maternal thought.
The epithet "controlling mother" is often unsympathetic, even
matriphobic. On the other hand, it may, in line with the insights
of maternal thought, remind us of what maternal thinking counts as
failure. To recognize excessive control as a liability sharply
distinguishes maternal from scientific practice.[18]

To a mother, "life" may well seem "terrible, hostile, and
quick to pounce on you if you give it a chance."[19] In response,
she develops a metaphysical attitude toward "Being as such," an
attitude which I call "holding," an attitude which is governed by
the priority of keeping over acquiring, of conserving the fragile,
of maintaining whatever is at hand and necessary to the child's
life. It is an attitude elicited by the work of "world-protect-
ion, world-preservation, world-repair. . . the invisible weaving
of a frayed and threadbare family life."[20]

The recognition of the priority of holding over acquiring
once again distinguishes maternal from scientific thought, as well
as from the instrumentalism of technocratic capitalism. In
recognizing resilient good humor and humility as achievements of
its practices, maternal thought takes issue both with contemporary
moral theory and with popular moralities of assertiveness.[21] Humility is a metaphysical attitude one takes toward a world beyond
one's control. One might conceive of the world as governed by
necessity and chance (as I do) or by supernatural forces that cannot be comprehended. In either case, humility implies a profound
sense of the limits of one's actions and of the unpredictability

of the consequences of one's work. As the philosopher Iris Murdoch puts it: "Every 'natural' thing, including one's own mind, is subject to chance. . . . One might say that chance is a subdivision of death. . . . We cannot dominate the world."[22] Humility which emerges from maternal practices accepts not only the facts of damage and death, but also the facts of the independent and uncontrollable, developing and increasingly separate existences of the lives it seeks to preserve. "Humility is not a peculiar habit of self-effacement, rather like having an inaudible voice, it is selfless respect for reality and one of the most difficult and central of virtues."[23]

If in the face of danger, disappointment, and unpredictability, mothers are liable to melancholy, they are also aware that a kind, resilient good humor is a virtue. This good humor must not be confused with the cheery denial which is both a liability and, unfortunately, a characteristic of maternal practice. Mothers are tempted to denial simply by the insupportable difficulty of passionately loving a fragile creature in a physically threatening, socially violent, pervasively uncaring, competitive world. Defensive denial is exacerbated as it is officially encouraged, when we must defend against perceptions of our own subordination. Our cheery denials are cruel to our children and demoralizing to ourselves.

Clear-sighted cheerfulness is the virtue of which denial is the degenerative form. It is clear-sighted cheerfulness that Spinoza must have had in mind when he said: "Cheerfulness is always a good thing and never excessive"; it "increases and assists the power of action."[24] Denying cheeriness drains intellectual energy and befuddles the will; the cheerfulness honored in maternal thought increases and assists the power of maternal action.

In a daily way, cheerfulness is a matter-of-fact willingness to continue, to give birth and to accept having given birth, to welcome life despite its conditions. When things fall apart, maternal cheerfulness becomes evident courage. There are many stories of mothers who, with resourcefulness and restraint, help their children to die well. The most common but disturbing stories concern mothers who accept their sons' wartime deaths, the most affecting, those which involve the deaths of small children in families.[25] These visible and accessible examples are but the manifestation of psychic strengths that have been developed in conditions of mothering which are invisible and frequently denied. Resilient good humor is a style of mothering "in the deepest sense of 'style' in which to discover the right style is to discover what you are really trying to do."[26]

Because in the dominant society "humility" and "cheerfulness" name virtues of subordinates, and because these virtues have in fact developed in conditions of subordination, it is difficult to credit them, easy to confuse them with the self-effacement and cheery denial which are their degenerative forms. Again and again, in attempting to articulate maternal thought, language is sicklied o'er by the pale cast of sentimentality and thought itself takes on a greeting card quality. Yet literature shows us many mothers who in their "holding" actions value the humility and resilient good humor I have described. One can meet such mothers, recognize their thought, any day one learns to listen. One can appreciate the efforts of their disciplined perseverance in the unnecessarily beautiful artifacts of the culture they created. "I made my quilt to keep my family warm. I made it beautiful so my heart would not break."[27]

Mothers not only must preserve fragile, existing life. They must also foster growth and welcome change. If the "being" which is preserved seems always to be endangered, undone, slipping away, the "being" which changes is always developing, building, purposively moving away. The "holding," preserving mother must, in response to change, be simultaneously a changing mother. Her conceptual scheme in terms of which she makes sense of herself, her child, and their common world will be more the Aristotelian biologist's than the Platonic mathematician's. Innovation takes precedence over permanence, disclosure, and responsiveness over clarity and certainty. The idea of "objective reality" itself "undergoes important modification when it is to be understood, not in relation to "the world described by science," but in relation to the progressing life of a person."[28]

Women are said to value open over closed structure, to eschew the clear-cut and unambiguous, to refuse a sharp division between inner and outer or self and other. We are also said to depend upon and to prize our private inner lives of the mind.[29] If these facets of the "female mind" are elicited by maternal practices, they may well be interwoven responses to the changeability of a growing child. A child is itself an "open structure" whose acts are irregular, unpredictable, often mysterious. A mother, in order to understand her child, must assume the existence of a conscious continuing person whose acts make sense in terms of perceptions and responses to a meaning-filled world. She knows that her child's fantasies and thoughts are not only connected to the child's power to act, but often the only basis for her under-standing of the child and for the child's self-understanding.[30]

A mother, in short, is committed to two philosophical posi-tions: she is a mentalist rather than a behaviorist, and she assumes the priority of personhood over action. Moreover, if her "mentalism" is to enable her to understand and to love, she must be realistic about the psyche whose growth she fosters. All psyches are moved by fear, lust, anger, pride, and defenses against them, by what Simone Weil called "natural movements of the soul" and likened to laws of physical gravity.[31] This is not to deny that the soul is also blessed by "grace," "light," and erotic hungering for goodness.[32] However, mothers cannot take grace for granted, nor force nor deny the less flattering aggrandizing and consolatory operations of childhood psychic life. A mother must again and again "regain the sense of the complexity and the reali-ty and the struggle . . . with some pity, some envy and much good will."[33]

Her realistic appreciation of a person's continuous mental life allows a mother to expect change, to change with change. As psychologist Jean Baker Miller puts it: "In a very immediate and day to day way women live for change."[34] Change requires a kind of learning in which what one learns cannot be applied exactly, and often not even by analogy, to a new situation. If science agrees to take as real the reliable results of repeatable experi-ments,[35] its learning will be quite different in kind from mater-nal learning. Miller is hopeful that if we attend to maternal practices, we can develop new ways of studying learning appropriate to the changing natures of all peoples and communities, for it is not only children who change, grow, and need help in growing. Most obviously those who care for children must change in response to changing reality. And we all might grow--as opposed to aging--if we could learn how. For everyone's benefit, "women must now face the task of putting their vast unrecognized experience with change into a new and broader level of operation."[36]

Miller writes of achievement, of women who have learned to change and respond to change. But she admits:

> Tragically in our society, women are prevented from
> fully enjoying these pleasures (of growth) themselves by
> being made to feel that fostering them in others is the
> only valid role for all women and by the loneliness,
> drudgery and isolated non-cooperative household setting
> in which they work.[37]

Similarly, in delineating maternal thought, I do not claim that mothers realize in themselves, the capacities and virtues which we learn to value as we care for others. Rather, mothers develop **conceptions** of abilities and virtues according to which they measure themselves and interpret their actions. It is no great sorrow that some mothers never acquire humility, resilient good humor, realism, respect for persons, and responsiveness to growth, that all of us fail often in many kinds of ways. What is a great sorrow is to find the task itself misdescribed, sentimentalized, and devalued.

Acting in the interests of preservation and growth, women have developed a maternal perspective. This perspective has its degenerative forms, such as the cheery denial that sometimes passes for cheerfulness. Preservation can turn into the fierce desire to foster one's own children's growth whatever the cost to other children. Holding--world-preservation and world-repair--can turn into frantic accumulating and storing, especially under the pressures of consumerism. Yet though liable to degenerative forms, this is a perspective which any moral or thinking person might profitably consider.

With regard to the third interest governing maternal practices, the interest in producing a child acceptable to the next generation, worthiness is quite problematic. Families and societies have an interest in reproducing their members in a manner and with a result they can appreciate. Women, themselves half of family and society, share that interest. Yet they act in a society in which they are relatively powerless in respect to men and governor-experts of both sexes. Powerlessness is exacerbated by the matraphobia I earlier described, by self-contempt, and by numerous demoralizing, frightening physical and psychological violences perpetrated against all women. In response to maternal powerlessness, to a society whose values it cannot determine, maternal thought has opted for inauthenticity and the "good" of others.

By "inauthenticity" I designate a double willingness--first a willingness to travailler pour l'armee,[38] to accept the uses to which others will put one's children; second a willingness to remain blind to the implications of those uses for the actual lives of women and children. Maternal thought embodies inauthenticity by taking on the values of the dominant culture. Like the "holding" of preservation, "inauthenticity" is a mostly nonconscious response to Being as Such. Only this attitude is not a caretaker's response to the natural exigencies of childtending, but a subordinate's reaction to a social reality essentially characterized by the domination and subordination of persons. Inauthenticity constructs and then assumes a world in which one's own values don't count. It is allied to fatalism and to some religious thought, some versions of Christianity, for example. As inauthenticity is lived out in maternal practice, it gives rise to the values of obedience and "being good;" that is, it is taken as an achievement to fulfill the values of the dominant culture. Obedience is related to humility in the face of the limits of one's powers. But unlike humility, which respects indifferent nature, the incomprehensible supernature, the human fallibility, obedience respects the actual control and preferences of dominant people.

Individual mothers, living out maternal thought, take on the values of the families and subcultures to which they belong and of the men with whom they are allied. Because some groups and many men are vibrantly moral, these values are not necessarily inadequate. However, even moral groups and men almost always accept the relative subordination of women, whatever other ideals of equality and autonomy they may hold. A "good" mother may well be praised for colluding in her own subordination with the destructive consequences to herself and her children that I've described. Moreover, most groups and men impose at least some values that are

psychologically and physically damaging to children. A mother
practiced in fostering growth will be able to "see" the effects
of, for example, injurious stratification, competitiveness, gender
stereotyping, hypocrisy, and conscription to war. Damage to a
child is as clear to her as the effect of a hurricane on a young
tree. Yet to be "good," a mother may be expected to endorse and
execute inimical commands. She is also the person principally
responsible for training her children in the ways and desires of
obedience. This may mean training her daughters for powerlessness, her sons for war, and both for crippling work in dehumani-
zing factories, businesses, and professions. It may mean training
both daughters and sons for defensive or arrogant power over
others in sexual, economic, or political life. A mother who
trains either for powerlessness or abusive power over others
betrays the very life she has preserved, whose growth she has
fostered. She denies her children even the possibility of being
both strong and good.

The strain of colluding in one's own powerlessness, coupled
with the frequent and much greater strain of betraying the children one has tended, would be insupportable if conscious. A mother
under strain may internalize as her own values those values which
are clearly inimical to her children. She has, after all, usually
been rewarded for just such protective albeit destructive inter-
nalization. Additionally, she may blind herself to the implications of her obedience, a blindness which is excused and exacerbated by the cheeriness of denial. For precariously but deeply
protected mothers, feminist accounts of power relations and their
cost call into question the worthiness of maternal work and the

genuiness of maternal love. Such women, understandably, fight insight as others fight bodily assault, revealing in their struggles a commitment to their own sufferings which may look "neurotic" but is in fact, given their options, realistic.

When I described maternal thought arising out of the interests in growth and preservation, I was not speaking of the actual achievement of mothers, but of a conception of achievement. Similarly, in describing the thought arising out of the interest in acceptability, I am not speaking of actual mothers' adherence to dominant values, but of a conception of their relation to those values in which obedience and "being good" is considered an achievement. There are many individual mothers who "fail," that is who insist on their own values, who will not remain blind to the implications of dominant values for the lives of their children. Moreover, I hope I have said enough about the damaging effects of the prevailing sexual arrangements and social hierarchies on maternal lives to make it clear that I do not blame mothers for their (our) obedience. Obedience is largely a function of social powerlessness. Maternal work is done according to the Law of the Symbolic Father and under His Watchful Eye, as well as, typically, according to the desires, even whims, of the father's house. "This is my Father's world/ Oh let me ne'er forget/ that though the wrong be oft so strong,/ He is the ruler yet." In these conditions of work, inauthentic obedience to dominant patriarchal values is as plausible a maternal response as respect for the results of experiment is in scientific work.

On the other hand, interest in producing an acceptable child provides special opportunities for mothers to explore, create, and

insist upon their own values, to train their children for strength
and moral sensitivity. For this opportunity to be realized,
either collectively or by individual mothers, maternal thought
will have to be transformed by feminist consciousness.

> Coming to have a feminist consciousness is the experi-
> ence of coming to know the truth about oneself and one's
> society. . . . The very meaning of what the feminist
> apprehends is illuminated by the light of what ought to
> be. . . . The feminist apprehends certain features of
> social reality as intolerable, as to be rejected in
> behalf of a transforming project for the future. . . .
> Social reality is revealed as deceptive. . . . What is
> really happening is quite different from what appears to
> be happening.[39]

Feminist consciousness will first transform inauthentic obedience
into wariness, uncertain reflection, at times, anguished confusion. The feminist becomes "marked by the experience of moral
ambiguity" as she learns new ways of living without betraying her
woman's past, without denying her obligations to others. "She no
longer knows what sort of person she ought to be, and therefore
she does not know what she ought to do. One moral paradigm is
called into question by the laborious and often obsure emergence
of another."[40]

Out of confusion, new voices will arise, voices recognized
not so much by the content of the truths they enunicate as by the
honesty and courage of enunciation. They will be at once familiar

and original, these voices arising out of maternal practice, affirming its own criteria of acceptability, insisting that the dominant values are unacceptable and need not be accepted.

How **does** the male child differentiate himself from his mother, and does this mean inevitably that he must "join the army," that is, internalize patriarchal values? Can the mother, in patriarchy, represent culture, and if so, what does this require of her?. . . . What do we want for our sons?. . . We want them to remain in the deepest sense, sons of the mother, yet also to grow into themselves, to discover new ways of being men as we are discovering new ways of being women.

What do we mean by the nurture of daughters? The most notable fact that the culture imprints on women is the sense of our limits. The most important thing one woman can do for another is to illuminate and expand her sense of actual possibilities. . . . The quality of the mother's life—however embattled and unprotected—is her primary bequest to her daughter.[41]

I have been arguing that maternal thought as it is governed by the interest in acceptability is clear and distinct enough to be expressed, but is not yet worthy of respect. The interest in acceptability will always shape maternal practices and provoke mothers to affirm and announce some values, their own or others.[42] The production of a child worthy of appreciation is a real demand

which a mother would impose on herself even if it were not demanded of her by her community. The only question is whether that
demand is met by acquiescence or the struggles of a conscience
attending clearly to the good of children. When mothers insist
upon the inclusion of their values and experiences in the public
world which children enter, when they determine what makes their
children acceptable, the work of growth and preservation will
acquire a new gaiety and joyfulness.

Finally, I would like to discuss a capacity-- "attention"--
and a virtue--love--which are central to the conception of
achievement that maternal thought as a whole. articulates. This
capacity and virtue, when realized, invigorate preservation and
enable growth. Attention and love again and again undermine a
mother's inauthentic obedience as she perceives and endorses a
child's experience though society finds it intolerable. The
identification of the capacity of attention and the virtue of love
is at once the foundation and the corrective of maternal thought.

The notion of "attention" is central to the philosophy of
Simone Weil and is developed, along with the related notion of
"love" by Iris Murdock, who was profoundly influenced by Weil.
Attention and love are fundamental to the construction of "objective reality" understood "in relation to the progressing life of a
person," a "reality which is revealed to the patient eye of
love."[43] Attention is an **intellectual** capacity connected even by
definition with love, a special kind of "knowledge of the individual."[44] "The name of this intense, pure, disinterested, gratui-
tous, generous attention is love."[45] Weil thinks that the capacity for attention is a "miracle," Murdoch ties it more closely to

familiar achievement. "The task of attention goes on all the time and at apparently empty and everyday moments we are 'looking,' making those little peering efforts of imagination which have such important cumulative results."[46]

For both Weil and Murdoch, the enemy of attention is what they call "fantasy," defined not as rich imaginative play, which does have a central role in maternal thnking, but as the "proliferation of blinding self-centered aims and images."[47] Fantasy, according to their original conception, is intellectual and imaginative activity in the service of consolation, domination, anxiety, and aggrandizement. It is reverie designed to protect the psyche from pain, self-induced blindness designed to protect it from insight. Fantasy, so defined, works in the service of inauthenticity. "The difficulty is to keep the attention fixed on the real situation"[48]--or, as I would say, on the real children. Attention to real children, children seen by the "patient eye of love" "teaches us how real things [real children] can be looked at and loved without being seized and used, without being appropriated into the greedy organism of the self."[49]

Much in maternal practices work against attentive love: intensity of identification, vicarious living through a child, daily wear of maternal work, harassment and indignities of an indifferent social order, the clamor of children themselves. Although attention is elicited by the very reality it reveals--the reality of a growing person--it is a discipline that requires effort and self-training. Love, the love of children at any rate, is not only the most intense of attachments; it is also a detachment, a giving up, a letting grow. To love a child without seizing or using it, to see **the child's** reality with the patient, loving eye of attention—such loving and attending might well describe the separation of mother and child from the mother's point of view. Of course, many of us who are mothers fail much of time in attentive love and loving attention. Many mothers also train themselves in the looking, self-restraining, and empathy that is loving attention. They can be heard being so in any playground or coffee klatch.

I am not saying that mothers, individually or collectively, are (or are not) especially wonderful people. My point is that out of maternal practices distinctive ways of conceptualizing, ordering, and valuing arise. We **think** differently about what it **means** and what it takes to be "wonderful," to be a person, to be real.

Murdoch and Weil, neither mothers themselves nor especially concerned with mothers, are clear about the absolute value of attentive love and the reality it reveals. Weil writes:

> In the first legend of the Grail, it is said that the Grail . . . belongs to the first comer who asks the guardian of the vessel, a king three quarters paralyzed by the most painful wound, "What are you going through?"

> The love of our neighbor in all its fullness simply means being able to say to him: "What are you going through?" . . . Only he who is capable of attention can do this.[50]

I do not claim absolute value but only that attentive love, the training to ask, "What are you going through?" is central to maternal practices. If I am right about its place in maternal thought, and if Weil and Murdoch are right about its absolute value, the self-conscious inclusion of maternal thought in the dominant culture will be of general intellectual and moral benefit.

I have described a "thought" arising out of maternal practices organized by the interests of preservation, growth, and acceptability. Although in some respects the thought is "contradictory," that is it betrays its own values and must be transformed by feminist consciousness, the thought as a whole, with its fulcrum and correction in attentive love, is worthy of being expressed and respected. This thought has emerged out of maternal practices that are oppressive to women and children. I believe that it has emerged largely in response to the relatively invariable requirements of children and despite oppressive circumstances. As in all women's thought, some worthy aspects of maternal thought may arise out of identification with the powerless and excluded. However, oppression is largely responsible for the defects rather than the strengths of maternal thought, as in the obedient goodness to which mothers find themselves "naturally" subscribing. When the oppressiveness of gender arrangements is combined with race, poverty, or the multiple injuries of class, it is a miracle that maternal thought can arise at all. On the other hand, that it does indeed arise, miraculously, is clear both from literature (Alice Walker, Tillie Olsen, Maya Angelou, Agnes Smedley, Lucille Clifton, Louisa May Alcott, Audre Lorde, Marilyn

French, Grace Paley, countless others) and from daily experience.
Maternal thought **identifies** priorities, attitudes, and virtues,
conceives of achievement. The more oppressive the institutions of
motherhood, the greater the pain and struggle in living out the
worthy and transforming the damaging aspects of thought.

It is now widely argued that the most liberating change we
can make in institutions of motherhood is to include men equally
in every aspect of maternal care. I am heartened to read that
"societies that do not elaborate the opposition of male and female
and place positive value on the conjugal relationship and involvement of both men and women in the home seem to be most egalitarian
in terms of sex role."[51] To prevent or excuse men from maternal
practice is to encourage them to separate public action from
private affection. Moreover, men's domination is present when
their absence from the nursery is combined with their domination
of every other room. To familiarize children with "natural"
domination at their earliest age in a context of primitive love,
assertion, and sexual passion is to prepare them to find equally
"natural" and exhaustive the division between exploiter and exploited which pervades the world. Although daughter and son alike
may internalize "natural" domination, neither, typically, can live
with it easily. Identifying with and imitating exploiters, we are
overcome with self-hate; aligning ourselves with the exploited, we
are fearful and manipulative. Again and again family power dramas
are repeated in psychic, interpersonal and professional dramas,
while they are institutionalized in economic, political, and
international life. Radically recasting the power-gender roles in
those dramas just might revolutionize social conscience.[52]

Assimilating men into childcare both inside and outside the home would also be conducive to serious social reform. Responsible, equal childcaring would require men to relinquish power and their own favorable position in the division between intellectual /professional and service labor as that division expresses itself domestically. Loss of preferred status at home might make socially privileged men more suspicious of unnecessary divisions of labor and damaging hierarchies in the public world. Moreover, if men were emotionally and practically committed to childcare, they would reform the work world in parents' interests. Once no one "else" was minding the child, there would be good daycare centers with flexible hours, daycare centers to which parents could trust their children from infancy on. These daycare centers, like the work week itself, would be managed "flexibly," in response to human needs as well as "productivity," with an eye to growth, rather than measurable "profit." Such moral reforms of economic life would probably begin with professionals and managers servicing themselves. However, even in nonsocialist countries, their benefits could be unpredictably extensive.

I would not argue, however, that the assimilation of men into childcare is the primary social goal for mothers to set themselves. Rather, we must work to bring a **transformed** maternal thought into the public realm, to make the preservation and growth of all children a work of public conscience and legislation. This will not be easy. Mothers are no less corrupted than anyone else by concerns of status and class. Often our misguided efforts on behalf of the success and purity of our children frighten them and everyone else around them. As we increase and enjoy our public effectiveness, we will have less reason to live vicariously through our children. We may then begin to learn to sustain a creative tension between our inevitable and fierce desire to foster our own children and the less compulsive desire that all children grow and flourish.

Nonetheless, it would be foolish to believe that mothers, just because they are mothers, can transcend class interest and implement principles of justice. All feminists must join in articulating a theory of justice shaped by and incorporating maternal thinking. Moreover, the generalization of attentive love to all children requires politics. The most enlightened thought is not enough.

Closer to home again, we must refashion our domestic life in the hope that the personal will in fact betoken the political. We must begin by resisting the temptation to construe "home" simplemindedly, as a matter of justice between mothers and fathers. Single parents, lesbian mothers, and coparenting women remind us that there are many ways to provide children with examples of caring, which do not incorporate sexual inequities of power and privilege. Those of us who do live with the fathers of our children will eagerly welcome shared parenthood--for overwhelming practical as well as ideological reasons. But in our eagerness, we mustn't forget that so long as a mother is not effective publicly and self-respecting privately, male presence can be harmful as well as beneficial. It does a woman no good to have the power of the Symbolic Father brought right into the nursery, often despite the deep, affectionate egalitarianism of an individual man. It takes a strong mother and father to resist the temptations to domination and subordination for which they have been trained and are socially rewarded. And whatever the hard-won equality and mutual respect an individual couple may achieve, so long as a mother—even if she is no more parent than father—is derogated and subordinate outside the home, children will feel angry, confused, and "wildly unmothered."[53]

Despite these reservations, I look forward to the day when men are willing and able to share equally and actively in transformed maternal practices. When that day comes, will we still identify some thought as maternal rather than merely parental? Might we echo the cry of some feminists—there shall be no more "women"—with our own—there shall be no more "mothers," only people engaging in childcare. To keep matters clear I would put the point differently. On that day, there will be no more "Fathers," no more people of either sex who have power over their children's lives and moral authority in their children's world, though they do not do the work of attentive love. There will be mothers of both sexes who live out transformed maternal thought in communities that share parental care—practically, emotionally, economically, and socially. Such communities will have learned from their mothers how to value children's lives.

FOOTNOTES

[1] From J. Echergray, "Severed Heart," quoted by Jessie Bernard, in **The Future of Motherhood** (New York: Dial, 1974), p. 4.

[2] Ruth Mack Brunswick, "The Preoedipal Phase of Libido Development," quoted by Nancy Chodorow, in **The Reproduction of Mothering** (Berkeley: University of California Press, 1978), p. 196, footnote.

[3] Adrienne Rich, **Of Woman Born** (New York: Norton, 1976), p. 11. My debt to this book is profound and pervasive.

[4] For an extensive discussion of the power of mothers, see Dorothy Dinnerstein, **The Mermaid and the Minotaur: Sexual Arrangements and Human Malaise** (New York: Harper & Row, 1976). In expressing our fears of maternal power Dinnerstein sometimes, unfortunately and unwittingly, gives voice to the very matriphobia she decries.

[5] In traditional heterosexual parenting, a returning father may distract even the nursing mother from her child, demanding attention and service which is frequently more alienating, more threatening to a mother's self-possession than childrens' demands. To the extent that the infant is sensitive to the gender of the mother, as Dinnerstein and others claim, to that extent it would be dimly aware of the gender-linked character of interruption. In any case, the child will soon become aware that females are caretakers whose work and caring is endlessly interruptible.

On the politics of interruption, see Michelle Cliff, "The Resonance of Interruption," **Chrysalis**, no 8 (Summer 1979); Pamela Fishman, "Interaction: The Work Women Do," **Social Problems** 25, no. 4 (April 1978); and Don Zimmerman and Candace West, "Sex Roles, Interruptions and Silences in Conversations," in **Language and Sex: Difference and Dominance**, ed. Barrie Thorne and Nancy Henley (Rowley, Mass., Newbury House, 1975).

Many fathers are of course, socially unappreciated. Poor, declassed, or "failing" fathers know the pain of introducing their children to a world in which they do not figure. Sometimes their powerlessness is visited directly upon the mothers. Even when it is not, mothers suffer a double powerlessness when the "fathers" of her kin and cultural group are degraded by the Laws of the Ruling Fathers; the "world of the fathers" belongs neither to her sons nor to the men her daughters will live among.

[6] I am indebted to Susan Harding for this point (personal conversation and lecture notes from the Residential College, University of Michigan).

[7] For an analysis of the evil of factory work which emphasizes workers' loss of control of their time, see Simone Weil, "Factory Work," in **Simone Weil Reader**, ed. George A. Panichas (New York: McKay, 1977). For a similar comparison of mothers' control over time compared with that of other workers, see Barbara Garson,

"Clerical," in **All the Livelong Day** (New York: Penguin Books, 1975). Of course, many mothers also work in factories, stores and fields; and some mothers work in managerial, professional, and executive positions. The issue is whether mothers have more control over time and order of their work (in the Weil sense) in their maternal than in their other working hours. Mothers do not have control over their **lives**, and this relative absence of self-determination has consequences which I will specify.

[8]Carol Pearson, "Women's Fantasies and Feminist Utopias," makes the general point that in several feminist utopias, "human kinship procedures can govern an entire society because the people in the society are mothers." See **Frontiers** 2, no. 3 (Fall 1977). Pearson quotes extensively from **Herland** (New York: Pantheon, 1979). For a clear discussion of significance of matriarchy, see Paula Webster, "Matriarchy: A Vision of Power," in **Toward an Anthropology of Women**, ed. Rayna R. Reiter (New York and London: Monthly Review Press, 1975), pp. 141-156.

[9]Lucille Clifton, "My Mama Moved Among the Days," in **Good Times** (New York: Random House, 1969), p. 2.

[10]Among other possible aspects of women's thought are those that might arise from our sexual lives, from our "homemaking," from the special conflict women feel between allegiance on the one hand to women and their world, and on the other hand, to all people of their kin and culture. Any identifiable aspect of women's thought will be interrelated to all of the others. Because women almost everywhere are relatively powerless in relation to men of their class, all aspects of women's thought will be affected by powerlessness. Whether we are discussing the thought arising from women's bodily, sexual, maternal, homemaking, linguistic, or any other experience, we are faced with a confluence of powerlessness and the "womanly" whatever that might be.

[11]The pervasive and false identification of womanhood and biological or adoptive motherhood injures both mothers and non-mothers. The identification obscures the many kinds of mothering performed by those who do not parent particular children in families. It frequently forces those labeled "nonmothers" to take a distance from their own mothers and the maternal lives of all women. Out of justified fear and resentment of the obligation to mother, these "nonmothers' may become caught up in socially induced but politically myopic efforts to divorce female identity from any connection with maternal practices. Meanwhile, mothers engage in parallel self-destructive efforts which further divide women from each other. In their fight to preserve their nonmaternal aspirations and projects, mothers may belittle the importance of maternal experience in their lives. Or out of fear of their own anger at a limiting social identity as well as out of legitimate fury at the devaluation of mothers and motherliness, they may overidentify with the maternal identification foisted upon them, letting their nonmaternal working and loving selves die. Whichever we mothers do, and frequently we do both, the cost to our maternal and nonmaternal works and loves is enormous.

242

[12]For the most complete and sensitive account of girls'
special relation to mothers' mothering, see Chodorow, **The Reproduction of Mothering.** See also Jane Flax, "The Conflict Between
Nurturance and Autonomy in Mother-Daughter Relationships and
Within Feminism," **Feminist Studies** 4, no. 2 (June 1978): 171-189.

[13]See Nancy Chodorow, "Feminism and Difference: Gender,
Relation, and Difference in Psychoanalytic Perspective," **Socialist
Review**, no 36 (July-August 1979). "We cannot know what children
would make of their bodies in a nongender or nonsexually organized
social world . . . .It is not obvious that there would be major
significance to biological sex differences, to gender difference
or to different sexualities" (p. 66).

[14]Examples of the invariant and **nearly** unchangeable include:
long gestation inside the mother's body; prolonged infant and
childhood dependence; physical fragility of infancy; radical
qualitative and quantitative change ("growth") in emotional and
intellectual capacities from infancy to adulthood; long development and psychological complexity of human sexual desire, of
memory and other cognitive capacities, and of "object relations."
Features which are **nearly** universal and certainly changeable
include: the identification of childbearing and childcaring, the
consequent delegation of childcare to natural mothers and other
women, the relative subordination of women in any social class to
men of that class.

[15]To see the universal in particulars, to assimilate differences and extend kinship is a legacy of the ecumenical Protestant-
ism in which I was raised. I am well aware that even nonviolent,
well-meaning Protestant assimilations can be obtuse and cruel for
others. Therefore I am dependent on others, morally as well as
intellectually, for the statement of differences, the assessment
of their effects on every aspect of maternal lives, and finally
for radical correction as well as for expansion of any general
theory I would offer. However, I do not **believe** that the thinking
I describe is limited only to "privileged white women," as one
reader put it. I first came to the notion of "maternal thinking"
and the virtues of maternal practices through personal exchange
with Tillie Olsen and then through reading her fiction. My debt
to her is pervasive. Similarly, I believe that "**Man Child: A
Black Lesbian Feminist's Response**" by Audre Lorde, **Conditions**, no.
4 (Winter 1979): 30-36, is an excellent example of what I call
"maternal thinking transformed by feminist consciousness." My
"assimilation" of Olsen's and Lorde's work in no way denies the
differences which separate us nor the biases that those differences may introduce into my account. These are only two of many
examples of writers in quite different social circumstances who
express what I take to be "maternal thinking."

[16]Nothing I say about maternal thought suggests that the
women who engage in it cannot engage in other types of intellectual discourse. A maternal thinker may also be an experimental
psychologist, a poet, a mathematician, an architect, a physicist.
I believe that because most thinkers have been men, most disciplines are partly shaped by "male" concepts, values, styles, and

strategies. However, unless we have identified "male" and "female" aspects of thought, the claim of gender bias is an empty one. I do not doubt that disciplines are also shaped by transgender interest, values, and concepts, which women, whether or not they engage in maternal practices, may fully share. To the extent that the disciplines are shaped by "male" thought, mothers and other women may feel alienated by the practices and thinking of their own discipline. Correctively, when thinkers are as apt to be women as men, thought itself may change.

[17] I derive the vocabulary most specifically from Jurgen Habermas, **Knowledge and Human Interests** (Boston: Beacon Press, 1971). However, I have been equally influenced by other philosophical relativists, most notably by Peter Winch, Ludwig Wittgenstein, and Susanne Kessler and Wendy McKenna. See, Winch, "Understanding a Primitive Society" and other papers, in **Ethics and Action** (London: Routledge & Kegan Paul, 1972); Wittgenstein, **Philosophical Investigations, Remarks on the Foundations of Mathematics, Zettel,** and **On Centainty** (Oxford: Blackwell, 1953, 1956, 1967, 1969). Kessler and McKenna, **Gender** (New York: Wiley, 1978). I am also indebted to the writings of Evelyn Keller, especially "Feminist Critique of Science: A Forward or Backward Move," "He, She and Id in Scientific Discourse" (unpublished manuscripts); and "Gender and Science," **Psychoanalysis and Contemporary Thought** 1, no. 3 (1978).

[18] See Habermas, **Knowledge and Human Interests** for the view that scientific knowledge is organized by its interests in control.

[19] The words are Mrs. Ramsay's in Virginia Woolf's **To the Lighthouse** (New York: Harcourt Brace & World, 1927), p. 92.

[20] Adrienne Rich, "Conditions for Work: The Common World of Women," in **Working It Out,** ed. Sara Ruddick and Pamela Daniels (New York: Pantheon, 1977). Italics mine.

[21] For the comparison, see Iris Murdoch, **The Sovereignty of Good** (New York: Schocken, 1971). Popular moralities as well as contemporary moral theory tend to emphasize decision, assertion, happiness, authenticity, and justification by principle.

[22] Iris Murdoch, **Sovereignty of Good,** p. 99.

[23] Ibid., p. 95.

[24] Spinoza, **Ethics,** Book 3, Proposition 42, demonstration. See also Proposition 40. Note and Proposition 45, both in Book 3.

[25] For an example of the first, see Virginia Woolf's **Mrs. Dalloway** (New York: Harcourt, Brace & World, 1925), in which Lady Bexborough opens a bazaar holding the telegram announcing her son's death. Her action is simultaneously admirable, repellent, and politically disturbing as I hope to show in the section on acceptability.

[26]Bernard Williams, **Morality** (New York: Harper Torchbooks, 1972), p. 11.

[27]The words are a Texas farmwoman's who quilted as she huddled with her family in a shelter as, above them, a tornado destroyed their home. The story was told to me by Miriam Schapiro.

[28]Murdoch, **Sovereignty of Good**, p. 26.

[29]These are differences often attributed to women both by themselves and by psychologists. For a critical review of the literature see Eleanor Maccoby and Carol Jacklin, **The Psychology of Sex Differences** (Stanford, Calif.: Stanford University Press, 1974). For a plausible account of women's valuing of inner life, see Patricia Meyer Spacks, **The Female Imagination** (New York: Knopf, 1975). Maccoby and Jacklin are critical both of the findings I mentioned and the adequacy of the psychological experiments they survey for testing or discovering these kinds of differences. I make little use of psychology, more of literature, in thinking about the kinds of cognitive sex differences I discuss. Psychologists are not, so far as I know, talking about women who have empathically identified with and assimilated maternal practices, either by engaging in them or by identifying with their own or other mothers. It would be hard to identify such a subgroup of women without circularity. But even if one could make the identification, tests would have to be devised that did not measure achievement, but conception of achievement. Mothers, to take one example, may well prize the inner life, but have so little time for it or be so self-protectively defended against their own insights (as I will discuss shortly) that they gradually lose the capacity for inner life. Or again, a mother may not maintain sharp boundaries between herself and her child or between her child's "outer" action and inner life. However, she **must** maintain some boundaries. We value what we are in danger of losing (e.g., inner life); we identify virtues because we recognize temptations to vice (e.g., openness because we are tempted to rigid control); we refuse what we fear giving way to (e.g., either pathological symbiotic identification or an unworkable division between our own and our children's interests). It is difficult to imagine tests sophisticated and sensitive enough to measure such conceptions, priorities, and values. I have found psychoanalytic theory the most useful of psychologies and Chodorow's **The Reproduction of Mothering** the most helpful in applying psychoanalytic theory to maternal practices.

[30]One reader has suggested that my account of a mother attuned to her own child's thoughts and fantasies is biased by my white, middle-class experience. By appreciation of a person's continuous mental life, I do not mean only the leisurely (and frequently intrusive) hovering over the child's psyche, hovering which is often the product of powerlessness and enforced idleness. The appreciation I think of is often a kind of pained groping for the meanings that a child is giving to its own experiences, including to its own sufferings. I believe I have heard these gropings both first-hand and in literary reflections of mothers who are not white and/or middle class. For two of many examples see Tillie

Olsen's "I Stand Here Ironing" from **Tell Me a Riddle** (New York: Delacorte Press, 1956) and Audre Lorde's "Man Child." If my interpretation of others' experiences is wrong, other women with different lives will correct me. Expressing maternal thinking is necessarily a collective project.

[31]Simone Weil, "Gravity and Grace," in **Gravity and Grace** (London: Routledge & Kegan Paul, 1952), first French edition, 1947), passim.

[32]Weil, "Gravity and Grace," and other essays in **Gravity and Grace**. Both the language and concepts are indebted to Plato.

[33]Bernard's words in the summing up of Virginia Woolf's **The Waves** (New York: Harcourt, Brace & World, 1931), p. 294.

[34]Jean Baker Miller, **Toward a New Psychology of Women** (Boston: Beacon Press, 1973), p. 54.

[35]As Habermas argues, **Knowledge and Human Interest**.

[36]Miller, **Toward a New Psychology of Women**, p. 56. This vast experience is unrecognized partly because psychologists assume that while mothers are responsible for preservation, fathers are responsible for growth. This view of psychologists "denies the possibility of a maternal nurturance which actually encourages autonomy. But what is nurturance if not the pleasure in the other's growth? if not the desire to satisfy the other's needs whether it be the need to cling or the need to be independent?" Jessica Benjamin, "Authority and the Family Revisted: or, A World Without Fathers?" **New German Critique**, no. 13 (Winter 1978): 35-57.

[37]Miller, **Toward a New Psychology of Women**, p. 40.

[38]I am indebted to Rich, **Of Women Born**, especially chap. 8, both for this phrase and for the working out of the idea of inauthenticity.

[39]Sandra Lee Bartky, "Toward a Phenomenology of Feminist Consciousness," in **Feminism and Philsophy**, ed. Mary Vetteeling-Braggin, Frederick A. Elliston and Jane English (Totowa, N.J.: Littlefield Adams, 1977), pp. 22-34, 33, 25, 28-29.

[40]Bartky, "Phenomenology of Feminist Consciousness," p. 31. On the riskiness of authenticity and the courage it requires of women see also Miller, **Toward a New Psychology of Women**, chap. 9.

[41]Rich, **Of Woman Born**, pp. 198, 211, 246, 247.

[42]For a discussion of the relative weight of parents' and children's values in determining children's lives, see William Ruddick, "Parents and Life Prospects," in **Having Children**, ed. Onora O'Neill and William Ruddick (New York: Oxford University Press, 1979).

[43]Murdoch, **Sovereignty of Good**, p. 40.

[44]Ibid., p. 28.

[45]Simone Weil, "Human Personality," in **Collected Essays,** chosen and translated by Richard Rees (London: Oxford University Press, 1962). Also, **Simone Weil Reader**, p. 333.

[46]Murdoch, **Sovereignty of Good**, p. 43.

[47]Ibid., p. 67.

[48]Ibid., p. 91.

[49]Ibid., p. 65.

[50]Simone Weil, "Reflections of the Right Use of School Studies With a View to the Love of God," in **Waiting for God** (New York: G. P. Putnam's Sons, 1951), p. 115.

[51]Michelle Zimbalist Rosaldo, "Woman, Culture and Society: A Theoretical Overview," in **Woman, Culture and Society,** ed. Michelle Zimbalist Rosaldo and Louise Lamphere (Stanford: Stanford University Press, 1974).

[52]Rich, **Of Woman Born**; Dinnerstein, **Mermaid and Minotaur,** passim.

[53]Rich, **Of Woman Born**, p. 225.

AUTHOR'S NOTE

I began circulating an early draft of this paper in the fall of 1978. Since then, the constructive criticism and warm response of readers has led me to believe that this draft is truly a collective endeavor. I would like especially to thank Sandra Bartky, Gail Bragg, Bell Chevigny, Nancy Chodorow, Margaret Comstock, Mary Felstiner, Berenice Fisher, Marilyn Frye, Susan Harding, Evelyn Fox Keller, Jane Lilienfeld, Jane Marcus, Adrienne Rich, Amelie Rorty, William Ruddick, Barrie Thorne, Marilyn Blatt Young, readers for **Feminist Studies,** and Rayna Rapp.

CHAPTER 7

THE IDEAL OF THE EDUCATED PERSON*
Jane Roland Martin

R. S. Peters calls it an ideal.[1] So do Nash, Kazemias and
Perkinson who, in their introduction to a collection of studies in
the history of educational thought, say that one cannot go about
the business of education without it.[2] Is it the good life? the
responsible citizen? personal autonomy? No, it is the educated
man.

The educated man! In the early 1960s when I was invited to
contribute to a book of essays to be entitled **The Educated Man**, I
thought nothing of this phrase. By the early 1970s I felt uncom-
fortable whenever I came across it, but I told myself it was the
thought not the words that counted. It is now the early 1980s.
Peters's use of the phrase "educated man" no longer troubles me
for I think it fair to say that he intended it in a gender-neutral
way.[3] Despite one serious lapse which indicates that on some
occasions he was thinking of his educated man as male, I do not
doubt that the ideal he set forth was meant for males and females
alike.[4] Today my concern is not Peters's language but his conception of the educated man--or person, as I will henceforth say.
I will begin by outlining Peters's ideal for you and will then

*Jane Roland Martin, "The Ideal of the Educated Person," **Educational Theory** 31, no. 2 (Spring 1981), pp.97-109. Copyright (c)
1982 by the Board of Trustees of the University of Illinois. Reprinted by permission of **Educational Theory**.

show that it does serious harm to women. From there I will go on to argue that Peters's ideal is inadequate for men as well as women and, furthermore, that its inadequacy for men is intimately connected to the injustice it does women. In conclusion I will explore some of the requirements an adequate ideal must satisfy.

Let me explain at the outset that I have chosen to discuss Peters's ideal of the educated person here because for many years Peters has been perhaps **the** dominant figure in philosophy of education. Moreover, although Peters's ideal is formulated in philosophically sophisticated terms, it is certainly not idiosyncratic. On the contrary, Peters claims to have captured our concept of the educated person, and he may well have done so. Thus, I think it fair to say that the traits Peters claims one must possess to be a truly educated person and the kind of education he assumes one must have in order to acquire those traits would, with minor variations, be cited by any number of people today if they were to describe their own conception of the ideal. I discuss Peters's ideal, then, because it has significance for the field of philosophy of education as a whole.

R. S. PETERS'S EDUCATED PERSON

The starting point of Peters's philosophy of education is the concept of the educated person. While granting that we sometimes use the term "education" to refer to any process of rearing, bringing up, instructing, etc., Peters distinguishes this very broad sense of "education" from the narrow one in which he is interested. The concept of the educated person provides the basis

for his distinction: whereas "education" in the broad sense refers
to any process of rearing, etc., "education" in the narrower, and
to him philosophically more important, sense refers to the family
of processes which have as their outcome the development of an
educated person.[5]

Peters set forth his conception of the educated person in
some detail in his book, **Ethics and Education.**[6] Briefly, an
educated person is one who does not simply possess knowledge. An
educated person has a body of knowledge and some kind of conceptual scheme to raise this knowledge above the level of a collection
of disjointed facts which in turn implies some understanding of
principles for organizing facts and of the "reason why" of things.
Furthermore, the educated person's knowledge is not inert: it
characterizes the person's way of looking at things and involves
"the kind of commitment that comes from getting on the inside of a
form of thought and awareness"; that is to say, the educated
person cares about the standards of evidence implicit in science
or the canons of proof inherent in mathematics. Finally, the
educated person has cognitive perspective. In an essay entitled
"Education and the Educated Man" published several years later,
Peters added to this portrait that the educated person's pursuits
can be practical as well as theoretical so long as the person
delights in them for their own sake, and that both sorts of pursuits involve standards to which the person must be sensitive.[7]
He also made it clear that knowledge enters into his conception of
the educated person in three ways, namely, depth, breadth and
knowledge of good.

In their book, **Education and Personal Relationships,** Downie,

Loudfoot and Telfer presented a conception of the educated person which is a variant on Peters's. I cite it here not because they too use the phrase "educated man," but to show that alternate philosophical connections of the educated person differ from Peters's only in detail. Downie, Loudfoot and Telfer's educated person has knowledge which is wide ranging in scope, extending from history and geography to the natural and social sciences and to current affairs. This knowledge is important, relevant and grounded. The educated person understands what he or she knows, knows how to do such things as history and science, and has the inclination to apply this knowledge, to be critical and to have curiosity in the sense of a thirst for knowledge. Their major departure from Peters's conception--and it is not, in the last analysis, very major--is to be found in their concern with knowledge by acquaintance; the educated person must not merely have knowledge **about** works or art--and, if I understand them correctly, about moral and religious theories--but must know these as individual things.

Consider now the knowledge, the conceptual scheme which raises this knowledge above the level of disjointed facts and the cognitive perspective Peters's educated person must have. It is quite clear that Peters does not intend that these be acquired through the study of cooking and driving. Mathematics, science, history, literature, philosophy--these are the subjects which constitute the curriculum for his educated person. In short, his educated person is one who has had--and profited from--a liberal education of the sort outlined by Paul Hirst in his famous essay, "Liberal Education and the Nature of Knowledge." Hirst describes what is sought in a liberal education as follows:

> first, sufficient immersion in the concepts, logic and
> criteria of the discipline for a person to come to know
> the distinctive way in which it 'works' by pursuing
> these in particular cases; and then sufficient generali-
> sation of these over the whole range of the discipline
> so that his experience begins to be widely structured in
> this distinctive manner. It is this coming to look at
> things in a certain way that is being aimed at, not the
> ability to work out in minute particulars all the de-
> tails that can be in fact discerned. It is the ability
> to recognise empirical assertions or aesthetic judgments
> for what they are, and to know the kind of consideration
> on which their validity will depend, that matters.[9]

If Peters's educated person is not in fact Hirst's liberally
educated person, he or she is certainly its identical twin.

Liberal education, in Hirst's view, consists in an initiation
into what he calls the forms of knowledge. There are, on his
count, seven of them. Although he goes to some lengths in his
later writings on the topic to deny that these forms are themselves intellectual disciplines, it is safe to conclude that his
liberally educated person, and hence Peters's educated person,
will acquire the conceptual schemes and cognitive perspectives
they are supposed to have through a study of mathematics, physical
science, history, the human sciences, literature, fine arts,
philosophy. These disciplines will not necessarily be studied

separately: an interdisciplinary curriculum is compatible with the Peters-Hirst ideal. But it is nonetheless their subject matter, their conceptual apparatus, their standards of proof and adequate evidence, their way of looking at things that must be acquired if the ideal is to be realized.

II. INITIATION INTO MALE COGNITIVE PERSPECTIVES

What is this certain way in which the educated person comes to look at things? What is the distinctive manner in which that person's experience is structured? A body of literature documenting the many respects in which the disciplines of knowledge ignore or misrepresent the experience and lives of women has developed over the last decade. I cannot do justice here to its range of concerns or its sophisticated argumentation. Through the use of examples, however, I will try to give you some sense of the extent to which the intellectual disciplines incorporate a male cognitive perspective, and hence a sense of the extent to which Hirst's liberally educated person and its twin--Peters's educated person-- look at things through male eyes.

Let me begin with history. "History is past politics" was the slogan inscribed on the seminar room wall at Johns Hopkins in the days of the first doctoral program.[10] In the late 1960s the historian, Richard Hofstaedter, summarized his field by saying: "Memory is the thread of personal identity, history of public identity." History has defined itself as the record of the public and political aspects of the past; in other words, as the record of the productive processes--man's sphere--of society. Small wonder that women are scarcely mentioned in historical narratives! Small wonder that they have been neither the objects nor the subjects of historical inquiry until very recently! The reproductive processes of society which have traditionally been carried on by women are excluded by **definition** from the purview of the discipline.

If women's lives and experiences have been excluded from the subject matter of history, the works women have produced have for the most part been excluded from literature and the fine arts. It has never been denied that there have been women writers and artists, but their works have not often been deemed important or significant enough to be studied by historians and critics. Thus, for example, Catherine R. Stimpson has documented the treatment accorded Gertrude Stein by two journals which exert a powerful influence in helping to decide what literature is and what books matter.[11] Elaine Showalter, pursuing a somewhat different tack, has documented the double standard which was used in the nineteenth century to judge women writers: all the most desirable aesthetic qualities--for example, power, breadth, knowledge of life, humor--were assigned to men; the qualities assigned to women, such as refinement, tact, precise observation, were not considered sufficient for the creation of an excellent novel.[12]

The disciplines are guilty of different kinds of sex bias. Even as literature and the fine arts exclude women's works from their subject matter, they include works which construct women according to the male image of her. One might expect this tendency to construct the female to be limited to the arts, but it is not. Naomi Weisstein has shown that psychology constructs the female personality to fit the preconceptions of its male practitioners, clinicians either accepting theory without evidence or finding in their data what they want to find.[13] And Ruth Hubbard has shown that this tendency extends even to biology where the stereotypical picture of the passive female is projected by the male practitioners of that field onto the animal kingdom.[14]

There are, indeed, two quite different ways in which a discipline can distort the lives, experiences and personalities of women. Even as psychology constructs the female personality out of our cultural stereotype, it holds up standards of development for women to meet which are derived from studies using male subjects.[15] Not surprisingly, long after the source of the standards is forgotten, women are proclaimed to be underdeveloped and inferior to males in relation to these standards. Thus, for example, Carol Gilligan has pointed out that females are classified as being at Stage 3 of Kohlberg's six stage sequence of moral development because important differences in moral development between males and females are ignored.[16]

In the last decade scholars have turned to the study of women. Thus, historical narratives and analyses of some aspects of the reproductive processes of society--of birth control, childbirth, midwifery, for example--have been published.[17] The existence of such scholarship is no guarantee, however, of its integration into the mainstream of the discipline of history itself, yet this latter is required if initiation into history as a form of knowledge is not to constitute initiation into a male cognitive perspective. The title of a 1974 anthology on the history of women, Clio's Consciousness Raised, is unduly optimistic.[18] Certainly, the consciousness of some historians has been raised, but there is little reason to believe that the discipline of history has redefined itself so that studies of the reproductive processes of society are not simply tolerated as peripherally relevant, but are considered to be as central to it as political, economic and military narratives are. Just as historians have begun to study women's past, scholars in literature and the fine arts have begun to bring works by women to our attention and to reinterpret the ones we have always known.[19] But there is still the gap between feminist scholarship and the established definitions of literary and artistic significance to be bridged, and until it is, the initiation into these disciplines provided by a liberal education will be an initiation into male perspectives.

In sum, the intellectual disciplines into which a person must be initiated to become an educated person **exclude** women and their works, **construct** the female to the male image of her and **deny** the truly feminine qualities she does possess. The question remains of whether the male cognitive perspective of the disciplines is integral to Peters's ideal of the educated person. The answer to this question is to be found in Hirst's essay, "The Forms of Knowledge Revisited."[20] There he presents the view that at any given time a liberal education consists in an initiation into **existing** forms of knowledge. Hirst acknowledges that new forms can develop and that old ones can disappear. Still, the analysis he gives of the seven distinct forms which he takes to comprise a liberal education today is based, he says, on our present conceptual scheme. Thus, Peters's educated person is not one who studies a set of ideal, unbiased forms of knowledge; on the contrary, that

person is one who is initiated into whatever forms of knowledge
exist in the society at that time. In our time the existing forms
embody a male point of view. The initiation into them envisioned
by Hirst and Peters is, therefore, one in male cognitive perspectives.

Peters's educated person is expected to have grasped the
basic structure of science, history and the like rather than the
superficial details of content. Is it possible that the feminist
critique of the disciplines therefore leaves his ideal untouched?
It would be a grave misreading of the literature to suppose that
this critique presents simply a surface challenge to the disciplines. Although the examples I have cited here may have suggested
to you that the challenge is directed at content alone, it is in
fact many pronged. Its targets include the questions asked by the
various fields of inquiry and the answers given them; the aims of
those fields and the ways they define their subject matter; the
methods they use, their canons of objectivity, and their ruling
metaphors. It is difficult to be clear on precisely which aspects
of knowledge and inquiry are at issue when Hirst speaks of initiation into a form of knowledge. A male bias has been found on so
many levels of the disciplines, however, that I think we can feel
quite confident that it is a property also of the education embodied in Peters's ideal.

III. GENDERIZED TRAITS

The masculinity of Peters's educated person is not solely a
function of a curriculum in the intellectual disciplines, however.

Consider the traits or characteristics Peters attributes to the educated person. Feelings and emotions only enter into the makeup of the educated person to the extent that being committed to the standards of a theoretical pursuit such as science or a practical one such as architecture, counts as such. Concern for people and for interpersonal relationships has no role to play: the educated person's sensitivity is to the standards immanent in activities, not to other human beings; an imaginative awareness of emotional atmosphere and interpersonal relationships need be no part of this person's makeup, nor is the educated person thought to be empathetic or supportive or nurturant. Intuition is also neglected. Theoretical knowledge and what Woods and Barrow--two more philosophers who use the phrase "educated man" --call "reasoned understanding" are the educated person's prime characteristics:[21] even this person's practical pursuits are to be informed by some theoretical perspectives; moreover, this theoretical bent is to be leavened neither by imaginative nor intuitive powers, for these are never to be developed.

The educated person as portrayed by Peters, and also by Downie, Loudfoot and Telfer, and by Woods and Barrow, coincides with our cultural stereotype of a male human being. According to that stereotype men are objective, analytic, rational; they are interested in ideas and things; they have no interpersonal orientation; they are neither nurturant nor supportive, empathetic or sensitive. According to the stereotype, nurturance and supportiveness, empathy and sensitivity are female attributes. Intuition is a female attribute too.[22]

This finding is not really surprising. It has been shown

that psychologists define moral development, adult development and even human development in male terms and that therapists do the same for mental health.[23] Why suppose that philosophers of education have avoided the androcentric fallacy?[24] Do not misunderstand! Females can acquire the traits and dispositions which constitute Peters's conception of the educated person; he espouses an ideal which, if it can be attained at all, can be by both sexes.[25] But our culture associates the traits and dispositions of Peters's educated person with males. To apply it to females is to impose on them a masculine mold. I realize that as a matter of fact some females fit our male stereotype and that some males do not, but this does not affect the point at issue, which is that Peters has set forth an ideal for education which embodies just those traits and dispositions our culture attributes to the male sex and excludes the traits our culture attributes to the female sex.

Now it might seem that if the mold is a good one, it does not matter that it is masculine; that if the traits which Peters's educated person possesses are desirable, then it makes no difference that in our society they are associated with males. Indeed, some would doubtless argue that in extending to women cognitive virtues which have long been associated with men and which education has historically reserved for men, Peters's theory of education strikes a blow for sex equality. It does matter that the traits Peters assigns the educated person are considered in our culture to be masculine, however. It matters because some traits which males and females can both possess are **genderized**; that is, they are appraised differentially according to sex.[26]

Consider aggressiveness. The authors of a book on assertive training for women report that in the first class meetings of their training courses they ask their students to call out the adjectives which come to mind when we say "aggressive woman" and "aggressive man." Here is the list of adjectives the women used to describe an aggressive man: "masculine," "dominating," "successful," "heroic," "capable," "strong," "forceful," "manly." Need I tell you the list of adjectives they used to describe an aggressive woman?: "harsh," "pushy," "bitchy," "domineering," "obnoxious," "emasculating," "uncaring." [27]

I submit to you that the traits Peters attributes to the educated person are, like the trait of aggressiveness, evaluated differently for males and females. Imagine a woman who is analytical and critical, whose intellectual curiosity is strong, who cares about the canons of science and mathematics. How is she described? "She thinks like a man," it is said. To be sure, this is considered by some to be the highest accolade. Still, a woman who is said to think like a man is being judged to be masculine, and since we take masculinity and femininity to lie at opposite ends of a single continuum, she is thereby being judged to be lacking in femininity.[28] Thus, while it is possible for a woman to possess the traits of Peters's education person, she will do so at her peril: her possession of them will cause her to be viewed as unfeminine, i.e., as an unnatural or abnormal woman.

IV. A DOUBLE BIND

It may have been my concern over Peters's use of the phrase

"educated man" which led me to this investigation in the first place, but as you can see, the problem is not one of language. Had Peters consistently used the phrase "educated person" the conclusion that the ideal he holds up for education is masculine would be unaffected. To be sure, Peters's educated person can be a male or female, but he or she will have acquired male cognitive perspectives and will have developed traits which in our society are genderized in favor of males.

I have already suggested that Peters's ideal places a burden on women because the traits constituting it are evaluated negatively when possessed by females. The story of Rosalind Franklin, the scientist who contributed to the discovery of the structure of DNA, demonstrates that when a woman displays the kind of critical, autonomous thought which is an attribute of Peters's educated person, she is derided for what are considered to be negative unpleasant characteristics.[29] Rosalind Franklin consciously opted out of "woman's sphere" and entered the laboratory. From an abstract point of view the traits she possessed were quite functional there. Nonetheless she was perceived to be an interloper, an alien who simply could not be taken seriously in relation to the production of new, fundamental ideas no matter that her personal qualities might be.[30]

But experiencing hostility and derision is the least of the suffering caused women by Peters's ideal. His educated person is one who will know nothing about the lives women have led throughout history and little if anything about the works or art and literature women have produced. If his educated person is a woman, she will have been presented with few female role models in her studies whereas her male counterpart will be able to identify with the doers and thinkers and makers of history. Above all, the certain way in which his educated man and woman will come to look at the world will be one in which men are perceived as they perceive themselves and women are perceived as men perceive them.

To achieve Peters's ideal one must acquire cognitive perspectives through which one sex is perceived on its own terms and one sex is perceived as the Other.[31] Can it be doubted that when the works of women are excluded from the subject matter of the fields into which they are being initiated, students will come to believe that males are superior and females are inferior human beings? That when in the course of this initiation the lives and experiences of women are scarcely mentioned, students will come to believe that the way in which women have lived and the things women have done throughout history have no value? Can it be doubted that these beliefs do female students serious damage? The woman whose self-confidence is bolstered by an education which transmits the message that females are inferior human beings is rare. Rarer still is the woman who, having been initiated into alien cognitive perspectives, gains confidence in her own powers without paying the price of self-alienation.

Peters's ideal puts women in a double bind. To be educated they must give up their own way of experiencing and looking at the world, thus alienating themselves from themselves. To be unalienated they must remain uneducated. Furthermore, to be an educated person a female must acquire traits which are appraised negatively when she possesses them. At the same time, the traits which are evaluated positively when possessed by her--for example, being nurturant and empathetic--are excluded from the ideal. Thus a female who has acquired the traits of an educated person will not be evaluated positively for having them, while one who has acquired those traits for which she will be positively evaluated will not have achieved the ideal. Women are placed in this double bind because Peters's ideal incorporates traits genderized in favor of males and excludes traits genderized in favor of females. It thus puts females in a no-win situation. Yes, men and women can both achieve Peters's ideal. However, women suffer, as men do not, for doing so.

Peters's masculine ideal of the educated person harms males as well as females, however. In a chapter of the 1981 NSSE Yearbook I argued at some length that Hirst's account of liberal education is seriously deficient.[32] Since Peters's educated person is to all intents and purposes Hirst's liberally educated person, let me briefly repeat my criticism of Hirst here. The Peters-Hirst educated person will have knowledge about others, but will not have been taught to care about their welfare, let alone to act kindly toward them. That person will have some understanding of society, but will not have been taught to feel its injustices or even to be concerned over its fate. The Peters-Hirst educated person is an ivory tower person: a person who can reason yet has no desire to solve real problems in the real world; a person who understands science but does not worry about the uses to which it is put; a person who can reach flawless moral conclusions but feels no care or concern for others.

Simply put, quite apart from the burden it places on women, Peters's ideal of the educated person is far too narrow to guide the educational enterprise. Because it presupposes a divorce of mind from body, thought from action, and reason from feeling and emotion, it provides at best an ideal of an educated **mind**, not an educated **person**. To the extent that its concerns are strictly cognitive however, even in that guise it leaves much to be desired.

V. EDUCATION FOR PRODUCTIVE PROCESSES

Even if Peters's ideal did not place an unfair burden on women it would need to be rejected for the harm it does men, but its inadequacy as an ideal for men and the injustice it does women are not unconnected. In my Yearbook essay I sketched in the rough outlines of a new paradigm of liberal education, one which would emphasize the development of persons and not simply rational minds; one which would join thought to action, and reason to feeling and emotion. I could just as easily have called it a new conception of the educated person. What I did not realize when I wrote that essay is that the aspects of the Peters-Hirst ideal which I found so objectionable are directly related to the role, traditionally considered to be male, which their educated person is to play in society.

Peters would vehemently deny that he conceives of education as production. Nonetheless, he implicitly attributes to education the task of turning raw material, namely the uneducated person, into an end product whose specifications he sets forth in his account of the concept of the educated person. Peters would deny even more vehemently that he assigns to education a societal function. Yet an examination of his conception of the educated person reveals that the end product of the education he envisions is designed to fit into a specific place in the social order; that he assigns to education the function of developing the traits and qualities and to some extent the skills of one whose role is to use and produce ideas.[33]

Peters would doubtless say that the production and consumption of ideas is everyone's business and that an education for this is certainly not an education which fits people into a particular place in society. Yet think of the two parts into which the social order has traditionally been divided. Theorists have put different labels on them, some referring to the split between work and home, others to the public and private domains and still others to productive and reproductive processes.[34] Since the public/private distinction has associations for educators which are not germane to the present discussion while the work/home distinction obscures some important issues, I will speak here of productive and reproductive processes. I do not want to make terminology the issue, however. If you prefer other labels, by all means substitute them for mine. My own is only helpful, I should add, if the term "reproduction" is construed broadly. Thus I use it here to include not simply biological reproduction of the species, but the whole process of reproduction from conception until the individual reaches more or less independence from the family.[35] This process I take to include not simply childcare and rearing, but the related activities of keeping house, running the household and serving the needs and purposes of all the family members. Similarly, I interpret the term "production" broadly to include political, social and cultural activities and processes as well as economic ones.

Now this traditional division drawn within the social order is accompanied by a separation of the sexes. Although males and females do in fact participate in both the reproductive and productive processes of society, the reproductive processes are considered to constitute "woman's sphere" and the productive processes "man's sphere." Although Peters's educated person is ill-equipped for jobs in trades or work on the assembly line, this person is tailor-made for carrying on certain of the productive processes of society, namely those which require work with heads, not hands. Thus his educated person is designed to fill a role in society which has traditionally been considered to be male. Moreover, he or she is not equipped by education to fill roles associated with the reproductive processes of society, i.e., roles traditionally considered to be female.

Once the functionalism of Peters's conception of the educated person is made explicit, the difficulty of including in the ideal feelings and emotions such as caring and compassion, or skills of cooperation and nurturance, becomes clear. These fall under our culture's female stereotype. They are considered to be appropriate for those who carry on the reproductive processes of society but irrelevant, if not downright dysfunctional, for those who carry on the productive processes of society. It would therefore be irrational to include them in an ideal which is conceived of solely in relation to productive processes.

I realize now, as I did not before, that for the ideal of the educated person to be as broad as it should be, the two kinds of societal processes which Peters divorces from one another must be joined together.[36] An adequate ideal of the educated person must give the reproductive processes of society their due. An ideal which is tied solely to the productive processes of society cannot readily accommodate the important virtues of caring and compassion, sympathy and nurturance, generosity and cooperation which are genderized in favor of females.

To be sure, it would be possible in principle to continue to conceive of the educated person solely in relation to the productive processes of society while rejecting the stereotypes which produce genderized traits. One could include caring and compassion in the ideal of the educated person on the grounds that although they are thought to be female traits whose home is in the reproductive processes of society, they are in fact functional in the production and consumption of ideas. The existence of genderized traits is not the only reason for giving the reproductive processes of society their due in an ideal of the educated person, however. These processes are themselves central to the lives of each of us and to the life of society as a whole. The dispositions, knowledge, skills required to carry them out well are not innate, nor do they simply develop naturally over time. Marriage, childrearing, family life: these involve difficult, complex, learned activities which can be done well or badly. Just as an educated person should be one in whom head, hand and heart are integrated, he or she should be one who is at home carrying on the reproductive processes of society, broadly understood, as well as the productive processes.

Now Peters might grant that the skills, traits, and knowledge necessary for carrying on reproductive processes are learned—in some broad sense of the term, at least—but argue that one does not require an education in them for they are picked up in the course of daily living. Perhaps at one time they were picked up in this way, and perhaps in some societies they are now. But it is far from obvious that, just by living, most adults in our society today acquire the altruistic feelings and emotions, the skills of childrearing, the understanding of what values are important to transmit and which are not, and the ability to put aside one's own projects and enter into those of others which are just a few of the things required for successful participation in the reproductive processes of society.

That education is needed by those who carry on the reproductive processes is not in itself proof that it should be encompassed by a conception of the educated person however, for this conception need not be all-inclusive. It need not be all inclusive but, for Peters, education which is not guided by his ideal of the educated person scarcely deserves attention. Moreover, since a conception of the educated person tends to function as an ideal, one who becomes educated will presumably have achieved something worthwhile. Value is attached to being an educated person: to the things an educated person knows and can do; to the tasks and activities that person is equipped to perform. The exclusion of education for reproductive processes from the ideal of the educated person thus carries with it an unwarranted negative value judgment about the tasks and activities, the traits and dispositions which are associated with them.

VI. REDEFINING THE IDEAL

An adequate ideal of the educated person must give the reproductive processes of society their due, but it must do more
than this. After all, these processes were acknowledged by Rousseau in Book V of **Emile**.[37] There he set forth two distinct ideals
of the educated person, the one for **Emile** tied to the productive
processes of society and the one for Sophie tied to the reproductive processes. I leave open here the question Peters never asks
of whether we should adopt one or more ideals of the educated
person.[38] One thing is clear, however. We need a conception
which does not fall into the trap of assigning males and females
to the different processes of society, yet does not make the
mistake of ignoring one kind of process altogether. We all
participate in both kinds of processes and both are important to
all of us. Whether we adopt one or many ideals, a conception of
the educated person which is tied only to one kind of process will
be incomplete.

An adequate ideal of the educated person must also reflect a
realistic understanding of the limitations of existing forms or
disciplines of knowledge. In my Yearbook chapter I made a case
for granting them much less "curriculum space" than Hirst and
Peters do. So long as they embody a male cognitive perspective,
however, we must take into account not simply the amount of space
they occupy in the curriculum of the educated person, but the
hidden messages which are received by those who are initiated into
them. An ideal of the educated person cannot itself rid the
disciplines of knowledge of their sex bias. But it can advocate

measures for counteracting the harmful effects on students of coming to see things solely through male eyes.

The effects of an initiation into male cognitive perspectives constitute a hidden curriculum. Alternative courses of action are open to us when we find a hidden curriculum and there is no reason to suppose that only one is appropriate. Let me say a few words here, however, about a course of action that might serve as at least a partial antidote to the hidden curriculum transmitted by an education in male biased disciplines.[39] When we find a hidden curriculum we can show it to its recipients; we can raise their consciousness, if you will, so that they will know what is happening to them. Raising to consciousness the male cognitive perspective of the disciplines of knowledge in the educated person's curriculum is no guarantee, of course, that educated females will not suffer from a lack of self-confidence and from self-alienation. Yet knowledge can be power. A curriculum which, through critical analysis, exposes the biased view of women embodied in the disciplines and which, by granting ample space to the study of women shows how unjust that view is, is certainly preferable to a curriculum which, by its silence on the subject, gives students the impression that the ways in which the disciplines look at the world are impartial and unbiased.

Now it might seem to be a relatively simple matter both to give the reproductive processes of society their due in an ideal of the educated person and to include in that ideal measures for counteracting the hidden curriculum of an education in the existing disciplines of knowledge. Yet given the way philosophy of education conceives of its subject matter today, it is not. The productive-reproductive dualism is built not simply into Peters's ideal but into our discipline.[40] We do not even have a vocabulary for discussing education in relation to the reproductive processes of society, for the distinction between liberal and vocational education which we use to cover the kinds of education we take to be philosophically important applies within productive processes: liberal and vocational education are both intended to fit people to carry on productive processes, the one for work with heads and the other to work with hands. The aims of education we analyze--critical thinking, rationality, individual autonomy, even creativity--are also associated in our culture with the productive, not the reproductive, processes of society. To give the reproductive processes their due in a conception of the educated person we will have to rethink the domain of philosophy of education.

Given the way we define our subject matter it is no more possible for us to take seriously the hidden curriculum I have set before you than the reproductive processes of society. Education, as we conceive of it, is an intentional activity.[41] Teaching is too.[42] Thus, we do not consider the unintended outcomes of education to be our concern. Moreover, following Peters and his colleagues, we draw a sharp line between logical and contingent relationships and treat the latter as if they were none of our business even when they are the expected outcomes of educational processes.[43] In sum, we leave it to the psychologists, sociologists and historians of education to worry about hidden curricula, not because we consider the topic unimportant--although perhaps some of us do--but because we consider it to fall outside our domain.

The redefinition of the subject matter of philosophy of education required by an adequate ideal of the educated person ought not to be feared. On the contrary, there is every reason to believe that it would ultimately enrich our discipline. If the experience and activities which have traditionally been considered to belong to women are included in the educational realm, a host of challenging and important issues and problems will present themselves for study. If the philosophy of education tackles questions about childrearing and the transmission of values, if it develops accounts of gender education to inform its theories of liberal education, if it explores the forms of thinking, feeling and acting associated with childrearing, marriage and the family, if the concepts of coeducation, mothering and nurturance become fair game for philosophical analysis, philosophy of education will be invigorated.

It would also be invigorated by taking seriously contingent as well as logical relationships. In divorcing educational processes from their empirical consequences and the mental structures which are said to be intrinsically related to knowledge from the empirical consequences of having them, we forget that education is a practical endeavor. It is often said that philosophy of education's concerns are purely conceptual, but the conclusion is inescapable that in analyzing such concepts as the educated person and liberal education we make recommendations for action. For these to be justified the contingent relationships which obtain between them and both the good life and the good society must be taken into account. A redefinition of our domain would allow us to provide our educational theorizing with the kind of justification it requires. It would also allow us to investigate the particularly acute and very challenging value questions that arise in relation to hidden curricula of all kinds.

CONCLUSION

In conclusion I would like to draw for you two morals which seem to me to emerge from my study of Peters's ideal of the educated person. The first is that Plato was wrong when, in Book V of the Republic, he said that sex is a difference which makes no difference.[44] I do not mean by this that there are inborn differences which suit males and females for separate and unequal roles in society. Rather, I mean that identical educational treatment of males and females may not yield identical results so long as that treatment contains a male bias. There are sex differences in the way people are perceived and evaluated and there may well be sex differences in the way people think and learn and view the world. A conception of the educated person must take these into account. I mean also that the very nature of the ideal will be skewed. When sex or gender is thought to make no difference, women's lives, experiences, activities are overlooked and an ideal is formulated in terms of men and the roles for which they have traditionally been considered to be suited. Such an ideal is necessarily narrow for it is rooted in stereotypical ways of perceiving males and their place in society.

For some time I assumed that the sole alternative to a sex-biased conception of the educated person such as Peters set forth was a gender-free ideal, that is to say an ideal which did not take sex or gender into account. I now realize that sex or gender **has** to be taken into account if an ideal of the educated person is not to be biased. To opt at this time for a gender-free ideal is to beg the question. What is needed is a **gender-sensitive** ideal, one which takes sex or gender into account when it makes a difference and ignores it when it does not. Such an ideal would truly be gender-just.

The second moral is that **everyone** suffers when an ideal of the educated person fails to give the reproductive processes of society their due. Ideals which govern education solely in relation to the productive processes of society will necessarily be narrow. In their failure to acknowledge the valuable traits, dispositions, skills, traditionally associated with reproductive processes, they will harm both sexes although not always in the same ways.[45]

FOOTNOTES

[1]R. S. Peters, "Education and the Educated Man," in R. F. Dearden, P. H. Hirst, and R.S. Peters, eds., **A Critique of Current Educational Aims** (London: Routledge and Kegan Paul, 1972), pp. 7, 9.

[2]Paul Nash, Andreas M. Kazemias, and Henry J. Perkinson, eds., **The Educated Man: Studies in the History of Educational Thought** (New York: John Wiley and Sons, 1965), p. 25.

[3]For a discussion of "man" as a gender neutral term see Janice Moulton, "The Myth of the Neutral Man," in Mary Vetterling-Braggin, Frederick A. Elliston, and Jane English, eds., **Feminism and Philosophy** (Totowa, N. J.: Littlefield, Adams, 1977), pp. 124-137. Moulton rejects the view that "man" has a gender-neutral use.

[4]Peters, "Education and the Educated Man," p. 11. Peters says in connection with the concept of the educated man: "For there are many who are not likely to go far with theoretical enquiries and who are unlikely to develop much depth or breadth of understanding to underpin and transform their dealings as workers, husbands and fathers" (emphasis added).

[5]Ibid., p. 7.

[6]R. S. Peters, **Ethics and Education** (London: George Allen and Unwin, 1966). Page references are to the American edition published by Scott, Foresman and Company, 1967.

[7]Peters, "Education and the Educated Man," pp. 9-11.

[8]R. S. Downie, Eileen M. Loudfoot, and Elizabeth Telfer, **Education and Personal Relationships** (London: Methuen and Co., 1974), p. 11ff.

[9]In Paul Hirst, **Knowledge and the Curriculum** (London: Routledge and Kegan Paul, 1974), p. 47.

[10]Nancy Schrom Dye, "Clio's American Daughters," in Julia A. Sherman and Evelyn Torton Beck, eds., **The Prism of Sex** (Madison: University of Wisconsin Press, 1979), p. 9.

[11]Catherine R. Stimpson, "The Power to Name," in Sherman and Beck, eds., **Prism**, pp. 55-77.

[12]Elaine Showalter, "Women Writers and the Double Standard," in Vivian Gornick and Barbara Moran, eds., **Women in Sexist Society** (New York: Basic Books, 1971), pp. 323-343.

[13]Naomi Weisstein, "Psychology Constructs the Female" in Gornick and Moran, eds., **Women in Sexist Society**, pp. 133-146.

[14]Ruth Hubbard, "Have Only Men Evolved?" in Ruth Hubbard, Mary Sue Henifin, and Barbara Fried, eds., **Women Look at Biology**

Looking at Women (Cambridge, Mass.: Schenkman Publishing Co., 1979), pp. 7-35.

[15]Carol Gilligan, "Women's Place in Man's Life Cycle," **Harvard Educational Review** 49, 4 (1979): 431-446.

[16]Carol Gilligan, "In a Different Voice: Women's Conceptions of Self and of Morality," **Harvard Educational Review** 47, 4 (1979): 481-517.

[17]See, for example, Linda Gordon, **Woman's Body, Woman's Right: A Social History of Birth Control in America** (New York: Viking, 1976); Richard W. Wertz and Dorothy C. Wertz, **Lying-In** (New York: Free Press, 1977); Jean Donnison, **Midwives and Medical Men: A History of Interprofessional Rivalries and Women's Rights** (New York: Schocken Books, 1977).

[18]Mary Hartman and Lois W. Banner, eds., **Clio's Consciousness Raised** (New York: Harper and Row, 1974).

[19]See, for example, Carolyn G. Heilbrun, **Toward a Recognition of Androgyny** (New York: Alfred A. Knopf, 1974); Patricia Meyer Spacks, **The Female Imagination** (New York: Avon, 1975); Ellen Moers, **Literary Women** (New York: Anchor Books, 1977); Elaine Showalter, **A Literature of Their Own: British Women Novelists from Bronte to Lessing** (Princeton, N. J.: Princeton University Press, 1977); Ann Sutherland Harris and Linda Nochlin, **Women Artists: 1550-1950** (New York: Alfred A. Knopf, 1976); Elsa Honig Fine, **Women and Art: A History of Women Painters and Sculptors from the Renaissance to the Twentieth Century** (Montclair and London: Allanheld and Schram/Prior, 1978); and Karen Peterson and J. J. Wilson, **Women Artists: Recognition and Reappraisal from the Early Middle Ages to the Twentieth Century** (New York: New York University Press, 1976).

[20]In Paul Hirst, **Knowledge and the Curriculum**, p. 92.

[21]R. G. Woods and R. St.C. Barrow, **An Introduction to Philosophy of Education** (Methuen and Co., 1975), Ch. 3.

[22]For discussions of our male and female stereotypes see, e.g., Alexandra G. Kaplan and Joan P. Bean, eds., **Beyond Sex-role Stereotypes** (Boston: Little, Brown, 1976); and Alexandra G. Kaplan and Mary Anne Sedney, **Psychology and Sex Roles** (Boston: Little, Brown, 1980).

[23]Carol Gilligan, "Women's Place"; I. Broverman, D. Broverman, F. Clarkson, P. Rosencrantz and S. Vogel, "Sex-role Stereotypes and Clinical Judgments of Mental Health," **Journal of Consulting and Clinical Psychology** 34 (1970): 1-7; Alexandra G. Kaplan, "Androgyny as a Model of Mental Health for Women: From Theory to Therapy," in Kaplan and Bean, eds., **Beyond Sex-role Stereotypes**, pp. 353-362.

[24]One commits the androcentric fallacy when one argues from the characteristics associated with male human beings to the

characteristics of all human beings. In committing it one often commits the naturalistic fallacy because the traits which are said to be natural to males are held up as ideals for the whole species.

[25] I say if it can be attained by all, because it is not entirely clear that the ideal can be attained by anyone insofar as it requires mastery of Hirst's seven forms of knowledge.

[26] See Elizabeth Beardsley, "Traits and Genderization," in Vetterling-Braggin, et al., eds., **Feminism and Philosophy**, pp. 117-123. Beardsley uses the term "genderization" to refer to language while I use it here to refer to traits themselves.

[27] Lynn Z. Bloom, Karen Coburn, Joan Pearlman, **The New Assertive Woman** (New York: Delacorte Press, 1975), p. 12.

[28] For discussion of the assumption that masculinity-femininity is a bipolar dimension see Anne Constantinople, "Masculinity-Femininity: An Exception to a Famous Dictum"; and Sandra L. Bem, "Probing the Promise of Androgyny" in Kaplan and Bean, eds., **Beyond Sex-role Stereotypes**.

[29] Anne Sayre, **Rosalind Franklin and DNA** (New York: W. W. Norton and Co., 1975). See also James D. Watson, **The Double Helix** (New York: Atheneum, 1968); and Horace Freeland Judson, **The Eighth Day of Creation** (New York: Simon and Schuster, 1979).

[30] It is important to note, however, that some colleagues did not take her seriously as a scientist; see Sayre, ibid. Adele Simmons cites historical evidence of the negative effects of having acquired such traits on women who did not opt out of "woman's sphere" in "Education and Ideology in Nineteenth-Century America: The Response of Educational Institutions to the Changing Role of Women," in Berenice A. Carroll, ed., **Liberating Women's History** (Urbana, Ill.: University of Illinois Press, 1976), p. 123. See also Patricia Meyer Spacks, **The Female Imagination** (New York: Avon Books, 1976). p. 25.

[31] See Simone de Beauvoir, **The Second Sex** (New York: Bantam Books, 1961) for an extended disccussion of woman as the Other.

[32] Jane Roland Martin, "Needed: A Paradigm for Liberal Education," in Jonas F. Soltis, ed., **Philosophy and Education** (Chicago: National Society for the Study of Education, 1981), pp. 37-59.

[33] For an account of education as production see Jane Roland Martin, "Sex Equality and Education: A Case Study," in Mary Vetterling-Braggin, ed., **"Femininity," "Masculinity," and "Androgyny"** (Totowa, N.J.: Littlefield, Adams, 1982). It should be noted that an understanding of the societal role for which Peters's educated person is intended illuminates both the sex bias and the class bias his ideal embodies.

[34] For an interesting discussion and criticism of the two-sphere analysis of society, see Joan Kelly, "The Doubled Vision of

Feminist Theory: A Postscript to the 'Women and Power Conference', **Feminist Studies** 5, 1 (1979): 216-227. Kelly argues that a
two-sphere analysis distorts reality and that feminist theory
shoud discard it. I use it here as a convenient theoretical
device.

[35] I am indebted here to Lorenne M. G. Clark, "The Rights of
Women: The Theory and Practice of the Ideology of Male Suprem-
acy," in William R. Shea and John King-Farlow, eds., **Contemporary
Issues in Political Philosophy** (New York: Science History Publications, 1976), pp. 49-65.

[36] In saying that an adequate conception of the educated person must reject a sharp separation of productive and reproductive
processes I do not mean that it must be committed to a specific
philosophical theory of the relationship of the two. An adequate
conception of the educated person should not divorce mind and
body, but it does not follow from this that it must be committed
to a specific view of the mind-body relationship; indeed, the
union of mind and body in a theory of education is quite compatible with a dualistic philosophical account of the relationship
between the two. Similarly, a theory of the educated person must
not divorce one kind of societal process from the other even if
the best account of the relationship of productive to reproductive
processes should turn out to be dualistic.

[37] Jean-Jacques Rousseau, **Emile**, trans., Allan Bloom (New
York: Basic Books, 1979). See also Lynda Lange, "Rousseau:
Women and the General Will," in Lorenne M. G. Clark and Lynda
Lange, eds., **The Sexism of Social and Political Theory** (Toronto:
University of Toronto Press, 1979), pp. 41-52; Susan Moller Okin,
Women in Western Political Thought (Princeton: Princeton Universi-
ty Press, 1979); and Jane Roland Martin "Sophie and Emile: A Case
Study of Sex Bias in the History of Educational Thought," **Harvard
Educational Review** 51, 3 (1981): 357-372.

[38] I also leave open the question of whether **any** ideal of the
educated person should guide and direct education as a whole.

[39] For more on this question see Jane Roland Martin, "What
Should We Do with a Hidden Curriculum When We Find One?" **Curriculum Inquiry** 6, 2 (1976): 135-151.

[40] On this point see Jane Roland Martin, "Excluding Women from
the Educational Realm."

[41] See, for example, Peters, **Ethics and Education**.

[42] See, for example, Israel Scheffler, **The Language of Education** (Springfield, Ill.: Charles C. Thomas, 1960), Chs. 4, 5.

[43] For a discussion of this point see Jane Roland Martin,
"Response to Roemer," in Jerrold R. Coombs, ed., **Philosophy of
Education 1979** (Normal, Ill.: Proceedings of the 35th Annual
Meeting of the Philosophy of Education Society, 1980).

[44]This point is elaborated on in Jane Roland Martin, "Sex Equality and Education: A Case Study."

[45]I wish to thank Ann Diller, Carol Gilligan, Michael Martin and Janet Farrell Smith for helpful comments on earlier versions of this address which was written while I was a Fellow at the Mary Ingraham Bunting Institute of Radcliffe College.

CHAPTER 8

NEW MAPS OF DEVELOPMENT:

NEW VISIONS OF MATURITY*

Carol Gilligan

That development is the aid of a liberal education seems
clear until we begin to ask what is a liberal education and what
constitutes development. The current spirit of reappraisal in the
field of education stems in part from the fact that some old
promises have failed and new practices must be found if the vision
of education for freedom and for democracy is to be realized or
sustained. But this current reappraisal in the field of education
finds its parallel in the field of developmental psychology where
a similar reassessment is taking place, a reassessment that began
in the early 1970s when developmental psychologists began to question the adulthood that formerly they had taken for granted and
when the exclusion of women from the research samples from which
developmental theories were generated began to be noticed as a
serious omission and one that pointed to the exclusion of other
groups as well. Thus, if the changing population of students,
particularly the large number of adults and especially of adult
women entering postsecondary education, has raised a series of
questions about the aims of education and the nature of

*Carol Gilligan, "New Maps of Development: New Visions of Maturi-
ty," **American Journal of Orthopsychiatry** 52, no. 2 (April 1982),
pp. 199-212. Copyright (c) 1982 by American Orthopsychiatric
Association, Inc. Reprinted by permission of American
Orthopsychiatric Association, Inc.

educational practice, the study of adulthood and of women has generated a new set of questions for theorists of human development.

To ask whether current developmental theories can be applied to understanding or assessing the lives of people who differ from those upon whose experience these theories were bases is only to introduce a problem of far greater magnitude, the adequacy of current theories themselves. The answer to the initial question is in one sense clear, given that these theories are used repeatedly in assessing the development of different groups. But the question asked in such assessment is how much like the original group is the different group being assessed. For example, if the criteria for development are derived from studies of males and these criteria are then used to measure the development of females, the question being asked is how much like men do women develop. The assumption underlying this approach is that there is a universal standard of development and a single scale of measurement along which differences found can be aligned as higher and lower, better and worse. Yet, the initial exclusion of women displays the fallacy of this assumption and indicates a recognition of difference, pointing to the problem I wish to address. While I will use the experience of women to demonstrate how the group left out in the construction of theory calls attention to what is missing in its account, my interest lies not only in women and the perspective they add to the narrative of growth but also in the problem that differences post for a liberal educational philosophy that strives toward an ideal of equality and for a developmental psychology that posits a universal and invariant sequence of growth. In joining the subjects of morality and women, I focus specifically on the questions of value inherent in education and in developmental psychology, and indicate how the lives of women call into question current maps of development and inform a new vision of human growth.

The repeated marking of women's experience as, in Freud's term, "a dark continent for psychology"[1] raises a question as to what has shadowed the understanding of women's lives. Since women in fact do not live on a continent apart from men but instead repeatedly engage with them in the activities of everyday life, the mystery deepens and the suggestion emerges that theory may be blinding observation. While the disparity between women's experience and the representation of human development, noted throughout the psychological literature, has generally been seen to signify a problem in women's development, the failure of women to fit existing models of human growth may point to a problem in the representation, a limitation in the conception of the human condition, an omission of certain truths about life. The nature of these truths and their implications for understanding development and thinking about education are the subjects of this paper.

CONSTRUCTION OF RELATIONSHIPS AND THE CONCEPT OF MORALITY

Evidence of sex differences in the findings of psychological research comes mainly from studies that reveal the way in which men and women construct the relation between self and others. While the differences observed in women's experience and understanding of relationships have posed a problem of interpretation recurs throughout the literature on psychoanalysis and personality psychology, this problem emerges with particular clarity in the field of moral judgment research. Since moral judgments pertain to conflicts in the relation of self to others, a difference in the construction of that relationship would lead to a difference in the conception of the moral domain. This difference would be manifest in the way in which moral problems are seen, in the questions asked which then serve to guide the judgment and resolution of moral dilemmas. While the failure to perceive this difference has led psychologists to apply constructs derived from research on men to the interpretation of women's experience and thought, the recognition of this difference points to the limitation of this approach. If women's moral judgments reflect a different understanding of social relationships, then they may point to a line of social development whose presence in both sexes is currently obscured.

THEORIES OF MORAL DEVELOPMENT

This discussion of moral development takes place against the background of a field where, beginning with Freud's theory that tied superego formation to castration anxiety, extending through Piaget's study of boys' conceptions of the rules of their games, and culminating in Kohlberg's derivation of six stages of moral development from research on adolescent males, the line of development has been shaped by the pattern of male experience and thought. The continual reliance on male experience to build the model of moral growth has been coupled with a continuity in the conception of morality itself. Freud's observation that "the first requisite of civilization is justice, the assurance that a rule once made will not be broken in favor of an individual,"[2] extends through Piaget's conception of morality as consisting in respect for rules[3] and into Kohlberg's claim that justice is the most adequate of moral ideals.[4] The imagery that runs through this equation of morality with justice depicts a world comprised of separate individuals whose claims fundamentally conflict but who find in morality a mode of regulating conflict by agreement that allows the development of life lived in common.

The notion that moral development witnesses the replacement of the rule of brute force with the rule of law, bringing isolated and endangered individuals into a tempered connection with one another, then leads to the observation that women, less aggressive and thus less preoccupied with rules, are as a result less morally developed. The recurrent observations of sex differences that mark the literature on moral development are striking not only in their concurrence but in their reiterative elaboration of a single theme. Whether expressed in the general statement that women show less sense of justice than men[5] or in the particular notation that girls, in contrast to boys, think it better to give back fewer blows than one has received,[6] the direction of these differences is always the same, pointing in women to a greater sense of connection, a concern with relationships more than rules. But this observation then yields to the paradoxical conclusion that women's preoccupation with relationships constitutes an impediment to the progress of their moral development.

THE MORAL JUDGMENTS OF TWO ELEVEN-YEAR-OLDS

To illustrate how a difference in the understanding of relationships leads to a difference in the conceptions of morality
and of self, I begin with the moral judgments of two 11-year-old
children, a boy and a girl who see in the same dilemma two very
different moral problems. Demonstrating how brightly current
theory illuminates the line and the logic of the boy's thought
while casting scant light on that of the girl, I will show how the
girl's judgments reflect a fundamentally different approach. I
have chosen for the purposes of this discussion a girl whose moral
judgments elude current categories of developmental assessment, in
order to highlight the problem of interpretation rather than to
exemplify sex differences per se. My aim is to show how, by
adding a new line of interpretation, it becomes possible to see
development where previously development was not discerned and to
consider differences in the understanding of relationships without
lining up these differences on a scale from better to worse.

The two children--Amy and Jake--were in the same sixth grade
class at school and participated in a study[7] designed to explore
different conceptions of morality and self. The sample selected
for study was chosen to focus the variables of gender and age
while maximizing developmental potential by holding constant, at a
high level, the factors of intelligence, education, and social
class that have been associated with moral development, at least
as measured by existing scales. The children in question were
both bright and articulate and, at least in their 11-year-old
aspirations, resisted easy categories of sex-role stereotyping

since Amy aspired to become a scientist wile Jake preferred English to math. Yet their moral judgments seemed initially to confirm previous findings of differences between the sexes, suggesting that the edge girls have on moral development during the early school years gives way at puberty with the ascendance of formal logical thought in boys.

The dilemma these children were asked to resolve was one in the series devised by Kohlberg to measure moral development in adolescence by presenting a conflict between moral norms and exploring the logic of its resolution. In this particular dilemma, a man named Heinz considers whether or not to steal a drug, which he cannot afford to buy, in order to save the life of his wife. In the standard format of Kohlberg's interviewing procedure, the description of the dilemma itself--Heinz's predicament, the wife's disease, the druggist's refusal to lower his price--is followed by the question, should Heinz steal the drug? Then the reasons for and against stealing are explored through a series of further questions, conceived as probes and designed to reveal the underlying structure of moral thought.

JAKE

Jake, at 11, is clear from the outset that Heinz should steal the drug. Constructing the dilemma as Kohlberg did as a conflict between the values of property and life, he discerns the logical priority of life and uses that logic to justify his choice:

For one thing, a human life is worth more than money,

and if the druggist only makes $1000, he is still going to live, but if Heinz doesn't steal the drug, his wife is going to die. [Why is life worth more than money?] Because the druggist can get a thousand dollars later from rich people with cancer, but Heinz can't get his wife again. [Why not?] Because people are all different, and so you couldn't get Heinz's wife again.

Asked if Heinz should steal the drug if he does not love his wife, Jake replies that he should, saying that not only is there "a difference between hating and killing," but also, if Heinz were caught, "the judge would probably think it was the right thing to do." Asked about the fact that, in stealing, Heinz would be breaking the law, he says that "the laws have mistakes and you can't go writing up a law for everything that you can imagine."

Thus, while taking the law into account and recognizing its function in maintaining social order (the judge, he says, "should give Heinz the lightest possible sentence"), he also sees the law as man-made and therefore subject to error and change. Yet his judgment that Heinz should steal the drug, like his view of the law as having mistakes, rests on the assumption of agreement, a societal consensus around moral values that allows one to know and expect others will recognize "the right thing to do."

Fascinated by the power of logic, this 11-year-old boy locates truth in math which, he says, is "the only thing that is totally logical." Considering the moral dilemma to be "sort of like a math problem with humans," he sets it up as an equation and proceeds to work out the solution. Since his solution is rationally derived, he assumes that anyone following reason would arrive at the same conclusion and thus that a judge would also consider stealing to be the right thing for Heinz to do. Yet he is also aware of the limits of logic; asked whether there is a right answer to moral problems, he says that "there can only be right and wrong in judgment," since the parameters of action are variable and complex. Illustrating how actions undertaken with the best of intentions can eventuate in the most disastrous of consequences, he says

. . .like if you give an old lady your seat on the trolley, if you are in a trolley crash and that seat goes through the window, it might be that reason that the old lady dies.

Theories of developmental psychology illuminate well the position of this child, standing at the juncture of childhood and adolescence, at what Piaget described as a pinnacle of childhood intelligence, and beginning through thought to discover a wider universe of possibility. The moment of preadolescence is caught by the conjunction of formal operational thought with a description of self still anchored in the factual parameters of his childhood world, his age, his town, his father's occupation, the substance of his likes, dislikes, and beliefs. Yet as his self-description radiates the self-confidence of a child who has arrived, in Erikson's terms, at a favorable balance of industry over inferiority--competent, sure of himself, and knowing well the rules of the game--so his emergent capacity for formal thought, his ability to think about thinking and to reason things out in a logical way, frees him from dependence on authority and allows him to find solutions to problems by himself.

This emergent autonomy then charts the trajectory that Kohlberg's six stages of moral development trace, a three-level progression from an egocentric understanding of fairness based on individual need (stages one and two), to a conception of fairness anchored in the shared conventions of societal agreement (stages three and four), and finally to a principled understanding of fairness that rests on the freestanding logic of equality and reciprocity (stages five and six). While Jake's judgments at 11 are scored as conventional on Kohlberg's scale, a mixture of stages three and four, his ability to bring deductive logic to bear on the solution of moral dilemmas, to differentiate morality from law, and to see how laws can be considered to have mistakes, points toward the principled conception of justice that Kohlberg equates with moral maturity.

AMY

In contrast, Amy's response to the dilemma conveys a very different impression, an image of development stunted by a failure of logic, an inability to think for herself. Asked if Heinz should steal the drug, she replies in a way that seems evasive and unsure:

Well, I don't think so. I think there might be other ways besides stealing it, like if he could borrow the

money or make a loan or something, but he really
shouldn't steal the drug, but his wife shouldn't die
either.

Asked why he should not steal the drug, she considers neither
property nor law but rather the effects that theft could have on
the relationship between Heinz and his wife. If he stole the
drug, she explains,

. . .he might save his wife then, but if he did, he
might have to go to jail, and then his wife might get
sicker again, and he couldn't get more of the drug, and
it might not be good. So, they should really just talk
it out and find some other way to make the money.

Seeing in the dilemma not a math problem with humans but a
narrative of relationships that extends over time, she envisions
the wife's continuing need for her husband and the husband's
continuing concern for his wife and seeks to respond to the druggist's need in a way that would sustain rather than sever connection. As she ties the wife's survival to the preservation of
relationships, so she considers the value of her life in a context
of relationships, saying that it would be wrong to let her die
because, "if she died, it hurts a lot of people and it hurts her."
Since her moral judgment is grounded in the belief that "if somebody has something that would keep somebody alive, then it's not
right not to give it to them," she considers the problem in the
dilemma to arise not from the druggist's assertion of rights but

from his failure of response.

While the interviewer proceeds with the series of questions that follow Kohlberg's construction of the dilemma, Amy's answers remain essentially unchanged, the various probes serving neither to elucidate nor to modify her initial response. Whether or not Heinz loves his wife, he still shouldn't steal or let her die; if it were a stranger dying instead, she says that "if the stranger didn't have anybody near or anyone she knew," then Heinz should try to save her life but he shouldn't steal the drug. But as the interviewer conveys through the repetition of questions that the answers she has given are not heard or not right, Amy's confidence begins to diminish and her replies become more constrained and unsure. Asked again why Heinz should not steal the drug, she simply repeats, "Because it's not right." Asked again to explain why, she states again that theft would not be a good solution, adding lamely, that, "if he took it, he might not know how to give it to his wife, and so his wife might still die." Failing to see the dilemma as a self-contained problem in moral logic, she does not discern the internal structure of its resolution: as she constructs the problem differently herself, Kohlberg's conception completely evades her.

Instead, seeing a world comprised of relationships rather than of people standing alone, a world that coheres through human connection rather than through systems of rules, she finds the puzzle in the dilemma to lie in the failure of the druggist to respond to the wife. Saying that "it is not right for someone to die when their life could be saved," she assumes that if the druggist were to see the consequences of his refusal to lower his

price, he would realize that "he should just give it to the wife
and then have the husband pay back the money later." Thus she
considers the solution to the dilemma to lie in making the wife's
condition more salient to the druggist or, that failing, in appealing to others who are in a position to help.

Just as Jake is confident the judge would agree that stealing
is the right thing for Heinz to do, so Amy is confident that, "if
Heinz and the druggist had talked it out long enough, they could
reach something besides stealing." As he considers the law to
"have mistakes," so she sees this drama as a mistake, believing
that "the world should just share things more and then people
wouldn't have to steal." Both children thus recognize the need
for agreement but see it as mediated in different ways: he im-
personally through systems of logic and law, she personally
through communication in relationship. As he relies on the conventions of logic to deduce the solution to this dilemma, assuming
these conventions to be shared, so she relies on a process of
communication, assuming connection and believing that her voice
will be heard. Yet while his assumptions about agreement are
confirmed by the convergence in logic between his answer and the
questions posed, her assumptions are belied by the failure in
communication, the interviewer's inability to understand her
response.

MEASURING MORAL DEVELOPMENT: ASSESSING DIVERSE PERCEPTIONS

While the frustration of the interview with Amy is apparent
in the repetition of questions and its ultimate circularity, the

problem of interpretation arises when it comes to assessing her development. Considered in the light of Kohlberg's conception of the stages and sequence of moral development, her moral judgments are a full stage lower in moral maturity than those of the boy. Scored as a mixture of stages two and three, they seem to reveal a feeling of powerlessness in the world, an inability to think systematically about the concepts of morality or law, a reluctance to challenge authority or to examine the logic of received moral truths, a failure even to conceive of acting directly to save a life or to consider that such action, if taken, could possibly have an effect. As her reliance on relationships seems to reveal a continuing dependence and vulnerability, so her belief in communication as the mode through which to resolve moral dilemmas appears naive and cognitively immature.

Yet her description of herself conveys a markedly different impression. Once again, the hallmarks of the preadolescent child depict a child secure in her sense of herself, confident in the substance of her beliefs, and sure of her ability to do something of value in the world. Describing herself at 11 as "growing and changing," Amy says that she "sees some things differently now, just because I know myself really well now, and I know a lot more about the world." Yet the world she knows is a different world from that refracted by Kohlberg's construction of Heinz's dilemma. Her world is a world of relationships and psychological truths, where an awareness of the connection between people gives rise to a recognition of responsibility for one another, a perception of the need for response. Seen in this light, her view of morality as arising from the recognition of relationship, her belief in communication as the mode of conflict resolution, and her conviction that the solution to the dilemma will follow from its compelling representation seem far from naive or cognitively immature; rather, her judgments contain the insights central to an ethic of care, just as Jake's judgments reflect the logic of the justice approach. Her incipient awareness of the "method of truth," central to nonviolent conflict resolution, and her belief in the restorative activity of care, lead her to see the actors in the dilemma arrayed not as opponents in a contest of rights but as members of a network of relationships on whose continuation they all depend. Consequently her solution to the dilemma lies in activating the network by communication, securing the inclusion of the wife by strengthening rather than severing connection.

But the different logic of Amy's response calls attention to a problem in the interpretation of the interview itself. Conceived as an interrogation, it appears as a dialogue that takes on moral dimensions of its own, pertaining to the interviewer's uses of power and to the manifestations of respect. With this shift in the conception of the interview, it immediately becomes clear that the interviewer's problem in hearing Amy's response stems from the fact that Amy is answering a different question from the one the interviewer thought had been posed. Amy is considering not **whether** Heinz should act in this situation (**Should** Heinz steal the drug?) but rather **how** Heinz should act in response to his awareness of his wife's need (Should Heinz **steal** the drug?). The interviewer takes the mode of action for granted, presuming it to be a matter of fact. Amy assumes the necessity for action and considers what form it should take. In the interviewer's failure to imagine a response not dreamt of in Kohlberg's moral philosophy lies the failure to hear Amy's question and to see the logic in her response, to discern that what from one perspective appears to be an evasion of the dilemma signifies in other terms a recognition of the problem and a search for a more adequate solution.

Thus in Kohlkberg's dilemma these two children see two very different moral problems--Jake a conflict between life and property that can be resolved by logical deduction, Amy a fracture of human relationship that must be mended with its own thread. Asking different questions that arise from different conceptions of the moral domain, they arrive at answers that fundamentally diverge, and the arrangement of these answers as successive stages on a scale of increasing moral maturity calibrated by the logic of the boy's response misses the different truth revealed in the judgment of the girl. To the question, "What does he see that she does not?", Kohlberg's theory provides a ready response, manifest in the scoring of his judgments a full stage higher than hers in moral maturity: to the question, "What does she see that he does not?", Kohlberg's theory has nothing to say. Since most of her responses fall through the sieve of Kohlberg's scoring system, her responses appear from his perspective to lie outside the moral domain.

Yet just as Jake reveals a sophisticated understanding of the logic of justification, so Amy is equally sophisticated in her understanding of the nature of choice. Saying that "if both the roads went in totally separate ways, if you pick one, you'll never know what would happen if you went the other way," she explains that "that's the chance you have to take, and like I said, it's

just really a guess." To illustrate her point "in a simple way,"
she describes how, in choosing to spend the summer at camp, she

> . . .will never know what would have happened if I had
> stayed here, and if something goes wrong at camp, I'll
> never know if I stayed here if it would have been bet-
> ter. There's really no way around it because there's no
> way you can do both at once, so you've got to decide,
> but you'll never know.

In this way, these two 11-year-old children, both highly
intelligent, though perceptive about life in different ways,
display different modes of moral understanding, different ways of
thinking about conflict and choice. Jake, in resolving the dilemma, follows the construction that Kohlberg has posed. Relying
on theft to avoid confrontation and turning to the law to mediate
the dispute, he transposes a hierarchy of power into a hierarchy
of values by recasting a conflict between people into a conflict
of claims. Thus abstracting the moral problem from the interpersonal situation, he finds in the logic of fairness an objective
means of deciding who will win the dispute. But this hierarchical
ordering, with its imagery of winning and losing and the potential
for violence which it contains, gives way in Amy's construction of
the dilemma to a network of connection, a network sustained by a
process of communication. With this shift, the moral problem
changes from one of unfair domination, the imposition of property
over life, to one of unnecessary exclusion, the failure of the
druggist to respond to the wife.

This shift in the formulation of the moral problem and the concomitant change in the imagery of relationships are illustrated as well by the responses of two eight-year-olds who participated in the same study[8] and were asked to describe a situation in which they weren't sure of the right thing to do:

Jeffrey (age 8): When I really want to go to my friends and my mother is cleaning the cellar, I think about my friends, and then I think about my mother, and then I think about the right thing to do. [But how do you know it's the right thing to do?] Because some things go before other things.

Karen (age 8): I have a lot of friends, and I can't always play with all of them, so everybody's going to have to take a turn, because they're all my friends. But like if someone's all alone, I'll play with them. [What kind of things do you think about when you are trying to make that decision?] Um, someone all alone, loneliness.

While Jeffrey sets up a hierarchical ordering in thinking about the conflict between desire and duty, Karen describes a network of relationships that include all of her friends. Both children deal with the issues of exclusion and priority created by choice, but while Jeffrey thinks about what goes first, Karen focuses on who is left out.

MORAL JUDGMENT AND SELF-DESCRIPTIONS

In illustrating a difference in children's thinking about moral conflict and choice, I have described two views that are complementary rather than sequential or opposed. In doing so, I go against the bias of developmental theory toward ordering differences in a hierarchical mode. This correspondence between the order of developmental theory and that manifest in the boys' responses contrasts with the disparity between the structure of theory and that manifest in the thought of the girls. Yet, in neither comparison does one child's thought appear as precursor of the other's position. Thus, questions arise about the relation between these perspectives; what is the significance of these differences, and how do these two modes of thinking connect? To pursue these questions, I return to the eleven-year-olds and consider the way they describe themselves.

[**How would you describe yourself to yourself?**]
Jake: Perfect. That's my conceited side. What do you want--any way that I choose to describe myself?

Amy: You mean my character? [**What do you think?**] Well, I don't know. I'd describe myself as, well, what do you mean?

[**If you had to describe the person you are in a way that you yourself would know it was you, what would you say?**]

Jake: I'd start off with eleven years old, Jake [last name]. I'd have to add that I live in [town] because that is a big part of me, and also that my father is a doctor because I think that does change me a little bit, and that I don't believe in crime, except for when your name is Heinz . . . that I think school is boring because I think that kind of changes your character a little bit. I don't sort of know how to describe myself, because I don't know how to read my personality. [If you had to describe the way you actually would describe yourself, what would you say?] I like corny jokes. I don't really like to get down to work, but I can do all the stuff in school. Every single problem that I have seen in school I have been able to do, except for ones that take knowledge, and after I do the reading, I have been able to do them, but sometimes I don't want to waste my time on easy homework. And also I'm crazy about sports. I think, unlike a lot of people, that the world still has hope . . . . Most people that I know I like, and I have the good life, pretty much as good as any I have seen, and I am tall for my age.

Amy: Well, I'd say that I was someone who likes school and studying, and that's what I want to do with my life. I want to be some kind of a scientist or something, and I want to do things, and I want to help people. And I think that's what kind of person I am, or what kind of

person I try to be. And that's probably how I'd describe myself. And I want to do something to help other
people. [**Why is that?**] Well, because I think that this
world has a lot of problems, and I think that everybody
should try to help somebody else in some way, and the
way I'm choosing is through science.

In the voice of the 11-year-old boy, a familiar form of
self-definition appears, resonating to the schoolbook inscription
of the young Stephen Daedalus ("himself, his name and where he
was")[9] and echoing the descriptions that appear in **Our Town**,[10]
laying out across the coordinates of time and space a hierarchical
order in which to define one's place. Describing himself as
distinct by locating his particular position in the world, Jake
sets himself apart from that world by his abilities, his beliefs,
and his height. Although Amy also enumerates her likes, her
wants, and her beliefs, she locates herself in relation to the
world, describing herself through actions that bring her into connection with others, elaborating ties through her ability to
provide help. To Jake's ideal of perfection against which he
measures the worth of himself, Amy counterposes an ideal of care
against which she measures the worth of her activity. While she
places herself in relation to the world and chooses to help others
through science, he places the world in relation to himself as it
defines his character, his position, and the quality of life.

CONCLUSION

As the voices of these children illuminate two modes of self-description and two modes of moral judgment, so they illustrate how readily we hear the voice that speaks of justice and of separation and the difficulty we encounter in listening to the voice that speaks of care and connection. Listening through developmental theories and through the structures of our educational and social system, we are attuned to a hierarchical ordering that represents development as a progress of separation, a chronicle of individual success. In contrast, the understanding of development as a progress of human relationships, a narrative of expanding connection, is an unimagined representation. The image of network or web thus seems more readily to connote entrapment rather than an alternative and nonhierarchical vision of human connection.

This central limitation in the representation of development is most clearly apparent in recent portrayals of adult life, where the insistent focus on self and on work provides scanty representation of an adulthood spent in the activities of relationship and care. The tendency to chart the unfamiliar waters of adult development with the familiar markers of adolescent separation and growth leads to an equation of development with separation; it results in a failure to represent the reality of connection both in love and in work. Levinson,[11] patterning the stages of adult development on the seasons of a man's life, defined the developmental process explicitly as one of individuation, yet reported his distress at the absence of friendships in men's lives.

Vaillant,[12] deriving his account of adaptation to life from the lives of the men who took part in the Grant study, noted that the question these men found most difficult to answer was, "Can you describe your wife?" In this light, the observation that women's embeddedness in lives of relationship, their orientation to inter-dependence, their subordination of achievement to care, and their conflicts over competitive success leave them personally at risk in mid-life, though generally construed as a problem in women's development, seems more a commentary on our society and on the representation of development itself.

In suggesting that the consideration of women's lives and of adulthood calls attention to the need for an expansion in the mapping of human development, I have pointed to a distinction between two modes of self-definition and two modes of moral judg-ment and indicated how these modes reflect different ways of imagining relationships. That these modes are tied to different experiences may explain their empirical association with gender, though that association is by no means absolute. That they re-flect different forms of thought--one relying on a formal logic whose development Piaget has described, the other on a narrative and contextual mode of thought whose development remains to be traced-- indicates the implication of this distinction for psy-chological assessment and education.

The experiences of inequality and of interdependence are embedded in the life cycle of life, universal because inherent in the relationship of parent and child. These experiences of in-equality and interdependence give rise to the ethics of justice and care, the ideals of human relationship--the vision that self and other will be treated as of equal worth, that despite differences in power, things will be fair; the vision that everyone will be responded to and included, that no one will be left alone or hurt. The adolescent, capable of envisioning the ideal, reflects on the childhood experiences of powerlessness and vulnerability and conceives a utopian world laid out along the coordinates of justice and care. This ability to conceive the hypothetical and to construct contrary-to-fact hypotheses has led the adolescent to be proclaimed a 'philosopher,"[13] a "metaphysican par excellence."[14] But the representation of the adolescent's moral philosophy in the literature of developmental psychology has been limited to the portrayal of changes in the conception of justice that supports the adolescent's claim to equality and the separation of other and self. My own work[15] has expanded this description by identifying two different moral languages, the language of rights that protects separation and the language of responsibilities that sustains connection. In dialogue, these languages not only create the ongoing tension of moral discourse, but also reveal how the dynamics of separation and attachment in the process of identity formation relate to the themes of justice and care in moral growth. This expanded representation of identity and moral development allows a more complex rendering of differences, and points to the need to understand and foster the development of both modes.

The old promise of a liberal education, of an education that frees individuals from blinding constraints and engenders a questioning of assumptions formerly taken for granted remains a compelling vision. But among the prevailing assumptions that need to be questioned are the assumptions about human development. The lives of women, in pointing to an uncharted path of human growth and one that leads to a less violent mode of life, are particularly compelling at this time in history and thus deserve particular attention. The failure to attend to the voices of women and the difficulty in hearing what they say when they speak has compromised women's development and education, leading them to doubt the veracity of their perceptions and to question the truth of their experience. This problem becomes acute for women in adolescence, when thought becomes reflective and the problem of interpretation thus enters the stream of development itself. But the failure to represent women's experience also contributes to the presentation of competitive relationships and hierarchical modes of social organization as the natural ordering of life. For this reason, the consideration of women's lives brings to the conception of development a much needed corrective, stressing the importance of narrative modes of thought and pointing to the contextual nature of psychological truths and the reality of interdependence in human life.

The process of selection that has shadowed this vision can be seen in Kohlberg's reading of Martin Luther King's letter from the Birmingham jail,[16] since Kohlberg extracted King's justification for breaking the law in the name of justice but omitted the way in which King's vision of justice was embedded in a vision of human connection. Replying to the clergy who criticized his action, King not only offered a justification of his action but also defended the necessity for action, anchoring that necessity in the realization of interdependence:

> I am in Birmingham because injustice is here. I cannot
> sit idly by in Atlanta and not be concerned about what
> happens in Birmingham. Injustice anywhere is a threat
> to justice everywhere. We are caught in an inescapable
> network of mutuality, tied in a single garment of desti-
> ny. Whatever affects one directly, affects all indi-
> rectly.

Thus, like Bonhoeffer,[17] who stated that action comes "not from thought but from a readiness for responsibility", King tied his responsiveness to a caring that arises from an understanding of the connection between people's lives, a connection not forged by systems of rules but by a perception of the fact of relationship, a connection not freely contracted but built into the very fabric of life.

The ideals of a liberal democratic society—of freedom and equality—have been mirrored in the developmental vision of auton-omy, the image of the educated man thinking for himself, the image of the ideal moral agent acting alone on the basis of his princi-ples, blinding himself with a Rawlsian "veil of ignorance," play-ing a solitary Kohlbergian game of "moral musical chairs." Yet the developmental psychologists who dared, with Erikson,[18] to "ask what is an adult," immediately began to see the limitations of this vision. Erikson himself has come increasingly to talk about the activity of caretaking and to identify caring as the virtue and strength of maturity.[19] When integrated into a developmental understanding, this insight should spur the search for the ante-cedents of this strength in childhood and in adolescence.

Kohlberg,[20] turning to consider adulthood, tied adult development to the experiences of "sustained responsibility for the welfare of others" and of the irreversible consequences of choice. The resonance of these themes of maturity to the voice of the 11-year-old girl calls into question current assumptions about the sequence of development and suggests a different path of growth.

The story of moral development, as it is presently told, traces the history of human development through shifts in the hierarchy of power relationships, implying that the dissolution of this hierarchy into an order of equality represents the ideal vision of things. But the conception of relationships in terms of hierarchies implies separation as the moral ideal--for everyone to stand alone, independent, self-sufficient, connected to others by the abstractions of logical thought. There is, then, a need to represent in the mapping of development a nonhierarchical image of human connection, and to embody in the vision of maturity the reality of interdependence. This alternate vision of the web of connection is the recognition of relationship that prevents aggression and gives rise to the understanding that generates response.

FOOTNOTES

[1] Sigmund Freud, "The Question of Lay Analysis" (1926), in **Standard Edition of the Complete Psychological Works of Sigmund Freud**, vol. 20, ed. James Strachey (London: Hogarth Press, 1961). Cf. Freud, "Some Physical Consequences of the Anatomical Distinction Between the Sexes" (1925), in **Standard Edition**, vol. 19.

[2] Freud, "Civilization and Its Discontents" (1929), in **Standard Edition**, vol. 21.

[3] Jean Piaget, **The Moral Judgment of the Child** (1932), trans. Marjorie Gabain (New York: Free Press, 1965).

[4] Lawrence Kohlberg, **The Philosophy of Moral Development** (San Francisco: Harper and Row, 1981).

[5] Freud, "The Question of Lay Analysis."

[6] Piaget, **The Moral Judgment of the Child**.

[7] Carol Gilligan, Sharry Langdale, and Nona Lyons, **The Contribution of Women's Thought to Developmental Theory: The Elimination of Sex-Bias in Moral Development Theory and Research** (Washington, D.C.: National Institute of Education, 1982).

[8] Ibid.

[9] James Joyce, **A Portrait of the Artist as a Young Man** (1916), (New York: Viking Press, 1956), p. 15.

[10] Thornton Wilder, **Our Town** (New York: Coward-McCann, 1938).

[11] Daniel J. Levinson, **The Seasons of a Man's Life** (New York: Alfred A. Knopf. 1978).

[12] George E. Vaillant, **Adaptation to Life** (Boston: Little, Brown, 1977).

[13] Kohlberg, "Continuities and Discontinuities in Childhood and Adult Moral Development Revisited," in **Life Span Developmental Psychology: Personality and Socialization**, eds. Paul Baltes and K. Warner Schaie (New York: Academic press, 1973).

[14] Barbel Inhelder and Jean Piaget, **The Growth of Logical Thinking from Childhood to Adolescence** (New York: Basic Books, 1958).

[15] Gilligan, **In a Difference Voice: Psychological Theory and Women's Development** (Cambridge, Mass.: Harvard University Press, 1982.

[16] Martin Luther King, Jr., **Why We Can't Wait** (New York: Harper and Row, 1964).

[17]Dietrich Bonhoeffer, **Letters and Papers from Prison** (New York: MacMillan, 1953).

[18]Erik H. Erikson, "Reflections on the Dissent of Contemporary Youth," **Daedalus** 99 (1970): 154-176.

[19]Erikson, "Reflections on Dr. Borg's Life Cycle," **Daedalus** 105 (1976): 1-29.

[20]Kohlberg, "Continuities and Discontinuities in Childhood and Adult Moral Development Revisted," in **Life Span Developmental Psychology: Personality and Socialization,** eds. Paul Baltes and K. Warner Schaie (New York: Academic Press, 1973).

NOTE

This essay was presented, in earlier versions, to the National Academy of Education, October 1981, and to the Conference on Adolescent Development and Secondary Schooling, Wisconsin Center for Education Research, November 1981. Research was supported by grant R03-MH31571 from the National Institute of Mental Health and grant G790131 from the National Institute of Education. Portions of this paper are contained in a full-length work, **In a Different Voice: Psychological Theory and Women's Development,** by Carol Gilligan, Harvard University Press, 1982.

CHAPTER 9

MORAL DEVELOPMENT AND EDUCATION: MEN'S
LANGUAGE OF RIGHTS AND WOMEN'S LANGUAGE OF RESPONSIBILITY*
Betty A. Sichel

Historically, adults have always been concerned about the
moral education of children and adolescents. During the contemporary period, however, a moral crisis has considerably increased
such concern. Many causes have been cited for the present moral
crisis. First, this crisis might be traced to the shift from the
gemeinschaft of extended families, agrarian society, and value
unity to the **gesellschaft** of nuclear families, urban or suburban
life, and value pluralism. More recently, an even move radical
shift occurred: Home no longer is where the heart can rest.[1]
With greater numbers of divorced and single-parent families, there
are new questions about moral education.

Second, the character and growth of science and technology
have spawned new moral problems (e.g., from questions about the
continuance of life support systems to those about abortions).
Actually, science and technology created moral dilemmas never even
dreamed of by older generations. Third, during the last few
decades, chicanery, crimes, lying, and other questionable acts

*Betty A. Sichel, "Moral Development and Education: Men's
Language of Rights and Women's Language of Responsibility,"
Contemporary Education Review 2, no. 1 (Spring 1983), pp. 33-42.
Copyright (c) 1983 by American Educational Research Association.
Reprinted by permission of American Educational Research
Association.

have been publicly identified as being committed by professionals, politicians, and business leaders. After criminal, unsavory skullduggery at every level of government shocked the nation, the public retained little confidence in the morality of elected and appointed government officials. The public has also expressed little confidence in many of society's institutions (e.g., whether business leaders benefit the public good and protect the environment). Fourth, mass media often presents and exacerbates a variety of unacceptable, illegal, sordid values and forms of behavior.

Schools are not immune from this moral crisis, the moral problems of the larger society often finding their way into schools. Vandalism and violent attacks on both teachers and other students are two of the more highly publicized problems facing schools. Recent Gallup Polls indicate that the public views discipline as one of the major problems facing schools and thus now favor moral education in schools.

Two of this generation's most insightful, provocative, and controversial books on the nature of moral development have recently been published. These works suggest aims for moral education programs and have far-reaching implications for school structure, curriculum, methodology, discipline, and the hidden curriculum. Lawrence Kohlberg's (1981) **The Philosophy of Moral Development** and Carol Gilligan's (1982) **In A Different Voice** are thus important books for psychologists, philosophers, educators, and the lay public.[2] The present essay review includes the following: (1) an introduction explaining the context in which these books were written and presenting the contrasting features of Gilligan's and Kohlberg's theories and findings; and (2) an examination of questions psychologists, philosophers, and educators might ask Kohlberg and Gilligan and the implications these works have for researchers and policymakers.

INTRODUCTION

The Hartshorne and May 1928-1930 studies marked a turning point in the understanding of the psychology of morality and moral development. As the result of their administration of 33 tests of deceit, the investigators questioned the efficiency of character traits and severely damaged the notion that moral character guarantees consistent, predictable moral behavior. According to Hartshorne and May, most people do not seem to possess unified character traits such as "honesty" or "cheating." Rather, honesty and dishonesty, and lying and cheating seemed dependent on the context of particular, unique situations.[3] Though their findings did not demonstrate the total absence of recognizable, consistent moral conduct and character traits, sufficient anomalies were created to all into question dominant assumptions underlying theories of moral behavior and educational assumptions. Thus, the time seemed appropriate for Piaget's (1932/1965) **The Moral Judgment of the Child.**[4]

However, of all Piaget's cognitive theories and studies, his moral development theory generated the least interest among educators and theorists. Though Europe during the 1930s was already confronted with social, political, and economic crises, only a few psychologists examined the validity of Piaget's moral cognitive developmental theory and conducted replicative studies with diverse samples.

In 1958, Lawrence Kohlberg posited a moral development theory that owes much to Piaget's seminal work but also includes elements from Dewey, Mead, and Baldwin. For many reasons, Kohlberg's theory not only met with a much warmer reception than Piaget's, but actually set in motion a Kuhnian paradigmatic revolution. First, Kohlberg's theory resolves anomalies created by the Hartshorne and May studies. Kohlberg also argues that identification and social-learning theories create other anomalies, which his theory overcomes. Second, consistent with Kuhn's explanation of why paradigmatic revolutions are accepted, Kohlberg's theory is aesthetically and even ethically pleasing. Its language and concepts are couched in an already accepted and popular framework, that of genetic structuralism. Furthermore, Kohlberg accepts and reinforces current dominant views about pluralistic democracy and justice as fairness. Third, the time was ripe for a moral developmental theory with realistic implications for educational practice. Radical changes in values and self-consciousness about social, political, and personal problems may have created a climate in which Kohlberg's theory could flourish. Thus, Kohlberg's revision of Piaget's theory met with a very different fate from its predecessor.

During the quarter century since its first appearance, numerous studies have ostensibly confirmed Kohlberg's theory and replicated its empirical findings. Simultaneously, however, there has been considerable criticism of Kohlberg's theory, experimental methods, and findings. At the very time that Kohlberg backed away from certain aspects of his theory and educational recommendations, the first volume of his early essays was published. About a year after the publication of these essays, Carol Gilligan's (1982) **In a Different Voice** challenged Kohlberg's assumptions and presented an alternative view. In particular, Gilligan claims that Kohlberg's stages of moral development are valid for men, but not for women.

Kohlberg's theory of the development of moral judgments posits three hierarchical, invariant, sequential levels: the preconventional, conventional, and postconventional. In turn, these three levels include a total of six stages. Moral judgments at the preconventional level are primarily egocentric and based on the welfare of the self. Punishment and obedience are the main focus of stage one and the limited reciprocity of "you scratch my back; I'll scratch yours" characterizes stage two. At the conventional level, the person looks outward and actively accepts what others and society believe. The stage three person wants to be considered a "good boy" or "nice girl," and stage four's reasoning is dominated by a concern with "law and order." Finally, with the postconventional level, the person's reasoning transcends egocentricity and outerdirectedness based on the beliefs of society and others. At the postconventional level individuals become autonomous, turn inward, and posit self-chosen principles and reasons for moral judgments. At stage five moral judgments are based on a social contract or utility and individual rights, and stage six embodies personally chosen and universalizable ethical principles of justice, equality of human rights, and respect for each person's dignity. Moral development from a lower to higher state is not additive, not the addition of discreet rules, standards, or

forms of behavior. Rather, similar to Piaget's cognitive structuralism, each higher, moral development stage requires a radical
transformation in the structure of thought processes and reasoning.

In addition to experiments in Taiwan, Israel, Turkey, and
Mexico, Kohlberg and his associates studied different socio-
economic and religious groups in the United States. They presented subjects with moral dilemmas, each followed by open-ended
but structured questioning. For example, in Kohlberg's well-known
dilemma, the Heinz case, a wife needs a drug for survival. Her
husband, Heinz, cannot raise sufficient money to buy it from the
only druggist who owns it. Should Heinz steal the drug?

Kohlberg has been criticized for omitting women from the
original sample that formed his ongoing longitudinal study. When
it was discovered that women generally scored a stage lower than
men, Kohlberg explained this tentative anomaly as follows: The
social roles women have traditionally been given and women's
education do not foster development to higher moral stages. Thus,
instead of reaching "law and order" stage 4 as many American men
do, women only reach stage 3 where the "conception of justice is
integrated with a conception of a good (positive and stable)
interpersonal relationship. The sociomoral order is conceived of
as primarily composed of dyadic relations of mutual role taking,
mutual affection, gratitude, and concern for one another's approval."[5] According to Kohlberg's explanation, when women achieve
equality and autonomy and are given (or take) the same roles as
men, their moral development stage will be identical with that of
men.

Gilligan's **In A Different Voice** challenges Kohlberg's interpretation of women's moral development. Instead of accepting his rationale for women's lower stage of moral development, Gilligan asserts that men and women speak different, equally valid moral languages: men a language of rights and women a language of responsibility. These two languages are instantiated in the way two 11-year-old children, Amy and Jake, resolve moral dilemmas. If Kohlberg's grading procedures and theory were used to interpret their stages of moral development, the boy would score a stage above the girl. This is surprising since Amy is articulate and has the realistic life goal of becoming a scientist. Amy's logical reasoning in mathematics would belie Kohlberg's grading of her responses to moral dilemmas. Whereas Jake resolves Kohlberg's Heinz dilemma in the same way he would tackle an algebraic equation, Amy hesitates, manifests uncertainty, and speaks of how the relationship between Heinz and his wife would suffer if Heinz steals the drug. Throughout the interchange between Amy and the interviewer, Amy seems unable to respond clearly and competently to the questions posed. But actually, Amy does not see the moral dilemma in the same way as Kohlberg assumes it should be interpreted. Instead of being a conflict of rights, between the right of property and the right of life, Amy concentrates on how one might resolve the problem.

In another set of interviews, an 8-year-old boy and girl, Jeffrey and Karen, relate actual, personal moral dilemmas. Jeffrey's problem reveals his lexical ordering and concern with rights. After telling of a conflict between playing with friends and helping his mother clean the basement, the boy notes that some things just go first (i.e., are ordered before other things). The girl relates a different problem, one about choosing which of many friends to play with. Instead of referring to conflicting rights and logical priority, Karen bases her judgment on people's feelings and whether someone is lonely.

Rather than only using hypothetical, moral problems of rights, Gilligan also questions women about personal moral problems, in particular, women debating whether to have abortions. From their reasoning and the standards for their judgments, Gilligan discerns a very different form of moral development. Here Gilligan distinguishes the women's language of responsibility as a "psychological logic" of relationships, while men's language of rights is a formal logic of fairness informing a justice position.[6] Just as Kohlberg's language of rights and formal logic of fairness delineate six stages of moral development, Gilligan's language of responsibility and "psychological logic" of relationships traces three moral perspectives. After the first focus on caring for the self and ensuring survival, a transitional period criticizes this as selfish. This then gives rise to a second focus with a new relationship between self and other. The second focus concentrates on responsibility and fuses it with the material characteristic of caring for dependent others. Finally, the third focus recognizes the dynamic interrelationship between self and other. Since caring is still the dominant quality, women at this third focus condemn exploitation and hurting relationships.[7]

PSYCHOLOGICAL ISSUES AND IMPLICATIONS

A considerable portion of the criticism leveled against Kohlberg's experimental methods and findings could also be applied to Gilligan's work. Criticism includes the following: (a) the question of whether moral action follows moral developmental stages;[8] (b) whether the theory is predictive; (c) whether the six stages are invariant and sequential;[9] (d) whether stage 5 and 6 even exist in the form first posited by Kohlberg;[10] and (e) the excessive time necessary to administer the dilemmas. Whereas Kohlberg has been criticized for ignoring the affective domain, Gilligan could equally be criticized for ignoring the affective domain, Gilligan could equally be criticized for creating a duality between the affective and cognitive.

Other equally serious problems confront Gilligan's work. First, what scale or measurement tools are used to interpret women's responses? Second, as Gilligan herself admits in another article, "The sample is small and nonrepresentative. Obviously, a Harvard sample cannot be equated with the general population."[11] Since most of Gilligan's subjects are upper-middle-class children or Radcliffe-Harvard students, how representative is her sample? Finally, is the perspective presented by Gilligan the result of acceptable research techniques? The reader has no way of knowing this. Though Gilligan's views seem intuitively correct, this is far different from an empirical study. Gilligan herself hesitates when she refers to women's development as "perspectives," "focuses," but not "stages." Thus, though a critical essay of considerable heuristic value, one must question whether Gilligan's views are based on empirical investigations. With these caveats, I proceed to the implications Kohlberg's and Gilligan's work may have for educational researchers.

1. Though recent theories (e.g., ethnology) rely on different methods of studying phenomena and reporting evidence, statistical studies are still dominant. As Kurtines and Greif (1974) assert, "Despite its demonstrated heuristic value, however, Kohlberg's model, like all theoretical systems, must ultimately be evaluated empirically."[12] Yet, Kohlberg and Gilligan both reject traditionally accepted statistical methods and instead rely on controlled, open-ended interview techniques. In itself, the warm reception given Kohlberg's and Gilligan's models must cause some uneasiness to those wedded to statistical and experimental methods. The question is not merely how valid Kohlberg's and Gilligan's methods are in relation to statistical methods. Rather, experimenters need to question whether this form of interviewing and its concomitant introspection have unexplored implications for educational research.

There is a larger question of the relationship between theories and their statistical validation. For example, Freud's psychoanalytical theory has a poor track record in the area of statistical validation and even practical implementation.[13] However, psychologists would be foolhardy to report the demise of Freud's theory. Thus, one must wonder under what circumstances and why continued allegiance should be given or withheld from a theory. Recent criticism, especially by Kurtines and Greif, and attempts at disconfirmation have been rejected by Kohlberg; "Kurtines. . . and Greif were in error in believing that defects in methodology can lead to a disconfirmation of a stage construct and in believing that the usual personality-test concepts of external validity (for example, predicting behavior) are appropriate for assessing the validity of a stage methodology."[14] How then can researchers disconfirm such a theory? Must one merely wait until it withers on the vine?

Another issue is implied by Gilligan's studies. Are educational research techniques and interviewing methods often unconsciously perceived by subjects as hostile or conflict situations? Does the separation of subjects from the personal existential life continuum, or the expectations and methods of experimenters, cause alienation and invalid experimental results?[15] Gilligan refers to this problem when the interviewer questions Amy about Kohlberg's Heinz dilemma. "As the interviewer conveys through the repetition of questions that the answers she gave were not heard or not right, Amy's confidence begins to diminish, and her replies become more constrained and unsure."[16] The interviewer is unable to "listen with a third ear" or understand Amy's interpretation of the moral dilemma. Though she does not explicitly criticize experimental methods, Gilligan's findings have implications for such a criticism.

2. Certain topics were rarely investigated and escaped theoretical nets of the behavioral sciences. Only during the last decade have experimental studies and theories focused on the unique experience and psychological life-cycle of women. Just as Eve was created from Adam's rib, psychology may have viewed women as an embarrassing appendage to male-dominated theories. Instead of only presenting anomalies in Kohlberg's theory or positing an

alternative moral language, Gilligan refers to "a problem of far greater magnitude, the adequacy of current theories themselves."[17] Whereas Freud saw women as "a dark continent for psychology" and Piaget wholly relied on boys' conceptions of games, Gilligan demonstrates that "life-cycle theorists [must] divide their attention and begin to live with women."[18] Only new visions which include the experiences of women and men can create more "fertile" psychological theories.[19] Though the recent work of Maccoby and Jacklin, Miller, Horner, Gilligan, and others contribute to an understanding of the psychology of women, psychology has not constructed theories to provide a holistic, unified vision of human development, of the life-cycle of men and women.

Finally, if women use a different moral language and progress through different moral perspectives, might there be a moral relativism and diversity in cross-cultural moral development that Kohlberg has been unwilling to accept?[20]

3. When Kohlberg posits stage development as a universal phenomenon, he makes two claims. First, human beings universally move sequentially through moral development stages though they may not reach the highest stages. Second, as with Piaget's notion of intelligence, the potential for moral development is a function of "something present from the start"[21] and an adequate social environment.

Gilligan's thesis and interviews challenge both these claims. First, Kohlberg's theory may not be universal, but only valid for part of the population, for men not women. Second, Kohlberg claims that moral development is not social learning, habituation, or an unfolding of innate wiring, but the result of an interaction between some potential and the environment. There are two explanations for differences in women's and men's moral development, which Kohlberg has not considered. First, the concept "potential" as applied to human beings or moral concepts might need enlargement. Any moral development theory that stresses the cognitive without the affective or vice versa may be an unfortunate narrowing of human potential, or the concept of potential needs to be enlarged. Second, moral development may be more dependent on the social environment than Kohlberg admits. Differing forms of attachment during infancy and childhood and the different relationships that male and female infants and children have with their mothers and fathers may contribute to differing forms of moral development. If environment has a greater influence on moral development, a fully articulated theory of moral development would have to combine Kohlberg's stage model with the insights of social-learning theory.

PHILOSOPHIC ISSUES AND IMPLICATIONS

One of the strengths of Kohlberg's theory is his serious examination of its philosophical underpinnings. In particular, the use of Rawls' widely accepted **A Theory of Justice**[22] adds to the attractiveness of Kohlberg's theory. The highest stage of moral development, for Kohlberg, is based on Rawls' principles of justice to guarantee fair distribution of limited goods and assure human rights. In the main, Rawls' principles provide lexical ordering of desired goods and the method by which to evaluate conflicting claims to goods and rights. Wolff (1977) emphasizes the conflict nature of Rawls' theory of justice by terming it a "bargaining game."[23]

This is exactly what Gilligan argues that women reject. In place of viewing moral dilemmas as bargaining games and rights conflicts between competing rational, self-interested players, women stress resolutions that include concern, care, continued attachment, responsibility, sacrifice, and the avoidance of hurting another. Gilligan would further reject Rawls' original position under a veil of ignorance. Whereas men search for abstract principles and a method that can be applied to any moral dilemma, women concentrate on particular situations, relationships, and people. Within these concrete relationships themselves, women discover their moral perspectives and "principles." Men accept the validity of examining hypothetical moral dilemmas extracted from the stream of their existential lives, while women reconstruct "the dilemma in its contextual particularity";[24] that is, women "reconstruct hypothetical dilemmas in terms of real (situations) . . . request or . . . supply missing information about the nature of the people and the places where they live."[25]

These differences between the philosophical underpinnings of men's and women's moral perspectives and methods of making moral judgments may require philosophers to reexamine currently accepted moral theories, for these theories primarily justify men's reasoning and have little to say about women's moral reasoning. In contrast to this stress on utilitarian and Kantian moral principles and reasoning, Blum argues that "morality is (not) of a unitary nature," but has two strains, one including "sympathy, compassion, and human concern," the other universalizability,

generality, and conflicts of rights.[26] However, Blum's own examples of the sympathy and compassion side of morality are
primarily limited to family matters, friendships, private concerns, and to an extent, relationships with colleagues. The wider
public domain where women struggle to gain a voice and equality
has not yet discovered women's moral language as articulated by
either Gilligan or Blum. Thus, philosophy must open new doors in
search of a wider vision of morality that includes not only women
or only men, but women and men.

EDUCATIONAL ISSUES AND IMPLICATIONS

In "Moral Stages and the Aims of Education," Part One of **The
Philosophy of Moral Development**, Kohlberg investigates the educational implications of his theory. Unfortunately, the first
essay, "Indoctrination Versus Relativity in Value Education" is
flawed in that it does not wholly represent Kohlberg's current
view. Kohlberg summarizes this first essay by stating that his
educational "approach differs from indoctrinative approaches
because it tries to move student's thinking in a direction that is
natural for the student rather than moving the student in the
direction of accepting the teacher's moral assumptions."[27] More
recently, Kohlberg advocates indoctrination.[28] In this he
hearkens back to Piaget's morality of constraint based on
Durkheim's theory of moral education as rule transmission.[29]
Though such a shift in Kohlberg's views has important
ramifications for his theory and educational recommendations, I
prefer at present to avoid muddying already tricky waters and

concentrate on Kohlberg's original insights and how they compare with the educational implications of Gilligan's theory and research. Since Kohlberg's first volume only includes educational theory and not his various educational intervention experiments, this section concentrates on educational theory and only peripherally practice. In "Development as the Aim of Education," Kohlberg contrasts romantic and cultural transmission conceptualizations of education with the one implied by his theory. Kohlberg maintains that only the cognitive-developmental psychology and interactionist epistemology of progressivism provide an adequate basis for understanding educational processes. Following the lead of Rousseau and A. S. Neill, the romantic tradition has been accepted by radical free schools and often by the open education movement. Unlike Kohlberg's progressivism, romanticism allows the innate goodness, spontaneity, and creativity of the child to unfold naturally. Diverse thinkers from Locke to Bereiter and Englemann, B. F. Skinner, and Thorndike form a core of behaviorists who advocate cultural transmission. Educational technology and behavior modification represent methods advocated by cultural transmission educators.

Kohlberg rejects both the romantic and cultural-transmission traditions and instead sides with Dewey and progressive education's tenants. According to Kohlberg, progressive education links cognitive processes and development with moral development and education. In addition, progressivism is an interactionist position that views moral development as occurring through transaction between individuals and the social environment. Because cognitive and moral development depend on the nature of social experience, Kohlberg advocates the stimulation of development "through discrepancy and match between experienced events and information-processing structures."[30]

Kohlberg accepts Festinger's notion of cognitive dissonance as the means of stimulating moral development and applies it in school settings.[31] First, when confronted with moral dilemmas and questions that cannot be resolved with present developmental stages, students experience cognitive dissonance and are motivated to use a higher stage reasoning. Second, in group discussions of moral dilemmas different students' responses are at different moral development stages. Students at lower stages experience cognitive dissonance when answers at a higher stage are given. A study by Turiel indicates that people prefer answers a stage higher than their own moral development stage.[32] Thus, the presence of higher stage resolutions provides an impetus for growth from a lower to higher stage. Education for cognitive, ego, and moral development cannot merely focus on the vertical growth in developmental stages, but also horizontal **decalage** that fosters a "spread or generalization across the range of basic physical and social actions, concepts, and objects to which the stage potentially applies."[33]

Both vertical moral stage development and horizontal **decalage**, according to Kohlberg, are stimulated through the explicit educational intervention of organized moral dilemma discussions and the formation of just community schools. Though the latter experiments seem radical departures from traditional school structure, both intervention approaches retain allegiance to men's language of rights. Thus, in one sense, Kohlberg's educational implications do not signify a radical transformation in the accepted, male-dominated public sphere or in the political and social environment. In specifically designed courses, the emphasis remains on the resolution of moral conflicts with stages that use higher forms of cognitive reasoning and more "differentiated" and "integrated" conceptualizations of rights.[34]

The just community school experiments stress "the importance of actual experiences of participation in a political community."[35] By taking participatory roles within a just community school, Kohlberg and others motivate students' moral development. Even though advocates of self-government in just community schools refer to trust, intimacy, team spirit, friendship, and belonging,[36] the impetus and rationale for the development of these schools has been that they lead to growth in moral development stages that emphasize men's language of rights. Many children, according to one report, "squirmed under the yoke of 'judging their friends'."[37] The character of such strain on interpersonal relationships conflicts with women's language of responsibility and their psychological logic of relationships.

Gilligan tangentially notes that her work should have implications for education, "the current reappraisal in the field of education finds its parallel in the field of developmental psychology where a similar reassessment is taking place."[38] Both these reassessments raise questions about the aims of education and educational practice. Also, the responses of women pursuing higher education for professional careers points to ways contemporary educational aims and practice are inimical to women's developmental cycle. Though Gilligan's findings could be related to more general concerns about "the ideal of the educated person,"[39] my comments are limited to the implications of Gilligan's views for moral education, how these compare with Kohlberg's recommendations, and then briefly how this might affect school and society.

What aspects of formal education contradict women's language of responsibility? First, the excessive competitiveness of schools rejects the caring, concerned, and responsible relationships underlying women's morality. Instead, students succeed when they accept and manifest the characteristics of the conflict model of men's language of rights. Also, the increased competitiveness of women's sports fosters the conflict model both in classrooms and other aspects of school life. In this type of educational environment, to succeed women must either lose their identity by abandoning the language of responsibility or equivocate by accepting both moral languages. Participatory, self-governing, just community schools and explicit moral education classes, as advocated by Kohlberg, do little to alleviate such identity dilemmas.

The Kohlbergean framework and its practical, educational manifestations accept academic and extracurricular competition as long as it is regulated by the principles of justice, fair distribution of scarce goods, and respect for the rights of all those within the educational community. To uphold her evidence and women's vision of the moral world, Gilligan must argue that this educational environment is not suitable for women's moral development. Whereas men's academic achievement focuses on "individual achievement" and only secondarily on "involvement with others,"[40] women in higher education "define their identity through relationships of intimacy and care."[41] But contemporary formal education, whether on the secondary or college level, does not foster or accept women's mode of discovering personal identity.

How could schools accommodate women's psychological life-cycle and foster their moral development? The following briefly note a few possible policy decisions and changes: (1) The competitive aspects of schooling would have to be severely reduced. (2) Schools would have to create and foster projects and practices that accept caring and concern. For example, peer tutoring, teaching, and counseling could foster such care. In addition, there might be greater concern with community projects that help the needy, lonely, and elderly. (3) Other aspects of knowledge outside traditional lexical ordering and analytical, hypothetical thought processes would have to be included (e.g., intuitive, non-verbal, and artistic forms of expression and understanding). (4) Instead of being concerned with the distribution of scarce goods among deserving and equal individuals, schools would question how communities of human beings can share such goods. (5)There would have to be modifications in the relationships between students and teacher, between teachers and administrators, and between students. This would include changes in behavior expectations and ways of maintaining discipline. (6) Finally, considerable change would have to be made in curriculum. The inclusion of successful women who speak men's language of right is not the answer. Rather, curriculum development also has to recognize the requirements of women's language of responsibility.

Gilligan's study and women's language provide a different

type of vision not merely for schools, but for society as well. Because contemporary schools educate people to become members of a society that stresses and accepts the conflict model of rights and fair distribution of scarce goods, people educated within a caring and concerned school environment might be at a distinct disadvantage in such a society. Therefore, Gilligan's work has even greater implications for which type of political and social environment ensures the greatest and most satisfactory development of women.

If a broader view of Gilligan's and Kohlberg's models is taken, educators and theorists might have a clue about the nature of moral development and moral education. First, Gilligan and Kohlberg may be speaking of the same phenomenon, but each is looking at one side of the coin. The fullest possible moral development may not be one view or the other, but both languages. In this case, the language of rights and the language of responsibility would have to be integrated for the development of the moral individual. If each language appears separately in men and women, this may be an unfortunate condition of present education and social and political life, not the reality of the fully moral life. Second, there are moral concepts and issues that neither Kohlberg nor Gilligan examines (e.g., the problems of will and weakness of will). Cross-fertilization from other psychological and philosophical theories may be necessary to discover a fully articulated theory and educational practice. In the end, however, no matter the problems confronting Kohlberg's and Gilligan's works, they remain important contemporary positions that must be studied by anyone interested in moral education.

FOOTNOTES

[1]Christopher Lasch, **Haven in a Heartless World: The Family Beseiged** (New York: Basic Books, 1977).

[2]Lawrence Kohlberg, **The Philosophy of Moral Development** (San Francisco: Harper and Row, 1981); and Carol Gilligan, **In a Different Voice: Psychological Theory and Women's Development** (Cambridge, Mass.: Harvard University Press, 1982).

[3]R. V. Burton, "Honesty and Dishonesty," in **Moral Development and Behavior: Theory, Research, and Social Issues,** ed. Thomas Lickona (New York: Holt, Rinehart and Winston, 1976).

[4]Jean Piaget, **The Moral Judgment of the Child,** trans. Marjorie Gabain (New York: Harcourt, Brace and World, 1932).

[5]Kohlberg, **The Philosophy of Moral Development,** p. 149.

[6]Gilligan, **In a Different Voice,** p. 73.

[7]Ibid., p. 74.

[8]William Kurtines and Esther B. Greif, "The Development of Moral Thought: Review and Evaluation of Kohlberg's Approach," **Psychological Bulletin** 81 (1974), 459-460; Betty A Sichel, "Can Kohlberg Respond to Critics?" **Educational Theory** 26 (1976): 337-347; and Sichel, "The Relation Between Moral Judgment and Moral Behavior in Kohlberg's Theory of the Development of Moral Judgments," **Educational Philosophy and Theory** 8 (1976): 55-67.

[9]Kurtines and Greif, "The Development of Moral Thought," pp. 460-466.

[10]John C. Gibbs, "Kohlberg's Stages of Moral Judgment: A Constructive Critique," **Harvard Educational Review** 47 (1977): 42-61; and John Michael Murphy and Carol Gilligan, "Moral Development in Late Adolescence and Adulthood: A Critique and Reconstruction of Kohlberg's Theory," **Human Development** 23 (1980): 77-104.

[11]Ibid., p. 84.

[12]Kurtines and Greif, "The Development of Moral Thought," p. 453.

[13]E. Rothstein, "The Scar of Sigmund Freud," **The New York Review of Books** 27 (October 9, 1980), pp. 14, 16-19.

[14]Kohlberg, "Revisions in the Theory and Practice of Moral Development," in **Moral Development,** ed. William Damon (San Francisco: Jossey-Bass, 1978), pp. 85-86.

[15]K. F. Riegel, "Subject-Object Alienation in Psychological Experiments and Testing," **Human Development** 18 (1975): 181-193.

[16]Gilligan, In a Different Voice, pp. 28-29.

[17]Gilligan, New Maps of Development: New Visions of Maturity," American Journal of Orthopsychiatry 52 (1982): 199-212.

[18]Gilligan, In a Different Voice, p. 23.

[19]Cf. ibid., p. 174.

[20]Elizabeth L. Simpson, "Moral Development Research: A Case Study of Scientific Cultural Bias," Human Development 17 (1974): 81-106; and J. A. Diorio, "Cognitive Universalism and Cultural Relativity in Moral Education," Educational Philosophy and Theory 8 (1976): 33-53.

[21]Kohlberg, The Philosophy of Moral Development, p. 133.

[22]John Rawls, A Theory of Justice (Cambridge, Mass.: Harvard University Press, 1971).

[23]Robert Paul Wolff, Understanding Rawls (Princeton, N.J.: Princeton University Press, 1977).

[24]Gilligan, In a Different Voice, p. 100.

[25]Ibid., pp. 100-101.

[26]Lawrence A. Blum, Friendship, Altruism and Morality (London: Routledge and Kegan Paul, 1980), p. 8.

[27]Kohlberg, The Philosophy of Moral Development, p. 28.

[28]Kohlberg, "Revisions in the Theory and Practice of Moral Development."

[29]Emile Durkheim, Moral Education: A Study in the Theory and Application of the Sociology of Knowledge (1925), trans. Everett K. Wilson and Herman Schnurer (New York: Free Press, 1961).

[30]Kohlberg, The Philosophy of Moral Development, p. 87.

[31]Ibid., pp. 145-147. Cf. L. Festinger, A Theory of Cognitive Dissonance (Stanford, Calif.: Stanford University Press, 1957).

[32]E. Turiel, "An Experimental Test of the Sequentiality of Developmental Stages of the Child's Moral Judgments," Journal of Personality and Social Psychology 3 (1966): 611-618.

[33]Kohlberg, The Philosophy of Moral Development, pp. 91-92.

[34]Ibid., pp. 214-219.

[35]Kohlberg, "High School Democracy and Educating for a Just Society," in Moral Development: A First Generation of Research and Development, ed. Ralph L. Mosher (New York: Praeger, 1980),

p. 34.

[36]J. Reimer and C. Power, "Educating for Democratic Community: Some Unresolved Dilemmas," in ibid., pp. 305, 331, 334.

[37]Thomas Lickona and M. Paradise, "Democracy in Elementary School," in ibid., p. 332.

[38]Gilligan, "New Maps of Development," p. 200.

[39]Jane Roland Martin, "The Ideal of the Educated Person," **Educational Theory** 32 (1981): 97–109.

[40]Gilligan, **In a Different Voice**, p. 163.

[41]Ibid, p. 164.

CHAPTER 10

AN ETHIC OF CARING*

Nel Noddings

FROM NATURAL TO ETHICAL CARING

David Hume long ago contended that morality is founded upon
and rooted in feeling--that the "final sentence" on matters
of morality, "that which renders morality an active virtue"-- " .
. .this final sentence depends on some internal sense or feeling,
which nature has made universal in the whole species. For what
else can have an influence of this nature?"[1]

What is the nature of this feeling that is "universal in the
whole species"? I want to suggest that morality as an "active
virtue" requires two feelings and not just one. The first is the
sentiment of natural caring. There can be no ethical sentiment
without the initial, enabling sentiment. In situations where we
act on behalf of the other because we want to do so, we are acting
in accord with natural caring. A mother's caretaking efforts in
behalf of her child are not usually considered ethical but natural. Even maternal animals take care of their offspring, and we
do not credit them with ethical behavior.

The second sentiment occurs in response to remembrance of the
first. Nietzsche speaks of love and memory in the context

*Nel Noddings, Caring: A Feminine Approach to Ethics and Moral
Education, pp. 79-103. Copyright (c) 1984 by The Regents of the
University of California. Reprinted by permission of the Univer-
sity of California Press.

of Christian love and Eros, but what he says may safely be taken
out of context to illustrate the point I wish to make here:

> There is something so ambiguous and suggestive about the
> word love, something that speaks to memory and to hope,
> that even the lowest intelligence and the coldest heart
> still feel something of the glimmer of this word. The
> cleverest woman and the most vulgar man recall the
> relatively least selfish moments of their whole life,
> even if Eros has taken only a low flight with them.[2]

This memory of our own best moments of caring and being cared
for sweeps over us as a feeling--as an "I must"--in response to
the plight of the other and our conflicting desire to serve our
own interests. There is a transfer of feeling analogous to transfer of learning. In the intellectual domain, when I read a certain kind of mathematical puzzle, I may react by thinking, "That
is like the sailors, monkey and coconuts problem," and then,
"Diophantine equations" or "modulo arithmetic" or "congruences."
Similarly, when I encounter an other and feel the natural pang
conflicted with my own desires--"I must--I do not want to"--I
recognize the feeling and remember what has followed it in my own
best moments. I have a picture of those moments in which I was
cared for and in which I cared, and I may reach toward this memory
and guide my conduct by it if I wish to do so.

Recognizing that ethical caring requires an effort that is
not needed in natural caring does not commit us to a position that
elevates ethical caring over natural caring. Kant has identified

the ethical with that which is done out of duty and not out of love, and that distinction in itself seems right. But an ethic built on caring strives to maintain the caring attitude and is thus dependent upon, and not superior to, natural caring. The source of ethical behavior is, then, in twin sentiments--one that feels directly for the other and one that feels for and with that best self, who may accept and sustain the initial feeling rather than reject it.

We shall discuss the ethical ideal, that vision of best self, in some depth. When we commit ourselves to obey the "I must" even at its weakest and most fleeting, we are under the guidance of this ideal. It is not just any picture. Rather, it is our best picture of ourselves caring and being cared for. It may even be colored by acquaintance with one superior to us in caring, but, as I shall describe it, it is both constrained and attainable. It is limited by what we have already done and by what we are capable of, and it does not idealize the impossible so that we may escape into ideal abstraction.

Now, clearly, in pointing to Hume's "active virtue" and to an ethical ideal as the source of ethical behavior, I seem to be advocating an ethic of virtue. This is certainly true in part. Many philosophers recognize the need for a discussion of virtue as the energizing factor in moral behavior, even when they have given their best intellectual effort to a careful explication of their positions on obligation and justification.[3] When we discuss the ethical ideal, we shall be talking about "virtue," but we shall not let "virtue" dissipate into "the virtues" described in abstract categories. The holy man living abstemiously on top of the

mountain, praying thrice daily, and denying himself human inter-
course may display "virtues," but they are not the virtues of
one-caring. The virtue described by the ethical ideal of one-caring is build up in relation. It reaches out to the other and
grows in response to the other.

Since our discussion of virtue will be embedded in an exploration of moral activity we might do well to start by asking whether or under what circumstances we are obligated to respond to the
initial "I must." Does it make sense to say that I am obliged to
heed that which comes to me as obligation?

OBLIGATION

There are moments for all of us when we care quite naturally.
We just do care; no ethical effort is required. "Want" and
"ought" are indistinguishable in such cases. I want to do what I
or others might judge I ought to do. But can there be a "demand"
to care? There can be, surely, no demand for the initial impulse
that arises as a feeling, an inner voice saying "I must do something," in response to the need of the cared-for. This impulse
arises naturally, at least occasionally, in the absence of pathology. We cannot demand that one have this impulse, but we shrink
from one who never has it. One who never feels the pain of
another, who never confesses the internal "I must" that is so
familiar to most of us, is beyond our normal pattern of understanding. Her case is pathological, and we avoid her.

But even if I feel the initial "I must," I may reject it. I
may reject it instantaneously by shifting from "I must do

something" to "Something must be done," and removing myself from the set of possible agents through whom the action should be accomplished. I may reject it because I feel that there is nothing I can do. If I do either of these things without reflection upon what I might do in behalf of the cared-for, then I do not care. Caring requires me to respond to the initial impulse with an act of commitment: I commit myself either to overt action on behalf of the cared-for (I pick up my crying infant) or I commit myself to thinking about what I might do. In the latter case, as we have seen, I may or may not act overtly in behalf of the cared-for. I may abstain from action if I believe that anything I might do would tend to work against the best interests of the cared-for. But the test of my caring is not wholly in how things turn out; the primary test lies in an examination of what I considered, how fully I received the other, and whether the free pursuit of his projects is partly a result of the completion of my caring in him.

But am I obliged to embrace the "I must"? In this form, the question is a bit odd, for the "I must" carries obligation with it. It come to us as obligation. But accepting and affirming the "I must" are different from feeling it, and these responses are what I am pointing to when I ask whether I am obliged to embrace the "I must." The question nags at us; it is a question that has been asked, in a variety of forms, over and over by moralists and moral theorists. Usually, the question arises as part of the broader question of justification. We ask something of the sort: Why must I (or should I) do what suggests itself to reason as "right" or as needing to be done for the sake of some other? We might prefer to supplement "reason" with "and/or feeling." This question is, of course, not the only thorny question in moral theory, but it is one that has plagued theorists who see clearly that there is no way to derive an "I ought" statement from a chain of facts. I may agree readily that "things would be better"--that is, that a certain state of affairs commonly agreed to be desirable might be attained--if a certain chain of events were to take place. But there is still nothing in this intellectual chain that can produce the "I ought." I may choose to remain an observer on the scene.

Now I'm suggesting that the "I must" arises directly and prior to consideration of what it is that I might do. The initial feeling is the "I must." When it comes to me indistinguishable from the "I want," I proceed easily as one-caring. But often it comes to me conflicted. It may be barely perceptible, and it may be followed almost simultaneously by resistance. When someone asks me to get something for him or merely asks for my attention, the "I must" may be lost in a clamor of resistance. Now a second sentiment is required if I am to behave as one-caring. I care about myself as one-caring and, although I do not care naturally for the person who has asked something of me--at least not at this moment--I feel the genuine moral sentiment, the "I ought," that sensibility to which I have committed myself.

Let me try to make plausible my contention that the moral imperative arises directly.[4] And, of course, I must try to explain how caring and what I am calling the "moral imperative" are related. When my infant cries in the night, I not only feel that I must do something but I want to do something. Because I love this child, because I am bonded to him, I want to remove his pain as I would want to remove my own. The "I must" is not a dutiful imperative but one that accompanies the "I want." If I were tied to a chair, for example, and wanted desperately to get free, I might say as I struggled, "I must do something; I must get out of these bonds." But this "must" is not yet the moral or ethical "ought." It is a "must" born of desire.

The most intimate situations of caring are, thus, natural. I do not feel that taking care of my own child is "moral" but, rather, natural. A woman who allows her own child to die of neglect is often considered sick rather than immoral; that is, we feel that either she or the situation into which she has been thrust must be pathological. Otherwise, the impulse to respond, to nurture the living infant, is overwhelming. We share the impulse with other creatures in the animal kingdom. Whether we want to consider this response as "instinctive" is problematic, because certain patterns of response may be implied by the term and because suspension of reflective consciousness seems also to be implied (and I am not suggesting that we have no choice), but I have no difficulty in considering it as innate. Indeed, I am claiming that the impulse to act in behalf of the present other is itself innate. It lies latent in each of us, awaiting gradual development in a succession of caring relations. I am suggesting that our inclination toward and interest in morality derives from caring. In caring, we accept the natural impulse to act on behalf of the present other. We are engrossed in the other. We have received him and feel his pain or happiness, but we are not compelled by this impulse. We have a choice; we may accept what we feel, or we may reject it. If we have a strong desire to be moral, we will not reject it, and this strong desire to be moral is derived, reflectively, from the more fundamental and natural desire to be and to remain related. To reject the feeling when it arises is either to be in an internal state of imbalance or to contribute willfully to the diminution of the ethical ideal.

But suppose in a particular case that the "I must" does not arise, or that it whispers faintly and disappears, leaving distrust, repugnance, or hate. Why, then, should I behave morally toward the object of my dislike? Why should I not accept feelings other than those characteristic of caring and, thus, achieve an internal state of balance through hate, anger, or malice?

The answer to this is, I think, that the genuine moral sentiment (our second sentiment) arises from an evaluation of the caring relation as good, as better than, superior to, other forms of relatedness. I feel the moral "I must" when I recognize that my response will either enhance or diminish my ethical ideal. It will serve either to increase or decrease the likelihood of genuine caring. My response affects me as one-caring. In a given situation with someone I am not fond of, I may be able to find all sorts of reasons why I should not respond to his need. I may be too busy. He may be undiscerning. The matter may be, on objective analysis, unimportant. But, before I decide, I must turn away from this analytic chain of thought and back to the concrete situation. Here is this person with this perceived need to which is attached this importance. I must put justification aside temporarily. Shall I respond? How do I feel as a duality about the "I" who will not respond?

I am obliged, then, to accept the initial "I must" when it occurs and even to fetch it out of recalcitrant slumber when it fails to awake spontaneously.[5] The source of my obligation is the value I place on the relatedness of caring. This value itself arises as a product of actual caring and being cared-for and my reflection on the goodness of these concrete caring situations.

Now, what sort of "goodness" is it that attaches to the caring relation? It cannot be a fully moral goodness, for we have already described forms of caring that are natural and require no moral effort. But it cannot be a fully nonmoral goodness either, for it would then join a class of goods many of which are widely separated from the moral good. It is, perhaps, properly described as a "premoral good," one that lies in a region with the moral good and shades over into it. We cannot always decide with certainty whether our caring response is natural or ethical. Indeed, the decision to respond ethically as one-caring may cause the lowering of barriers that previously prevented reception of the other, and natural caring may follow.

I have identified the source of our obligation and have said that we are obligated to accept, and even to call forth, the feeling "I must." But what exactly must I do? Can my obligation be set forth in a list or hierarchy of principles? So far, it seems that I am obligated to maintain an attitude and, thus, to meet the other as one-caring and, at the same time, to increase my own virtue as one-caring. If I am advocating an ethic of virtue, do not all the usual dangers lie in wait: hypocrisy, self-righteousness, withdrawal from the public domain? We shall discuss these dangers as the idea of an ethical ideal is developed more fully.

Let me say here, however, why it seems preferable to place an ethical ideal above principle as a guide to moral action. It has been traditional in moral philosophy to insist that moral principles must be, by their very nature as moral principles, universifiable. If I am obligated to do **X** under certain conditions, then under sufficiently similar conditions you also are obligated to do **X**. But the principle of universifiability seems to depend, as Nietzsche pointed out, on a concept of "sameness."[6] In order to accept the principle, we should have to establish that human predicaments exhibit sufficient sameness, and this we cannot do without abstracting away from concrete situations those qualities that seem to reveal the sameness. In doing this, we often lose the very qualities or factors that gave rise to the moral question in the situation. That condition which makes the situation different and thereby induces genuine moral puzzlement cannot be satisfied by the application of principles developed in situations of sameness.

This does not mean that we cannot receive any guidance from an attempt to discover principles that seem to be universifiable. We can, under this sort of plan, arrive at the doctrine of "prima facie duty" described by W. D. Ross.[7] Ross himself, however, admits that this doctrine yields no real guidance for moral conduct in concrete situations. It guides us in abstract moral thinking; it tells us, theoretically, what to do, "all other thing being equal." But other things are rarely if ever equal. **A** and **B**, struggling with a moral decision, are two different persons with different factual histories, different projects and aspirations, and different ideals. It may indeed be right, morally right, for A to do X and B to do not -X. We may, that is, connect "right" and "wrong" to faithfulness to the ethical ideal. This does not cast us into relativism, because the ideal contains at its heart a component that is universal: Maintenance of the caring relation.

Before turning to a discussion of "right" and "wrong" and their usefulness in an ethic of caring, we might try to clear up the problem earlier mentioned as a danger in any ethic of virtue: the temptation to withdraw from the public domain. It is a real danger. Even though we rejected the sort of virtue exhibited by the hermit-monk on the mountaintop, that rejection may have been one of personal choice. It still remains possible that an ethic of caring is compatible with the monk's choice, and that such an ethic even induces withdrawal. We are not going to be able to divide cases clearly. The monk who withdraws only to serve God is clearly under the guidance of an ehic that differs fundamentally from the ethic of caring. The source of his ethic is not the source of ours, and he might deny that any form of human related- ness could be a source for moral behavior. But if, when another intrudes upon his privacy, he receives the other as one-caring, we cannot charge him with violating our ethic. Further, as we saw in our discussion of the one-caring, there is a legitimate dread of the proximate stranger--of that person who may ask more than we feel able to give. We saw there that we cannot care for everyone. Caring itself is reduced to mere talk about caring when we attempt to do so. We must acknowledge, then, that an ethic of caring implies a limit on our obligation.

Our obligation is limited and delimited by relation. We are

never free, in the human domain, to abandon our preparedness to care; but, practically, if we are meeting those in our inner circles adequately as ones-caring and receiving those linked to our inner circles by formal chains of relation, we shall limit the calls upon our obligation quite naturally. We are not obligated to summon the "I must" if there is no possibility of completion in the other. I am not obliged to care for starving children in Africa, because there is no way for this caring to be completed in the other unless I abandon the caring to which I am obligated. I may still choose to do something in the direction of caring, but I am not obligated to do so. When we discuss our obligation to animals, we shall see that this is even more sharply limited by relation. We cannot refuse obligation in human affairs by merely refusing to enter relation; we are, by virtue of our mutual human- ity, already and perpetually in potential relation. Instead, we limit our obligation by examining the possibility of completion. In connection with animals, however, we may find it possible to refuse relation itself on the grounds of a species-specific im- possibility of any form of reciprocity in caring.

Now, this is very important, and we should try to say clearly what governs our obligation. On the basis of what has been devel- oped so far, there seem to be two criteria: the existence of or potential for present relation, and the dynamic potential for growth in relation, including the potential for increased reci- procity and, perhaps, mutuality. The first criterion establishes an absolute obligation and the second serves to put our obliga- tions into an order of priority.

If the other toward whom we shall act is capable of

responding as cared-for and there are no objective conditions that prevent our receiving this response—if, that is, our caring can be completed in the other—then we must meet that other as one-caring. If we do not care naturally, we must call upon our capacity for ethical caring. When we are in relation or when the other has addressed us, we must respond as one-caring. The imperative in relation is categorical. When relation has not yet been established, or when it may properly be refused (when no formal chain or natural circle is present), the imperative is more like that of the hypothetical: I must if I wish to (or am able to) move into relation.

The second criterion asks us to look at the nature of potential relation and, especially, at the capacity of the cared-for to respond. The potential for response in animals, for example, is nearly static; they cannot respond in mutuality, nor can the nature of their response change substantially. But a child's potential for increased response is enormous. If the possibility of relation is dynamic—if the relation may clearly grow with respect to reciprocity—then the possibility and degree of my obligation also grows. If response is imminent, so also is my obligation. This criterion will help us to distinguish between our obligation to members of the nonhuman animal world and, say, the human fetus. We must keep in mind, however, that the second criterion binds us in proportion to the probability of increased response and to the imminence of that response. Relation itself is fundamental in obligation.

I shall give an example of thinking guided by these criteria, but let us pause for a moment and ask what it is we are trying to accomplish. I am working deliberately toward criteria that will preserve our deepest and most tender human feelings. The caring of mother for child, of human adult for human infant, elicits the tenderest feelings in most of us. Indeed, for many women, this feeling of nurturance lies at the very heart of what we assess as good. A philosophical position that has difficulty distinguishing between our obligation to human infants and, say, pigs is in some difficulty straight off. It violates our most deeply cherished feeling about human goodness. This violation does not, of course, make the position logically wrong, but it suggests that especially strong grounds will be needed to support it. In the absence of such strong grounds, . . . we might prefer to establish a position that captures rather than denies our basic feelings. We might observe that man (in contrast to woman) has continually turned away from his inner self and feeling in pursuit of both science and ethics. With respect to strict science, this turning outward may be defensible; with respect to ethics, it has been disastrous.

Now let's consider an example: the problem of abortion. Operating under the guidance of an ethic of caring, we are not likely to find abortion in general either right or wrong. We shall have to inquire into individual cases. An incipient embryo is an information speck--a set of controlling instructions for a future human being. Many of these specks are created and flushed away without their creators' awareness. From the view developed here, the information speck is an information speck; it has no given sanctity. There should be no concern over the waste of "human tissue," since nature herself is wildly prolific, even profligate.[8] The one-caring is concerned not with human tissue but with human consciousness--with pain, delight, hope, fear, entreaty, and response.

But suppose the information speck is mine, and I am aware of it. This child-to-be is the product of love between a man deeply cared-for and me. Will the child have his eyes or mine? His stature or mine? Our joint love of mathematics or his love of mechanics or my love of language? This is not just an information speck; it is endowed with prior love and current knowledge. It is sacred, but I--humbly, not presumptuously--confer sacredness upon it. I cannot, will not destroy it. It is joined to loved others through formal chains of caring. It is linked to the inner circle in a clearly defined way. I might wish that I were not pregnant, but I cannot destroy this known and potentially loved person-to-be. There is already relation albeit indirect and formal. My decision is an ethical one born of natural caring.

But suppose, now, that my beloved child has grown up; it is she who is pregnant and considering abortion. She is not sure of the love between herself and the man. She is miserably worried about her economic and emotional future. I might like to convey sanctity on this information speck; but I am not God--only mother to this suffering cared-for. It is she who is conscious and in pain, and I as one-caring move to relieve the pain. This information speck is an information speck and that is all. There is no formal relation, given the breakdown between husband and wife, and with the embryo, there is no present relation; the possibility of future relation--while not absent, surely--is uncertain. But what of this possibility for growing response? Must we not consider it? We must indeed. As the embryo becomes a fetus, and, growing daily, becomes more nearly capable of response as cared-for, our obligation grows from a nagging uncertainty--an "I must if I wish"--to an utter conviction that we must meet this small other as one-caring.

If we try to formalize what has been expressed in the concrete situations described so far, we arrive at a legal approach to abortion very like that of the Supreme Court; abortions should be freely available in the first trimester, subject to medical determination in the second trimester, and banned in the third, when the fetus is viable. A woman under the guidance of our ethic would be likely to recognize the growing possibility of relation; the potential is clearly dynamic. Further, many women recognize the relation as established when the fetus begins to move about. It is not a question of when life begins but of when relation begins.

But what if relation is never established? Suppose the child is born and the mother admits no sense of relatedness. May she commit infanticide? One who asks such questions misinterprets the concept of relatedness that I have been struggling to describe. Since the infant, even the near-natal fetus, is capable of relation--of the sweetest and most unselfconscious reciprocity--one who encounters the infant is obligated to meet it as one-caring. Both parts of this claim are essential; it is not only the child's capability to respond but also the encounter that induces obligation. There must exist the possibility for our caring to be completed in the other. If the mother does not care naturally, then she must summon ethical caring to support her as one-caring. She may not ethically ignore the child's cry to live.

The one-caring, in considering abortion as in all other matters, cares first for the one in immediate pain or peril. She might suggest a brief and direct form of counseling in which a young expectant mother could come to grips with her feelings. If the incipient child has been sanctified by its mother, every effort must be made to help the two to achieve a stable and hopeful life together; if it has not, it should be removed swiftly and mercifully with all loving attention to the woman, the conscious patient. Between these two clear reactions is a possible confused one: the young woman is not sure how she feels. The one-caring probes gently to see what has been considered, raising questions and retreating when the questions obviously have been considered and are now causing great pain. Is such a view "unprincipled"? If it is, it is boldly so; it is at least connected with the world as it is, at its best and at its worst, and it requires that we -- in espousing a "best" --stand ready to actualize that preferred condition. The decision for or against abortion must be made by those directly involved in the concrete situation, but it need not be made alone. The one-caring cannot require everyone to behave as she would in a particular situation. Rather, when she dares to say, "I think you should do X," she adds, also, "Can I help you?" The one under her gaze is under her support and not her judgment.

One under the guidance of an ethic of caring is tempted to retreat to a manageable world. Her public life is limited by her insistence upon meeting the other as one-caring. So long as this is possible, she may reach outward and enlarge her circles of caring. When this reaching out destroys or drastically reduces her actual caring, she retreats and renews her contact with those

who address her. If the retreat becomes a flight, an avoidance of
the call to care, her ethical ideal is diminished. Similarly, if
the retreat is away from human beings and toward other objects of
caring--ideas, animals, humanity-at-large, God--her ethical ideal
is virtually shattered. This is not a judgment, for we can understand and sympathize with one who makes such a choice. It is more
in the nature of a perception: we see clearly what has been lost
in the choice.

Our ethic of caring--which we might have called a "feminine
ethic"--begins to look a bit mean in contrast to the masculine
ethics of universal love or universal justice. But universal love
is illusion. Under the illusion, some young people retreat to the
church to worship that which they cannot actualize; some write
lovely poetry extolling universal love; and some, in terrible
disillusion, kill to establish the very principles which should
have entreated them not to kill. Thus are lost both principles
and persons.

RIGHT AND WRONG

How are we to make judgments of right and wrong under this
ethic? First, it is important to understand that we are not
primarily interested in judging but, rather, in heightening moral
perception and sensitivity. But "right" and "wrong" can be useful.

Suppose a mother observes her young child pulling the kitten's tail or picking it up by the ears. She may exclaim, "Oh,
no, it is not nice to hurt the kitty," or, "You must not hurt the

kitty." Or she may simply say, "Stop. See--you are hurting the kitty," and she may then take the kitten in her own hands and show the child how to handle it. She holds the kitten gently, stroking it, and saying, "See? Ah, ah, kitty, nice kitty. . . ." What the mother is supposing in this interaction is that the realization that his act is hurting the kitten, supplemented by the knowledge of how to avoid inflicting hurt, will suffice to change the child's behavior. If she believes this, she has no need for the statement, "It is wrong to hurt the kitty." She is not threatening sanctions but drawing dual attention to a matter of fact (the hurting) and her own commitment (I will not hurt). Beyond this, she is supposing that her child, well-cared-for himself, does not want to inflict pain.

Now, I am not claiming through use of this illustration that moral statements are mere expressions of approval or disapproval, although they do serve an expressive function. A. J. Ayer, who did make a claim of this sort before modifying his position somewhat, uses an illustration very like the one just given to support an emotivist position.[9] But even if it were possible to take a purely analytic stance with respect to moral theory, as Ayer suggests he has done, that is certainly not what I intend to do. One who labels moral statements as expressions of approval or disapproval, and takes the matter to be finished with that, misses the very heart of morality. He misses the commitment to behave in a fashion compatible with caring. Thus he misses both feeling and content. I may, after all, express my approval or disapproval on matters that are not moral. Thus it is clear that when I make a moral judgment I am doing more than simply expressing approval or disapproval.   I am both expressing my own commitment to behave in a way compatible with caring and appealing to the hearer to consider what he is doing. I may say first to a child, "Oh! Don't hurt the kitty!" And I may then add, "It is wrong to hurt the kitty."   The word is not necessary , strictly speaking, but I may find it useful.

What do I mean by this? I certainly mean to express my own commitment, and I show this best by daily example. But I may mean to say more than this. I may explain to the child that not only do I feel this way but that our family does, that our community does, that our culture does. Here I must be very careful. Our community may say one thing and do quite another. Such contradiction is even more likely at the level of "our culture."   But I express myself doubly in words and in acts, and I may search out examples in the larger culture to convince the child that significant others do feel this way. The one-caring is careful to distinguish between acts that violate caring, acts that she herself holds wrong, and those acts that "some people" hold to be wrong. She need not be condescending in this instruction. She is herself so reluctant to universalize beyond the demands of caring that she cannot say, "It is wrong," to everything that is illegal, church-forbidden, or contrary to a prevailing etiquette.   But she can raise the question, attempt to justify the alien view, express her own objections, and support the child in his own exploration.

Emotivists are partly right, I think, when they suggest that we might effectively substitute a statement describing the fact or event that triggers our feeling or attitude for statements such as "It is wrong to do X." When I say to my child, "It is wrong to hurt the kitty," I mean (if I am not threatening sanctions) to inform him that he is hurting the kitten and, further, that I believe that if he perceives he is doing so, he will stop. I am counting on his gradually developing ability to feel pain in the other to induce a decision to stop. To say, "It is wrong to cause pain needlessly," contributes nothing by way of knowledge and can hardly be thought likely to change the attitude or behavior of one who might ask, "Why is it wrong?" If I say to someone, "You are hurting the cat," and he replies, "I know it--so what? I like hurting cats," I feel "zero at the bone." Saying to him, "It is wrong to hurt cats," adds little unless I intend to threaten sanctions. If I mean to equate "It is wrong to hurt cats" with "There will be a sure and specific punishment for hurting cats," then it would be more honest to say this. One either feels a sort of pain in response to the pain of others, or one does not feel it. If he does feel it, he does not need to be told that causing pain is wrong. If he does not feel it in a particular case, he may remember the feeling--as one remembers the sweetness of love on hearing a certain piece of music--and allow himself to be moved by this remembrance of feeling. For one who feels nothing, directly or by remembrance, we must prescribe reeducation or exile. Thus, at the foundation of moral behavior--as we have already pointed out--is feeling or sentiment. But, further, there is commitment to remain open to that feeling, to remember it, and to put one's thinking in its service. It is the particular commitment underlying genuine expressions of moral judgment--as well as the special content--that the emotivist misses.

The one-caring, clearly, applies, "right" and "wrong" most

confidently to her decisions. This does not, as we have insisted
before, make her a relativist. The caring attitude that lies at
the heart of all ethical behavior is universal; . . . In general
the one-caring evaluates her own acts with respect to how faith-
fully they conform to what is known and felt through the recep-
tivity of caring. But she also uses "right" and "wrong" instruc-
tively and respectfully to refer to the judgments of significant
others. If she agrees because the matter at hand can be assessed
in light of caring, she adds her personal commitment and example;
if she has doubts--because the rule appealed to seems irrelevant
or ambiguous in the light of caring--she still acknowledges the
judgment but adds her own dissent or demurrer. Her eye is on the
ethical development of the cared-for and, as she herself withholds
judgment until she has heard the "whole story," she wants the
cared-for to encounter others, receive them, and reflect on what
he has received. Principles and rules are among the beliefs he
will receive, and she wants him to consider these in the light of
caring.

But is this all we can say about right and wrong? Is there
not a firm foundation in morality for our legal judgments? Surely, we must be allowed to say, for example, that stealing is wrong
and is, therefore, properly forbidden by law. Because it is so
often wrong--and so easily demonstrated to be wrong--under an
ethic of caring, we may accede that such a law has its roots
partly in morality. We may legally punish one who has stolen, but
we may not pass moral judgment on him until we know why he stole.
An ethic of caring is likely to be stricter in its judgment, but
more supportive and corrective in following up it judgment, than

ethics otherwise grounded. For the one-caring, stealing is almost always wrong:

Ms. A talks with her young son. **But, Mother, the boy pleads, suppose I want to make you happy and I steal something you want from a big chain store. I haven't hurt anyone, have I? Yes, you have,** responds his mother, and she points to the predicament of the store managers who may be accused of poor stewardship and to the higher prices suffered by their neighbors. **Well, suppose I steal from a rich, rich person? He can replace what I take easily, and . . .** Wait, says Ms. A. **Is someone suffering? Are you stealing to relieve that suffering, and will you make certain that what you steal is used to relieve it? . . .But can't I steal to make someone happy?** her son persists. Slowly, patiently, Ms. A. explains the position of one-caring. **Each one who comes under our gaze must be met as one-caring. When I want to please X and I turn toward Y as a means for satisfying my desire to please X, I must now meet Y as one-caring. I do not judge him for being rich--for treasuring what I, perhaps, regard with indifference. I may not cause him pain by taking or destroying what he possesses. But what if I steal from a bad guy--someone who stole to get what he has?** Ms. A smiles at her young son, struggling to avoid his ethical responsibility: **Unless he is an immediate threat to you or someone else, you must meet him, too, as one-caring.**

The lessons in "right" and "wrong" are hard lessons--not swiftly accomplished by setting up as an objective the learning of some principle. We do not say: It is wrong to steal. Rather, we consider why it was wrong or may be wrong in this case to steal. We do not say: It is wrong to kill. By setting up such a principle, we also imply its exceptions, and then we may too easily act on authorized exceptions. The one-caring wants to consider, and wants her child to consider, the act itself in full context. She will send him into the world skeptical, vulnerable, courageous, disobedient, and tenderly receptive. The "world" may not depend upon him to obey its rules or fulfill its wishes, but you, the individual he encounters, may depend upon him to meet you as one-caring.

THE PROBLEM OF JUSTIFICATION

Since I have chided the emotivist for not digging beneath the expressive layer of moral sentiment to the nature of the feeling itself and the commitment to act in accord with the feeling, one might ask whether I should not dig beneath the commitment. Why should I be committed to not causing pain? Now, clearly, in one sense, I cannot answer this better than we already have. When the "Why?" refers to motivation, we have seen that the one-caring receives the other and acts in the other's behalf as she would for herself; that is, she acts with a similar motive energy. Further, I have claimed that, when natural caring fails, the motive energy in behalf of the other can be summoned out of caring for the ethical self. We have discussed both natural caring and ethical caring. Ethical caring, as I have described it, depends not upon rule or principle but upon the development of an ideal self. It does not depend upon just any ideal of self, but the ideal developed in congruence with one's best remembrance of caring and being cared-for.

So far, in recommending the ethical ideal as a guide to ethical conduct, I have suggested that traditional approaches to the problem of justification are mistaken. When the ethical theorist asks, "Why should I behave thus-and-so?" his question is likely to be aimed at justification rather than motivation and at a logic that resides outside the person. He is asking for reasons of the sort we expect to find in logical demonstration. He may expect us to claim that moral judgments can be tested as claims to facts can be tested, or that moral judgments are derived from divine commandment, or that moral truths are intuitively apprehended. Once started on this line of discussion, we may find ourselves arguing abstractly about the status of relativism and absolutism, egoism and altruism, and a host of other positions that, I shall claim, are largely irrelevant to moral conduct. They are matters of considerable intellectual interest, but they are distractions if our primary interest is in ethical conduct.

Moral statements cannot be justified in the way that statements of fact can be justified. They are not truths. They are derived not from facts or principles but from the caring attitude. Indeed, we might say that moral statements come out of the moral view or attitude, which, as I have described it, is the rational attitude built upon natural caring. When we put it this way, we see that there can be no justification for taking the moral viewpoint--that in truth, the moral viewpoint is prior to any notion of justification.

But there is another difficulty in answering the request for

justification. Consideration of problems of justification requires us to concentrate on moral judgments, on moral statements.
Hence we are led to an exploration of the language and reasoning
used to discuss moral conduct and away from an assessment of the
concrete events in which we must choose whether and how to behave
morally. Indeed, we are often led far beyond what we feel and
intuitively judge to be right in a search for some simple and
absolute guide to moral goodness.

For an ethic of caring, the problem of justification is not
concentrated upon justified action in general. We are not "justified"--we are **obligated**--to do what is required to maintain and
enhance caring. We must "justify" not-caring; that is, we must
explain why, in the interest of caring for ourselves as ethical
selves or in the interest of others for whom we care, we may
behave as ones-not-caring toward this particular other. In a
related problem, we must justify doing what this other would not
have us do to him as part of our genuine effort to care for him.
But even in these cases, an ethic of caring does not emphasize
justification. As one-caring, I am not seeking justification for
my action; I am not standing alone before some tribunal. What I
seek is completion in the other--the sense of being cared-for and,
I hope, the renewed commitment of the cared-for to turn about and
act as one-caring in the circles and chains within which he is
defined. Thus, I am not justified but somehow fulfilled and completed in my own life and in the lives of those I have thus influenced.

It sounds all very nice, says my male colleague, but can you
claim to be doing "ethics"? After all, ethics is the study of

justified action. . . . Ah, yes. But, "after-all," I am a woman, and I was not party to that definition. Shall we say then that I am talking about "how to meet the other morally"? Is this part of ethics? Is ethics part of this?

WOMEN AND MORALITY: VIRTUE

Many of us in education are keenly aware of the distortion that results from undue emphasis on moral judgments and justification. Lawrence Kohlberg's theory, for example, is widely held to be a model for moral education, but it is actually only a hierarchical description of moral reasoning.[10] It is well known, further, that the description may not be accurate. In particular, the fact that women seem often to be "stuck" at stage three might call the accuracy of the description into question. But perhaps the description is accurate within the domain of morality conceived as moral justification. If it is, we might well explore the possibility that feminine nonconformity to the Kohlberg model counts against the justification/judgment paradigm and not against women as moral thinkers.

Women, perhaps the majority of women, prefer to discuss moral problems in terms of concrete situations. They approach moral problems not as intellectual problems to be solved by abstract reasoning but as concrete human problems to be lived and to be solved in living. Their approach is founded in caring. Carol Gilligan describes the approach:

. . . women not only define themselves in a context of

human relationship but also judge themselves in terms of
their ability to care. Woman's place in man's life cycle
has been that of nurturer, caretaker, and helpmate, the
weaver of those networks of relationships on which she
in turn relies.[11]

Faced with a hypothetical moral dilemma, women often ask for
more information. It is not the case, certainly, that women cannot arrange principles hierarchically and derive conclusions logically. It is more likely that they see this process as peripheral
to or even irrelevant to moral conduct. They want more information, I think, in order to form a picture. Ideally, they need to
talk to the participants, to see their eyes and facial expressions, to size up the whole situation. Moral decisions are, after
all, made in situations; they are qualitatively different from the
solution of geometry problems. Women, like act-deontologists in
general, give reasons for their acts, but the reasons point to
feelings, needs, situational conditions, and their sense of personal ideal rather than universal principles and their application.

As we have seen, caring is not in itself a virtue. The
genuine ethical commitment to maintain oneself as caring gives
rise to the development and exercise of virtues, but these must be
assessed in the context of caring situations. It is not, for
example, patience itself that is a virtue but patience with respect to some infirmity of a particular cared-for or patience in
instructing a concrete cared-for that is virtuous. We must not
reify virtues and turn our caring toward them. If we do this, our
ethic turns inward and is even less useful than an ethic of

principles, which at least remains indirectly in contact with the acts we are assessing. The fulfillment of virtue is both in me and in the other.

A consideration of caring and an ethic built upon it give new meaning to what Kohlberg assesses as "stage three" morality. At this stage, persons behave morally in order to be thought of--or to think of themselves as --"good boys" or "good girls." Clearly, it makes a difference whether one chooses to be good or to be thought of as good. One who chooses to be good may not be "stuck," as Kohlberg suggests, in a stage of moral reasoning. Rather, she may have chosen an alternative route to moral conduct.

It should be clear that my description of an ethic of caring as a feminine ethic does not imply a claim to speak for all women nor to exclude men. . . There is reason to believe that women are somewhat better equipped for caring than men are. This is partly a result of the construction of psychological deep structures in the mother-child relationship. A girl can identify with the one caring for her and thus maintain relation while establishing identity. A boy must, however, find his identity with the absent one--the father--and thus disengage himself from the intimate relation of caring.[12]

There are many women who will deplore my insistence on locating the source of caring in human relations. The longing for something beyond is lovely--alluring--and it persists. It seems to me quite natural that men, many of whom are separated from the intimacy of caring, should create gods and seek security and love in worship. But what ethical need have women for God? I do not mean to suggest that women can brush aside an actually existing

God but, if there is such a God, the human role in Its maintenance must be trivial. We can only contemplate the universe in awe and wonder, study it conscientiously, and live in it conservatively. Women, it seems to me, can accept the God of Spinoza and Einstein. What I mean to suggest is that women have no need of a conceptualized God, one wrought in the image of man. All the love and goodness commanded by such a God can be generated from the love and goodness found in the warmest and best human relations.

Let me say a little more here, because I know the position is a hard one for many--even for many I love. In [a]. . . discussion of Abraham, we saw a fundamental and deeply cut chasm between male and female views. We see this difference illustrated again in the New Testament. In Luke 16, we hear the story of a rich man who ignored the suffering of Lazarus, a beggar. After death, Lazarus finds peace and glory, but the rich man finds eternal torment. He cries to Abraham for mercy:

> Father Abraham, have mercy on me, and send Lazarus, that he may dip the tip of his finger in water, and cool my tongue; for I am tormented in this flame.
>
> But Abraham said, Son, remember that thou in thy lifetime receivedst thy good things, and likewise Lazarus evil things: but now he is comforted and thou are tormented.
>
> And beside all this, between us and you there is a great gulf fixed: so that they which would pass from hence to you cannot; neither can they pass to us, that would come from thence.[13]

But what prevents their passage? The judgmental love of the harsh father establishes the chasm. This is not the love of the mother, for even in despair she would cast herself across the chasm to relieve the suffering of her child. If he calls her, she will respond. Even the wickedest, if he calls, she must meet as one-caring. Now, I ask again, what ethical need has woman for God?

In the stories of Abraham, we hear the tragedy induced by the traditional, masculine approach to ethics. When Kierkegaard defends him in an agonized and obsessive search for "something beyond" to which he can repeatedly declare his devotion, he reveals the emptiness at the heart of his own concrete existence. If Abraham is lost, he, Kierkegaard, is lost. He observes: "So either there is a paradox, that the individual as the individual stands in an absolute relation to the absolute/or Abraham is lost."[14]

Woman, as one-caring, pities and fears both Abraham and Kierkegaard. Not only are they lost, but they would take all of us with them into the lonely wilderness of abstraction.

THE TOUGHNESS OF CARING

An ethic built on caring is thought by some to be tenderminded. It does involve construction of an ideal from the fact and memory of tenderness. The ethical sentiment itself requires a prior natural sentiment of caring and a willingness to sustain tenderness. But there is no assumption of innate human goodness and, when we move to the construction of a philosophy of education, we shall find enormous differences between the view

developed here and that of those who find the child innately good.
I shall not claim that the child is "innately wise and good," or
that the aim of life is happiness, or that all will be well with
the child if we resist interfering in its intellectual and moral
life.[15] We have memories of caring, of tenderness, and these lead
us to a vision of what is good--a state that is good-in-itself and
a commitment to sustain and enhance that good (the desire and
commitment to be moral). But we have other memories as well, and
we have other desires. An ethic of caring takes into account
these other tendencies and desires; it is precisely because the
tendency to treat each other well is so fragile that we must
strive so consistently to care.

Far from being romantic, an ethic of caring is practical,
made for this earth. Its toughness is disclosed in a variety of
features, the most important of which I shall try to describe
briefly here.

First, since caring is a relation, an ethic built on it is
naturally other-regarding. Since I am defined in relation, I do
not sacrifice myself when I move toward the other as one-caring.
Caring is, thus, both self-serving and other-serving. Willard
Gaylin describes it as necessary to the survival of the species:
"If one's frame of reference focuses on the individual, caring
seems self-sacrificing. But if the focus is on the group, on the
species, it is the ultimate self-serving device--the sine qua non
of survival."[16]

Clearly, this is so. But while I am drawn to the other,
while I am instinctively called to nurture and protect, I am also
the initiator and chooser of my acts. I may act in accordance

with that which is good in my deepest nature, or I may seek to avoid it--either by forsaking relation or by trying to transform that which is feeling and action into that which is all propositional talk and principle. If I suppose, for example, that I am somehow alone and totally responsible for either the apprehension or creation of moral principles, I may find myself in some difficulty when it comes to caring for myself. If moral principles govern my conduct with respect to others, if I must always regard the other in order to be moral, how can I properly meet my own needs and desires? How can I, morally, care for myself?

An ethic of caring is a tough ethic. It does not separate self and other in caring, although of course, it identifies the special contribution of the one-caring and the cared-for in caring. In contrast to some forms of agapism, for example, it has no problem in advocating a deep and steady caring for self. In a discussion of other-regarding forms of agapism, Gene Outka considers the case of a woman tied to a demanding parent. He explores the possibility of her finding justification for leaving in an assessment of the greatest good for all concerned, and he properly recommends that her own interests be included. In discussing the insistence of some agapists on entirely other-regarding justification, he explores the possibility of her breaking away "to become a medical doctor," thereby satisfying the need for multilateral other-interests.[17] The one-caring throws up her hands at such casting about for reasons. She needs no special justification to care for herself for, if she is not supported and cared-for, she may be entirely lost as one-caring. If caring is to be maintained, clearly, the one-caring must be maintained. She must be strong, courageous, and capable of joy.

When we look at the one-caring in conflict (e.g., Mr. Jones and his mother), we saw that he or she can be overwhelmed by cares and burdens. The ethical responsibility of the one-caring is to look clear-eyed on what is happening to her ideal and how well she is meeting it. She sees herself, perhaps, as caring lovingly for her parent. But perhaps he is cantankerous, ungrateful, rude, and even dirty. She sees herself becoming impatient, grouchy, tired, and filled with self-pity. She can stay and live by an honestly diminished ideal--"I am a tired, grouchy, pitiful caretaker of my old father"--or she can free herself to whatever degree she must to remain minimally but actually caring. The ethical self does not live partitioned off from the rest of the person. Thinking guided by caring does not seek to justify a way out by means of a litany of predicted "goods," but it seeks a way to remain one-caring and, if at all possible, to enhance the ethical ideal. In such a quest, there is no way to disregard the self, or to remain impartial, or to adopt the stance of a disinterested observer. Pursuit of the ethical ideal demands impassioned and realistic commitment.

We see still another reason for accepting constraints on our ethical ideals. When we accept honestly our loves, our innate ferocity, our capacity for hate, we may use all this as information in building the safeguards and alarms that must be part of the ideal. We know better what we must work toward, what we must prevent, and the conditions under which we are lost as ones-caring. Instead of hiding from our natural impulses and pretending that we can achieve goodness through lofty abstractions, we accept what is there—all of it—and use what we have already assessed as good to control that which is not-good.

Caring preserves both the group and the individual and, as we have already seen, it limits our obligation so that it may realistically be met. It will not allow us to be distracted by visions of universal love, perfect justice, or a world unified under principle. It does not say, "Thou shalt not kill," and then seek other principles under which killing is, after all, justified. If the other is a clear and immediate danger to me or to my cared-fors, I must stop him, and I might need to kill him. But I cannot kill in the name of principle or justice. I must meet this other—even this evil other—as one-caring so long as caring itself is not endangered by my doing so. I must, for example, oppose capital punishment. I do not begin by saying, "Capital punishment is wrong." Thus I do not fall into the trap of having to supply reasons for its wrongness that will be endlessly disputed at a logical level. I do not say, "Life is sacred," for I cannot name a source of sacredness. I may point to the irrevocability of the decision, but this is not in itself decisive, even for me, because in many cases the decision would be just and I could not regret the demise of the condemned. (I have, after all, confessed my own ferocity; in the heat of emotion, I might have torn him to shreds if I had caught him molesting my child.)

My concern is for the ethical ideal, for my own ethical ideal and for whatever part of it others in my community may share. Ideally, another human being should be able to request, with expectation of positive response, my help and comfort. If I am not blinded by fear, or rage, or hatred, I should reach out as one-caring to the proximate stranger who entreats my help. This is the ideal one-caring creates. I should be able to respond to the condemned man's entreaty, "Help me." We must ask, then, after the effects of capital punishment on jurors, on judges, on jailers, on wardens, on newspapers "covering" the execution, on ministers visiting the condemned, on citizens affirming the sentence, on doctors certifying first that the condemned is well enough to be executed and second that he is dead. What effects have capital punishment on the ethical ideals of the participants? For me, if I had to participate, the ethical ideal would be diminished. Diminished. The ideal itself would be diminished. My act would either be wrong or barely right--right in a depleted sense. I might, indeed, participate ethically--rightly-- in an execution but only at the cost of revising my ethical ideal downward. If I do not revise it and still participate, then my act is wrong, and I am a hypocrite and unethical. It is the difference between "I don't believe in killing, but . . ." and "I did not believe in killing cold-bloodedly, but now I see that I must and for these reasons." In the latter case, I may retain my ethicality, but at considerable cost. My ideal must forever carry with it not only what I would be but what I am and have been. There is no un-bridgeable chasm between what I am and what I will be. I build the bridge to my future self, and this is why I oppose capital punishment. I do not want to kill if other options are open to me, and I do not want to ask others in the community to do what may diminish their own ethical ideals.

While I must not kill in obedience to law or principle, I may not, either, refuse to kill in obedience to principle. To remain

one-caring, I might have to kill. Consider the case of a woman
who kills her sleeping husband. Under most circumstances, the
one-caring would judge such an act wrong. It violates the very
possibility of caring for the husband. But as she hears how the
husband abused his wife and children, about the fear with which
the woman lived, about the past efforts to solve the problem
legally, the one-caring revises her judgment. The jury finds the
woman not guilty by reason of an extenuated self-defense. The
one-caring finds her ethical, but under the guidance of a sadly
diminished ethical ideal. The woman has behaved in the only way
she found open to protect herself and her children and, thus, she
has behaved in accord with the current vision of herself as one-
caring. But what a horrible vision! She is now one-who-has-
killed once and who would not kill again, and never again simply
one who would not kill. The test of ultimate blame or blameless-
ness, under an ethic of caring, lies in how the ethical ideal was
diminished. Did the agent choose the degraded vision out of
greed, cruelty, or personal interest? Or was she driven to it by
unscrupulous others who made caring impossible to sustain?

We see that our own ethicality is not entirely "up to us."
Like Winston in **Nineteen Eighty-Four**, we are fragile; we depend
upon each other even for our own goodness. This recognition casts
some doubt on Immanuel Kant's position:

It is contradictory to say that I make another person's
perfection my end and consider myself obliged to promote
this. For the **perfection** of another man, as a person,
consists precisely of **his own** power to adopt his end in

accordance with his own concept of duty; and it is self-contradictory to demand that I do (make it my duty to do) what only the other person himself can do.[18]

In one sense, we agree fully with Kant. We cannot define another's perfection; we, as ones-caring, will not even define the principles by which we should live, nor can we prescribe the particular acts he should perform to meet that perfection. But we must be exquisitely sensitive to that ideal of perfection and, in the absence of a repugnance overwhelming to one-caring, we must as ones-caring act to promote that ideal. As parents and educators, we have perhaps no single greater or higher duty than this.

The duty to enhance the ethical ideal, the commitment to caring, invokes a duty to promote skepticism and noninstitutional affiliation. In a deep sense, no institution or nation can be ethical. It cannot meet the other as one-caring or as one trying to care. It can only capture in general terms what particular ones-caring would like to have done in well-described situations. Laws, manifestos, and proclamations are not, on this account, either empty or useless; but they are limited, and they may support immoral as well as moral actions. Only the individual can be truly called to ethical behavior, and the individual can never give way to encapsulated moral guides, although she may safely accept them in ordinary, untroubled times.

Everything depends, then, upon the will to be good, to remain in caring relation to the other. How may we help ourselves and each other to sustain this will?

FOOTNOTES

[1] David Hume, "An Enquiry Concerning the Principles of Morals," in **Ethical Theories**, ed. A. I. Melden (Englewood Cliffs, N.J.: Prince-Hall, Inc., 1967), p. 275.

[2] Friedrich Nietzsche, "Mixed Opinions and Maxims," in **The Portable Nietzsche**, ed. by Walter Kaufmann (New York: The Viking Press, Inc., 1954), p. 65.

[3] See, for example, William F. Frankena, **Ethics** (Englewood Cliffs, N.J.: Prentice-Hall, Inc., 1973), pp. 63-71.

[4] The argument here is, I think, compatible with that of Philippa Foot, "Reasons for Action and Desires," in **Virtues and Vices**, ed. Philippa Foot (Berkeley, Los Angeles, London: University of California Press, 1978), pp. 148-156. My argument, however, relies on a basic desire, universal in all human beings, to be in relation—to care and be cared for.

[5] The question of "summonability" is a vital one for ethicists who rely on good or altuistic feelings for moral motivation. Note treatment of this program in Lawrence R. Blum, **Friendship, Altuism, and Morality** (London: Routledge & Kegan Paul, 1980), pp 20-23 and pp. 194-203. See, also, Henry Sedgwick, **The Methods of Ethics** (Indianapolis: Hackett, 1981), and Philip Mercer, **Sympathy and Ethics** (Oxford: Clarendon Press, 1962).

[6] Friedrich Nietzsche, **The Will to Power**, trans. Walter Kaufmann (New York: Random House, 1967), pp. 476, 670. For a contemporary argument against strict application of universalizability, see Peter Winch, **Ethics and Action** (London: Routledge & Kegan Paul, 1972).

[7] W. D. Ross, **The Right and the Good** (Oxford: Clarendon Press, 1930). See also Frankena, **Ethics**.

[8] Paul Ramsey raises this concern in **Fabricated Man** (New Haven and London: Yale University Press, 1970).

[9] See the discussion in James Rachels, ed., **Understanding Moral Philosophy** (Encino, Calif.,: Dickenson Publishing Company, Inc., 1976), pp. 38-39.

[10] See Lawrence Kohlberg and R. Kramer, "Continuities and Discontinuities in Childhood and Adult Moral Development," **Human Development** 12 (1969), 93-120. See also Lawrence Kohlberg, "Stages in Moral Development as a Basis for Moral Education," in **Moral Education: Interdisciplinary Approaches**, ed. C. M. Beck, B. S. Crittenden, and E. V. Sullivan (Toronto: Toronto University Press, 1971).

[11] Carol Gilligan, "Woman's Place in Man's Life Cycle," **Harvard Educational Review** 49 (1979), 440.

[12] See Nancy Chodorow, **The Reproduction of Mothering** (Berkeley, Los Angeles, London: University of California Press, 1978).

[13] Luke 16: 24-26.

[14] Soren Kierkegaard, **Fear and Trembling**, trans. Walter Lowrie (Princeton: Princeton University Press, 1954), p. 129.

[15] For a lovely exposition of this view, see A. S. Neill, **Summerhill** (New York: Hart Publishing Company, 1960).

[16] Willard Gaylin, **Caring** (New York: Alfred A. Knopf, 1976), p. 115.

[17] Gene Outka, **Agape**: **An Ethical Analysis** (New Haven and London: Yale University Press, 1972), pp. 300-305.

[18] Immanuel Kant, **The Metaphysics of Morals**, Part II: **The Doctrine of Virtue** (New York: Harper and Row, 1964), pp. 44-45.

CHAPTER 11

OUR PREFERENCES, OURSELVES*

George Sher

In broadest outline, feminist social theory makes two main
normative claims. It contends that (1) whatever their preferences
happen to be, women should have as much opportunity to realize
those preferences as men, and (2) there is something badly wrong
with women's traditional preferences (and certain associated
traits), at least insofar as they are induced by sexual stereotypes and conditioning. Of these claims, (1) is used to justify
antidiscrimination laws and the provision of various supporting
services; (2) is used to justify "consciousness-raising"--revis-
ions of language, alterations in the images of women (and men) in
books and media, and the provision of "role models" to encourage
preferences which would not otherwise develop. Although these
claims occasionally seem to converge on the same policies (for
example, Affirmative Action), they are conceptually quite distinct.

In recent years, philosophers have shed a good deal of light
on (1). They have said much that is illuminating about equality of
opportunity and the delicate balancing of interests that it
requires. But discussion of (2) has been much less useful.

* George Sher, "Our Preferences, Ourselves," **Philosophy & Public
Affairs** 12, no. 1 (Winter 1983), pp. 34-50. Copyright (c) 1983 by
Princeton University Press. Reprinted by permission of Princeton
University Press.

Although many have asserted that perpetuating women's traditional preferences is wrong, the reasoning behind this assertion has not been worked out in great detail. There have been ritual gestures toward utility, equality, and autonomy; but no appeal to one of these notions which does not itself presuppose the superiority of some preferences (or something equally problematical) has yet been produced. As a result, the arguments against the traditional preferences have been either inconclusive or question-begging. The main aim of the present article is to demonstrate this in some detail. A secondary aim is to suggest a different and more promising approach to the problem.

It will be helpful to begin by delineating both the range of preferences and the range of arguments to be discussed. Although women's traditional preferences take a variety of forms, the central cases include preferences to devote one's time to one's tasks as housewife and mother, preferences to promote the career of one's husband and the well-being of one's children, and preferences for such traditionally female occupations as nurse and teacher. By extension, I shall also take them to include the personality traits apt to yield success in these roles such as gentleness, concern for others, and lack of (certain sorts of) aggressiveness. Of the popular arguments for altering these preferences or their manner of acquisition, one is that doing so would maximize overall utility by providing various new benefits. Another is that it would promote justice by equalizing the distribution of important goods, including the crucial good of self-respect. A third is that it would increase liberty and autonomy by allowing women the fullest possible range of life choices. In addition, each argument is sometimes supplemented by claims that the traditional preferences inhibit personal growth or are exploitative. Although the arguments all assume that the relevant preferences and traits are environmentally determined, and that different environmental stimuli would produce different psychological characteristics, I shall not question this controversial assumption here. Instead, I shall accept it in order to assess its normative consequences.

To see the problem with such arguments, consider first the appeal to utility. Because the principle of utility says that we should always maximize value, and because utilitarians generally believe that only happiness has value, most versions of this argument maintain that perpetuating women's traditional preferences would bring less overall happiness than altering them. Although various reasons for believing this have been proposed, two of the most important are brought out by Jane English. According to English, within the traditional system "a woman who might lead a happy life as a pilot and a man who would find nursing rewarding are steered into professions they may not enjoy so much nor do so well. They lose happiness, and so do the rest of us in that we do not have the most talented people in society performing each job."[1] Paraphrasing somewhat, we may say that women's traditional preferences reduce both social productivity and women's individual enjoyment. Since both are important determinants of overall happiness, the utilitarian argument against the traditional preferences may seem very strong.

In fact, however, the situation is considerably more complicated than this. Although altering women's preferences would indeed promote the development of new talents, it would also drastically change the traditional division of society's labor. Because efficiency requires specialization as well as developed talents, it is far from obvious that such a change would increase overall productivity. Moreover, and more importantly for our purposes, it is also not clear that the change would increase women's individual enjoyment. On the standard assumptions of formal utility theory, enjoyment or happiness is not something over and above the satisfaction of preferences. Instead, one's happiness is defined by a utility function which is assigned on the basis of one's preferences as expressed under different assignments of probability to different states of affairs. On these assumptions, a woman whose utility function assigns a high ranking to her domestic life must be precisely as happy as a nontraditional woman whose life occupies a similar position in her utility function. Thus, to show that nontraditional preferences would bring more overall enjoyment, one must establish that they are on the whole more likely to be satisfied than traditional ones. But while this may be true in isolated instances, it is surely unlikely as a general rule. At the very least, no reason for accepting it has been provided. Of course, this problem would not arise if the utilitarian were to drop either the assumption that happiness is defined in terms of satisfied preference, or else the deeper assumption that only happiness has value. However, given the difficulty of providing a criterion of happiness that does not involve preference, the first suggestion does not seem promising. Moreover, if one adopts the second, then one must hold that of two equally satisfied sets of preferences one may be worth more than the other.

Since whether nondomestic preferences are worth more than domestic ones is precisely what is at issue, to assume this without argument would merely beg the question.

If the only preferences whose satisfaction could determine happiness were actual ones, then these objections to the utilitarian argument would be decisive. However, even if formal utility theory does imply this, a different tradition within utilitarianism connects happiness to preference-satisfaction in a more sophisticated way. In a famous passage in **Utilitarianism**, John Stuart Mill writes that "if one of. . .two [pleasures] is, by those who are competently acquainted with it, placed so far above the other that they prefer it, even though knowing it to be attended with a greater amount of discontent . . .we are justified in ascribing to the preferred enjoyment a superiority in quality so far outweighing quantity as to render it, in comparison, of small account."[2] Purged of rhetorical excess and restricted to single individuals, what this comes to is that the value of one's situation may depend not merely on how strongly one **does** prefer it, but on how strongly one **would** prefer it if one were "competently acquainted" with some alternative. The value of one's situation may depend not on its position in one's actual utility function, but rather on its position in the different utility function that would grow out of broader experience or more balanced judgment. If this "choice criterion of value" is acceptable, it will be of obvious application to women's traditional preferences. Although it will not guarantee that nontraditional lives are worth more than traditional ones for traditional women, it will at least open up this possibility. According to it, the value of a traditional life for a particular woman will depend not on her actual preferences, but rather on the preferences she would acquire if competently acquainted with nontraditional as well as traditional life styles. Moreover, whatever those preferences would be, the natural way of discovering them is simply to **make** her acquainted with the competing options. Thus, even where the choice criterion does favor a traditional life, it may still condemn any mode of social conditioning that precludes a competent acquaintance with other possibilities.

Although the issue is seldom framed in quite these terms, it seems clear that something like the choice criterion provides the appeal to utility with its best chance of success. However, even if that criterion is defensible in some contexts, its viability here is dubious at best. The "competent acquaintance" requirement is easy to satisfy when the competing alternatives are activities or states that can be sequentially performed or undergone and then compared from a neutral vantage point. However, when the alternatives are entire ways of life, the situation is vastly more problematical. The objection that some ways of life require lifelong immersion may perhaps be met by allowing that one's 'acquaintance' with one or both competitors may be merely imaginative. However, even so, the ideal of the genuinely neutral standpoint will still be defeated whenever one of the competing ways of life requires a commitment which from the inside renders the other unattractive but from the outside seems merely incomprehensible. This is true of some forms of religious life, and it holds for at least some forms of domestic life as well. Because it does, no appeal to the choice criterion can succeed unless it disallows such committed lives as illegitimate. But to do this without further argument would again assume a version of what is to be shown. Thus embellished, the augmented appeal to utility would again be question-begging.[3]

I suspect that few feminists would be disturbed by this. Although utility is often invoked as a supporting consideration, a more basic complaint against the traditional preferences is that their perpetuation produces inequalities that are unjust. A widely accepted principle of justice states that all persons should be treated equally except when there is a relevant basis for inequality; and a system producing preferences that lead men and women to live very different lives may seem a blatant violation of this.[4] Yet here too problems arise. The strong presumption for equality applies only to modes of treatment which allocate benefits and burdens. Hence, to succeed, the egalitarian argument must assume that the traditional preferences deny women benefits or impose burdens upon them. But this assumption only reraises the difficulties encountered above. If benefiting someone is just raising his position as determined by his own utility function, then merely altering women's traditional preferences will not benefit them. On the other hand, if benefit involves more than this, then it implies a ranking of preferences which itself requires defense. Since this ranking is presupposed by the appeal to equality, it cannot be defended in terms of equality. Hence, the egalitarian argument threatens to be just as question-begging as the appeal to utility.

This objection applies not only to appeals to utility and equality, but also to appeals to all other principles for distributing goods. Hence, any criticism of women's preferences that appeals to such a principle may appear to confuse the question of how goods should be distributed with the question of which things are goods. But this conclusion, though tempting, is premature. The proponent of, say, equality may attempt to connect his distributional principle to a favored conception of the good by deriving the latter from the same considerations that support the former. If this can be done, and if women's traditional preferences do deprive them of equal amounts of the goods thus defended, then the egalitarian attack on those preferences will succeed after all. There is, moreover, at least one (moderately) egalitarian framework which seems to yield precisely this result. That framework is introduced by John Rawls; and it is to his account that we must now turn.

In a **Theory of Justice** Rawls explicitly acknowledges that arguments for particular principles of justice should not presuppose any special conception of the good.[5] However, because he holds that the principles of justice depend on the choices that would be made by rational and self-interested parties who did not know their actual life circumstances or preferences, Rawls also cannot say that what counts as a good or benefit for a person is directly determined by that person's preferences. To resolve this dilemma, and to provide a definite motivation for those in the "original position," Rawls introduces the notion of primary goods--of things whose possession can only help us to realize whatever (other) preferences we have. These primary goods, which include rights and liberties, powers and opportunities, income and wealth, and the social bases of self-respect, are things it is rational for us to want whatever else we want. They would invariably be chosen by rational individuals in the original position, and it is this that confers on them their status as goods. Because that status flows from the same hypothetical choice procedure which yields Rawls's substantive principles of justice, the result is an egalitarian theory whose conception of benefit is internal to it. If this theory is correct, it may indeed allow egalitarians to criticize socially induced preferences without begging the question. In particular, it suggests (though Rawls himself does not assert) that women are treated unjustly if they are caused to develop preferences that prevent them from acquiring equitable shares of primary goods. Since primary goods acquire their status from choices made under ideal rather than actual conditions, this claim is not undercut by the fact that women with traditional preferences neither prefer more primary goods than they have, nor have other preferences whose realization requires additional amounts of such goods.

Many feminists maintain that women's traditional preferences have caused them to acquire far less power than men.[6] Although power is a complicated notion, this claim may well be correct if power is interpreted politically and economically. If it is, the traditional preferences may indeed prevent women from acquiring equitable shares of an important primary good. The situation is complicated by the fact that Rawls himself does not include political and economic power among the primary goods. By "powers" he means only Hohfeldian abilities "to create by certain procedures a structure of rights and duties that courts will enforce."[7] Nevertheless, the idea that political and economic power are also primary goods is not implausible. Because it is not, the extension of Rawls's framework to demonstrate injustice in women's disinclination to seek such power is not implausible either.

Should we then agree that the conditioning which women undergo deprives them of their fair share of the primary good of power? Despite appearances, I believe we should not; for the idea that power is something it is rational to want whatever else one wants is belied by women's traditional preferences themselves. It is true that having more power outside her marriage would allow a woman with traditional preferences to satisfy some preferences which would otherwise go unsatisfied. However, it is also true that one cannot have such power without pursuing it, and that the character traits necessary for its pursuit are themselves incompatible with many sorts of traditional preferences. The successful pursuit of power demands aggressiveness and a taste for competition, and so would require drastic changes in the temperament and preferences of many traditional women. However, any such changes would inevitably preclude many quieter and more domestic pursuits and relationships. Hence, given the necessities of human psychology, any gains in political and economic power would be more than offset by what are, to many traditional women, satisfactions of far greater moment. Similarly, even if power is quite unequally distributed within many marriages, many traditional women will regard any rearrangement of this pattern as precluding the sort of relationship they value most deeply. Hence, here again any shift in power may actually bring a net loss in preference-satisfaction. In view of this, the parties in the original position cannot automatically assume that their preferences in the actual world are best served by social arrangements which maximize their power. At best, they can assume this if they know that their actual preferences are not women's traditional ones. However, to build this assumption into the original position would of course be illegitimate. To do so would again beg the question against the very preferences whose value is at issue.

These considerations do not entirely discredit the idea that political and economic power should play an important role in any list of primary goods. Such power is often extremely helpful in getting what one wants and nothing said here suggests that those in the original position should ignore this. However, given the sacrifices that acquiring power may involve, it does seem that what those in the original position should desire is not power **simpliciter**, but rather the absence of impediments to its acquisition when it is desired. Properly speaking, it is not power itself but rather access to it, which really satisfies Rawls's definition of a primary good. Thus, Rawls's framework does not show that power should be distributed equally (or in a way which maximizes the power of the least powerful). At best, it shows that all persons should have equal access to power (or that any inequalities in access should maximize the access of those with least access). Of course, the notion of equal access is itself problematical, and may be read as demanding anything from formal equality of opportunity to something much stronger. However, for our purposes the crucial point is that it does not demand that all people's preferences should either require or yield similar amounts of power. A fortiori, it does not condemn women's traditional preferences for failing to require or yield as much power as others.

These remarks concern only inequalities of power, but similar considerations obviously hold for inequalities of wealth and income. Moreover, rights and liberties, as Rawls understands them, are basically absences of restraint on action (or protections against such restraint), and so are not made unequal by women's traditional preferences. In view of this, the only primary good whose unequal distribution may still tell against the traditional preferences is self-respect. According to Rawls, self-respect includes two main elements. It includes first "a person's sense of his own value, his secure conviction his conception of his good, his plan of life, is worth carrying out. And, second, [it] implies a confidence in one's ability, so far as it is within one's power, to fulfill one's intentions."[8] If we lack self-respect, "then nothing may seem worth doing, or if some things have value for us, we lack the will to strive for them. All desire and activity becomes empty and vain, and we sink into apathy and cynicism."[9] Because self-respect thus affects not only one's ability to pursue one's goals, but also the value one attaches to them, it comes closer than the other primary goods to being something it is always rational to want whatever else one wants. Hence, if women's traditional preferences do bring significantly less self-respect than others, then the Rawlsian framework may indeed imply that they should be altered.

Do women's traditional preferences bring them less self-respect than men's? Given Rawls's account of self-respect, the operative questions here are (a) whether the traditional preferences cause women to downgrade their goals or themselves, and

(b) whether those preferences reduce the likelihood that women will actually achieve their goals. Of these questions, the second can immediately be answered in the negative; for a woman whose central goals concern her home, husband, and family is surely no less likely to achieve them than a man (or woman) who prefers to be a corporate executive or an athlete. However, the answer to the first question is less clear; for the importance which women with traditional preferences attach to their goals (and them-selves) may be said to be affected by several distinct factors. These factors include (1) the relative lack of difficulty of the tasks which the traditional preferences generate, and (2) the internal structure of the traditional preferences, and (3) the fact that society attaches little prestige to women's domestic activities. Let us now consider each factor in turn.

The first factor, the relative lack of difficulty of the tasks generated by women's traditional preferences, is relevant to their self-respect because of a general principle of motivation, which Rawls calls the Aristotelian Principle. This principle asserts "that, other things equal, human beings enjoy the exercise of their realized capacities (their innate or trained abilities), and that this enjoyment increases the more the capacity is realized or the greater its complexity."[10] According to Rawls, activities which fail to satisfy the Aristotelian Principle "are likely to seem dull and flat, and to give us no feeling of compe-tence or sense that they are worth doing."[11] Such activities are likely to reduce one's self-respect. Hence, if the traditional preferences do not generate tasks which tax women's ingenuity and skill, then the charge that they reduce women's self-respect may indeed go through.

This version of the appeal to self-respect has some initial plausibility. However, despite its plausibility, it does not succeed. It is true that some of the tasks required by women's traditional preferences are routine and mechanical. However, it is also true that many of these tasks, such as cooking and child raising, can be performed in ways which are creative and interesting. For this reason, the Aristotelian Principle will at best predict not that women with traditional preferences must tend to find life dull and flat, but rather that they must tend to do these things in increasingly interesting and complicated ways.[12] But in fact it is doubtful whether the principle predicts even this much. Although the Aristotelian Principle is proposed as a near universal description of how humans behave, it is very easy to find common-sense counterexamples, both male and female, to it. As Vinit Haksar has observed, "there are plenty of people who live well-regulated simple lives without becoming bored"[13] (and, we may add, without believing that they are less worthwhile than others). In view of this, the Aristotelian Principle at best describes a weak and easily overcome tendency in human behavior. But if this is so, then it is hardly strong enough to establish **any** conclusions about how women with traditional preferences are likely to act or feel.

The second way of working out the appeal to self-respect is very different. On this account, the crucial aspect of women's traditional preferences is not the complexity of the tasks they require, but rather the content of the goals they generate. It is often noted that a woman with traditional preferences aims largely at furthering the interests of other people. She is most concerned to support her husband's career and to look after the health and well-being of her children. Because she does arrange her life to further the interests of others, it is tempting to describe her as minimizing or sacrificing her own interests. It is tempting to say, with Thomas Hill, Jr., that she "tends not to form her own interests, values, and ideals; and when she does, she counts them as less important than her husband's."[14] If this is so, there is indeed a sense in which such a woman does not believe that she is as important as other people. This is true at least in that she systematically subordinates her own interests to those of others.

The claim that women with traditional preferences neglect or ignore their own interests is very common. It underlies not only many assertions that those preferences undermine self-respect, but also many assertions that those preferences are exploitative.[15] Yet despite its pervasiveness, the claim does not really take us any further forward. The difficulty is that its central assumption--that a preference to advance the interests of her husband and children cannot itself be an important element of a woman's own interest--is just as problematical as the disputed claim that a woman's traditional preferences are harmful or not worthwhile. We often do say that one's interests are constituted by one's basic religious, moral, or even recreational preferences; and so it is hardly obvious that they cannot also be determined by a preference to care for one's family. Thus, the proposed argument only replaces the question of how women are harmed by their traditional preferences with the equally difficult question of why such preferences cannot themselves determine women's interests. If we lack an answer to the latter question, we cannot invoke the content of women's traditional preferences to show that they reduce women's (Rawlsian) self-respect. If we have one, the appeal to diminished self-respect is no longer necessary.[16]

These considerations suggest that no intrinsic features of women's traditional preferences undermine self-respect. However, even so, it may still be held that those preferences have social accompaniments which produce the same effect. In particular, self-respect may be said to be undermined by the fact that women's traditional preferences bring them little prestige and few other social rewards. Because such rewards go largely to those whose activities are outside the home and family, they serve as a public announcement that our society places little value on women's traditional tasks and relationships. Thus, it may seem only natural for many traditional women to believe that they themselves have little value as well.

Unlike other versions of the appeal to self-respect, this one focuses squarely on the **social bases** of self-respect. It thus comes closer than the others to addressing what Rawls himself considers the relevant primary good. Moreover, although the notions of prestige and reward are themselves complex, there is clearly something right about the idea that our society does not currently place a high value on women's traditional preferences. The prevailing reward structure may indeed lead many traditional women to think less of themselves; and so too, ironically, may the recent pronouncements of some feminists. But what, exactly, should we conclude from this? The conclusion often advocated is that the determinants of the traditional preferences should be altered or abolished. However, if those preferences are not in themselves harmful, and if the tasks to which they lead are worth doing and important, then this conclusion is perverse. Under these conditions, the more reasonable conclusion is that we should strive to change the inadequate and destructive reward structure which is presently **associated** with those preferences. If the only complaint against women's traditional preferences is that they reduce self-respect because they are inadequately rewarded, then the proper response is surely not to abolish them, but rather to reward them more adequately.

With this conclusion, we may finally abandon the claim that women's traditional preferences deprive them of equitable shares of primary goods. Because no other conception of the good which is internally connected to a distributional principle is available, the prospects for a successful appeal to equality or a related principle do not seem bright. However, even so, one other major argument against women's traditional preferences does remain. It is often held that the real problem with those preferences lies not in their distributional effects, but rather in the way they are acquired and perpetuated. What is really objectionable, it is said, is not the decisions they yield, but rather the fact that they are relentlessly conditioned by various aspects of the social environment. On this account nothing wrong occurs when a woman rationally weighs her options under conditions of equal opportunity and then freely chooses to live a domestic life. However, when her decision stems from preferences shaped by expectations encountered since early childhood, then it is in an important sense not autonomously made. Since autonomous choice is among the most precious and distinctive of human activities, women are greatly harmed by being denied a capacity for it. Hence, to set things right, the forces that render women incapable of autonomy--the forces that cause them to acquire a single, stereotyped set of preferences--must now be altered.

If anything, this appeal to autonomy is even more common than the appeal to equality. However, even so, it is hard to assess; for its central notion is notoriously unclear. In this context, of course, autonomy must involve something more than merely doing what one prefers; but what that 'something more' could be is far from obvious. To appreciate the difficulty, consider first the claim that women only choose autonomously if the basic preferences motivating their choices have not themselves been produced by social conditioning. As Sharon Bishop Hill puts it, women's autonomous choices must "express genuine interests of theirs which arise spontaneously under certain conditions [of psychological strength and rationality]."[17] There is an obvious danger that Hill's notations of psychological strength and rationality will covertly assume the very normative claims she wants to establish. However, given the recent emphasis on the effects of sex role stereotyping, Hill's central contention--that autonomy requires preferences which arise spontaneously rather than through social conditioning--does strike a familiar chord.

Can an appeal to autonomy, thus conceived, support a general attack on women's traditional preferences? Despite its familiarity, I believe it cannot. For one thing, if women's traditional preferences are largely or entirely shaped by sexual stereotypes, then one's character and preferences must be extremely malleable when one is young. But if so, then abolishing the prevailing stereotypes is likely only to clear the way for other, less systematic forms of conditioning. Hence, abolishing those stereotypes is unlikely to increase women's autonomy as Hill defines it.[18] In addition, even if eliminating stereotypes did increase autonomy in Hill's sense, the moral import of this would remain unclear. We value autonomy because we believe that people should control their own destinies; and Hill's definition at first seems attractive precisely because a conditioned preference is so plainly not within one's control. But on second glance, this is inconclusive; for however we interpret 'spontaneous', it seems clear that a preference which arises spontaneously is also not within one's control. Whether it is caused by the agent's innate psychological tendencies or simply by nothing at all, the fact remains that such a preference arrives unbidden. Thus, replacing conditioned preferences by spontaneous ones would bring no real increase in women's control over their lives.

Given these considerations, those who argue that traditional preferences reduce women's autonomy cannot interpret autonomous action as action grounded in unconditioned preferences. Instead, they must interpret it as action grounded in preferences which stem more positively from the agent's choice or will. Generally speaking, such positive accounts of autonomy have taken two main forms. On the one hand, since choices concerning preferences are always grounded in further preferences, some philosophers have maintained that autonomous agents must be motivated by preferences which accord with their higher-order preferences--by preferences which they prefer to have.[19] On the other hand, since higher-order preferences are themselves embedded in a broader context of interests, abilities, beliefs, and circumstances, other philosophers have understood autonomy as requiring reflection of a more broad-gauged sort. Because genuine control requires an understanding of all the values and presuppositions supporting one's preferences, these philosophers contend that one cannot act autonomously unless this entire complex of attitudes has been subjected to rational assessment.[20]

The first of these accounts will plainly not support the claim that women's traditional preferences must render them non-autonomous. If one accepts the two-level approach, one must concede that women with traditional preferences do not lack autonomy as long as they prefer to have and be motivated by those preferences, and there is no reason to deny that this may occur.[21] However, the second approach seems more promising. Women socialized to prefer domestic roles are often said to be incapable of ascending to higher planes of reflective awareness. Because they are so firmly anchored in a single view of their lives and themselves, they cannot raise questions about the appropriateness or desirability of their plans and aspirations. They cannot fully imagine alternative possibilities. Hence, they may indeed appear to lack autonomy in its second positive sense.

This version of the appeal to autonomy is plainly the strongest we have seen. Even so, I do not think it succeeds; for like the other arguments we have examined, it tacitly prejudges the very question it seeks to answer. The argument assumes that women with traditional preferences lack control of their lives because they cannot examine the presuppositions and values upon which their preferences depend. It is only by raising questions about these attitudes, and by imagining alternative ways of life, that they can freely decide to accept or alter their preferences. But if we accept the argument's premise that the traditional preferences preclude such questioning and imagining, then we must surely challenge its further assumption that such activity, if undertaken, would make possible a genuine choice between traditional and nontraditional preferences. If traditional preferences do involve a commitment which make radical questioning impossible, then no woman can engage in such questioning unless her erstwhile traditional preferences are already so altered that a decision to retain them is no longer possible. To question in this way is already to have made one's choice; and so its justification cannot be that it alone makes real choice possible. Instead, the justification must again be that the resulting preferences are superior in some other dimension. If autonomy requires this sort of questioning, then Haksar may well be correct in asserting that the idea that people should be autonomous is itself a form of perfectionism.[22]

This point can be made in another way. To see that some alternatives must always lie outside the boundaries of genuine choice, consider a feminist attempting to imagine herself living a traditional life. Such a woman may indeed imagine herself remaining at home with her children while her husband works, but she can surely not imagine herself accepting all aspects of the traditional role. Given her penchant for exhaustive self-scrutiny, she cannot imagine herself entertaining a simpler and less self-conscious commitment to domestic life; and many related attitudes and values will elude her as well. A fully traditional outlook is no more a genuine option for her than her own outlook is for a more traditional woman. Hence, the difference between traditional and non-traditional preferences cannot be that only the former impose genuine restrictions on choice. The claim that such preferences interfere with autonomy may yet succeed; but the argument's center of gravity must again be shifted to another place.

It is, however, no longer clear what that other place could be. We have not examined all of the familiar arguments against women's traditional preferences; and each argument has been found to be either inconclusive or question- begging. In view of this, it seems safe to conclude that the case against those preferences has not yet been made. The possibility of making it receives con-tinuing support from our common abhorrence of conditioned prefer-ences for slavery and certain other forms of servitude. However, until this abhorrence is satisfactorily analyzed and accounted for, we cannot tell whether it stems from moral principle or simply from a deeply held ideal of the person. In the latter case, the reaction might still be defensible, but the strategy of attacking women's traditional preferences by invoking moral prin-ciples would be fundamentally misguided. Moreover, and even more important, until this abhorrence is explained, we also cannot tell whether consistency demands that we condemn the preferences of contented housewives as well as contented slaves. At least prima facie, the analogy seems very far from complete; for the traditional male-female relation is grounded in bonds of mutual attraction and affection, and in shared purposes and concern for common dependents which the master-slave relation utterly lacks. However, many feminists will reply that the similarities outweigh the differences. Without a well-motivated account of what is relevant, the situation remains obscure.

In the end, its obscurity may not matter. Whatever we believe about well-integrated traditional preferences, there is clearly a problem when a woman's traditional preferences do not cohere with her other attitudes. When a woman is strongly attached to domesticity yet hopelessly unsatisfied by it, or when she aspires to independence but lacks the drive or aggressiveness to achieve it, then the conditions which have shaped her character and preferences may indeed be criticized. Moreover, although there is no reason to believe that such tensions are inherent in women's traditional preferences, they do seem to be increasingly associated with them. Given the overwhelming testimony of unhappiness and bitterness that feminism has called forth, it seems clear that women with unmixedly traditional preferences are increasingly rare. Given the swirl of influences to which women are exposed, this is hardly surprising. Yet surprising or not, it suggests an important insight in the feminist position. We saw above that there is good reason to increase the prestige and rewards which attach to women's traditional preferences. However, if the traditional preferences are seriously at odds with other attitudes which many women hold, then some changes of a rather different sort may also be required. If the determinants of the other attitudes are pervasive and intractable, and if the lack of coherence produces deep conflict and unhappiness in many women, then there may indeed be a reason to alter some of the conditions which produce the traditional preferences at an early age. In that case, at least some efforts to change our traditional expectations and stereotypes may be called for on grounds of simple humanity. This way of justifying efforts to alter the determinants of women's traditional preferences resembles some of the arguments considered above; but it also differs importantly from them. Unlike the earlier arguments, it appeals not to the nature or effects of the traditional preferences themselves but to their incompatibility with certain other preferences; not to timeless considerations but to the peculiarities of the historical moment; not to principles of distributive justice or respect for autonomy but to the humbler principle that suffering should be relieved. If it lacks the moral grandeur of the rejected arguments, it is at least grounded in a principle whose content and validity are uncontroversial. To be fully convincing, the argument would have to be supplemented by evidence that the current malaise will not dissipate on its own, and that particular efforts to relieve it will not cause unintended harm to women, their children, or others. These matters cannot be considered here. However, what can be said is that given the degree of self-consciousness which many women have already reached, neither stasis nor a return to past attitudes seems likely. The final irony is that some of the changes so often advocated in the name of freedom may be best defended as ways of accommodating a shift about which there is no real choice at all.

FOOTNOTES

[1] Jane English, ed., **Sex Equality** (Englewood Cliffs, N. J.: Prentice-Hall, 1977), p. 8. For remarks in a similar vein, see Altson Jaggar, "On Sexual Equality", ibid., p. 106.

[2] John Stuart Mill, **Utilitarianism** (Indianapolis: Hackett, 1979), pp. 8-9.

[3] For related criticism of the choice criterion, see Vinit Haksar, **Equality, Liberty, and Perfectionism** (Oxford: Oxford University Press, 1969), pp. 206-231.

[4] In "On Sexual Equality," Jaggar goes so far as to claim that a feminist must by definition believe "that justice requires equality between men and women" (p. 94).

[5] John Rawls, **A Theory of Justice** (Cambridge, Mass.: Harvard University Press, 1971), p. 94; see also pp. 325-332.

[6] See, for example, B. C. Postow, "Thomas on Sexism," **Ethics** 90 (1980): 254.

[7] John Rawls, "Fairness to Goodness," **The Philosophical Review** 84 (1975): 542-543, n.

[8] Rawls, **A Theory of Justice**, p. 440.

[9] Ibid.

[10] Ibid., p. 414.

[11] Ibid., p. 440.

[12] As Rawls himself notes, "the forms of life which absorb men's energies, whether they be religious devotions or purely practical matters or even games and pastimes, tend to develop their intricacies and subtleties almost without end" (Rawls, **A Theory of Justice**, p. 429).

[13] Haksar, **Equality, Liberty, and Perfectionism**, p. 200.

[14] Thomas Hill, Jr., "Servility and Self-Respect," in **Today's Moral Problems**, ed. Richard A. Wasserstrom (New York: Macmillan Co., 1979, p 135.

[15] See, for example, Judith Farr Tormey, "Exploitation, Oppression, and Self-Sacrifice," in **Women and Philosophy**, ed. Carol C. Gould and Marx Wartofsky (New York: Capricorn, 1976), pp. 206-221.

[16] There may appear to be an alternative route to the conclusion that women with traditional preferences believe themselves to be less important than other people. Instead of deriving this conclusion from the fact that such women neglect their own

interests, one may attempt to derive it from the fact that the preferences which generate those interests are logically parasitic on the preferences of others. However, it is simply a non sequitor to infer from "X's preferences are logically parasitic upon Y's" to "X believes himself to be less important than Y."

[17] Sharon Bishop Hill, "Self-Determination and Autonomy," in **Today's Moral Problems,** ed. Richard A. Wasserstrom (New York: Macmillan Co., 1979), p. 132.

[18] Irving Thalberg makes a similar point in "Socialization and Autonomous Behavior," **Tulane Studies in Philosophy** (1979): 30-32. Thalberg, however, does accept a different version of the autonomy argument.

[19] See Gerald Dworkin, "Acting Freely," **Nous** 4 (1970): 367-383; Harry Frankfurt, "Freedom of the Will and the Concept of a Person," **The Journal of Philosophy** 68 (1971): 5-20; and Gary Watson, "Free Agency," **The Journal of Philosophy** 72 (1975): 205-220.

[20] For a clear statement of this view, see William E. Connolly, **The Terms of Political Discourse** (Lexington, Mass.: Heath, 1974), pp. 140-178.

[21] Again, see Thalberg, "Socialization and Autonomous Behavior," pp. 22-27.

[22] See Haksar, **Equality, Liberty, and Perfectionism,** pp. 172-184.

AUTHOR'S NOTE

This paper has been greatly improved by the astute suggestions of Emily Sher, Alan Wertheimer, the Editors of **Philosophy and Public Affairs,** and especially, Arthur Kullik.

CONTRIBUTORS

JOSEPH L. DeVITIS is Professor of Education at The University of Tennessee at Martin.

CAROL GILLIGAN is Associate Professor of Education and Psychology at Harvard University.

EDWARD JONES is Assistant Professor of Psychology at the Fuller Graduate School of Psychology.

JANE ROLAND MARTIN is Professor of Philosophy and Education at the University of Massachusetts, Boston.

NEL NODDINGS is Associate Professor of Education at Stanford University.

SUSAN MOLLER OKIN is Associate Professor of Politics at Brandeis University.

CAROLE PATEMAN is Professor of Government at the University of Sydney, New South Wales, Australia.

SARA RUDDICK teaches philosophy, biology, and literature at the New School for Social Research.

GEORGE SHER is Professor of Philosophy at the University of Vermont.

BETTY A. SICHEL is Professor of Education at C. W. Post Center, Long Island University.

CARROLL SMITH-ROSENBERG is Professor of History and Psychiatry at the University of Pennsylvania.

351, 356 (**See Language**)
Expressive leader, 55 (**See also** Parsons, Talcott)
Expressive roles, 54 (**See also** Parsons, Talcott)

Factory system, 180, 240-241
Fairness, 141, 288, 295, 302, 312, 316, 327 (**See** Justice)
Family, 4-5, 17, 21-22, 26-29, 35, 39-47 **passim**, 51-58 **passim**, 68-75 **passim** 78-84, 92-97 **passim**, 100, 105, 109-118, 131-133, 139-141, 145-146, 151-168 **passim**, 172-173, 177-200 **passim** 214, 222, 226-227, 236-245 **passim** 264-266, 271, 301, 309, 321-323, 352, 365-366, 370, 385-388 (**See also** Children and child-rearing; Domestic functions; Father; Husband; Marriage; Mother; Nuclear family; Sex role; Wife)
Family therapy, 139, 147 (**See also** Psychotherapy; Therapy)
Fantasy, 127, 143, 158, 171-172, 207-208, 212, 224, 233, 244
Father, xix, 25-26, 30, 55, 75-79 **passim**, 108-111, 114, 131-132, 167, 172-174, 180, 190, 199, 209, 217, 237-240, 245, 274, 287, 321, 361-363 (**See also** Children and child-rearing; Domestic functions; Husband; Marriage; Mother; Nuclear family; Sex role; Wife)
Fear, 98, 114, 132, 147, 210, 219, 224, 236, 241, 346-347, 367-369
Feinberg, Walter, 2, 11
Feminine psychology, 6-8, 48-49, 159-165 **passim**
Femininity, x, xii-xiii, 48-49, 92-93, 108, 111, 116, 132, 138, 145, 155-157, 161-163, 167-168,

171-174, 241, 255, 259, 276-277, 350, 359, 361, 398
Feminism, xi-xiii, xvi-xviii, 1-3, 7, 10, 46-48, 52-54, 57, 80-85 **passim**, 132, 159, 176, 185, 190, 209, 212-213, 228-230, 235, 238-245 **passim**, 255-256, 350, 359-361, 373, 379-381, 389, 394-396
Ferguson, John, 38-39, 62
Festinger, L., 325, 331
Fetishism, 170-171
Feudalism, 180
Fine arts, 251-255
Fine, Elsa Honig, 275
Firestone, Shilamuth, 84-85
Fischer-Homburger, Esther, 119
Fisher, Berenice, 246
Fishman, Pamela, 240
Flax, Jane, 242
Flexner, Eleanor, 119-120
Foote, E. B., 123
Foot, Philippa, 371
Formal operational thought, 287-288 (**See also** Piaget, Jean)
Forms: of knowledge, 24, 251-252, 255-256
Fox, Renee, 119
Fragility, 108, 220-223, 242, 364, 369
Frankena, William F., 371
Frankfurt, Harry, 399
Franklin, Rosalind, 260, 276
Freedom, 37-38, 44-46, 66, 81, 131, 185-186, 189, 279, 304, 397
Free will, 115
French, Marilyn, 235-236
Freud, Sigmund, xi, xiii, 5-6, 47-48, 65, 71-80 **passim**, 83, 86-92 **passim**, 119, 127-149, 153, 159-162, 166, 174-175, 183, 187-192 **passim**, 198, 202, 209, 281-283, 306, 318, 320 (**See also** Psychiatry; Psychoanalysis; Psychology)
Friday, Nancy, 166, 202
Friedman, Cornelia, 119

Frances E. Mascia-Lees

TOWARD A MODEL OF WOMEN'S STATUS

American University Studies: Series XI (Anthropology/Sociology). Vol. 1
146 pages   paperback US $ 14.60*

*Recommended price - alterations reserved

Many difficulties have been encountered by researchers attempting to assess women's status in contemporary societies. One major obstacle has to do with the problems encountered in developing indices of status that can be used as objective measures of women's position. Due to such obstacles, many, if not most, studies of women's status have concentrated on qualitative analyses of single cultures or culture areas, making comparisons across societies unsystematic and, therefore, of limited applicability. Yet it is just such systematic studies that are required if the conditions perpetuating women's status around the world are to be identified and changed. This work presents a first attempt to develop measures of women's status using existing statistics, that are applicable across nations and make possible comparisons in time and space. This volume reviews the literature on the determinants of women's status in contemporary societies, analyzes the range of variation in women's position in the public sector, provides quantitative measures of women's status in the political, económic, educational, and family spheres, and identifies factors important in explaining and predicting women's position on a world-wide scale.

PETER LANG PUBLISHING, INC.
62 West 45th Street
USA – New York, NY 10036

Douglas R. Austrom

THE CONSEQUENCES OF BEING SINGLE

American University Studies: Series XI (Anthropology/Sociology). Vol. 6
ISBN 0-8204-0095-5   246 pages   paperback US $ 24.70*

*Recommended price - alterations reserved

As a result of contemporary trends in marriage and divorce, the proportion of single adults has risen quite dramatically. Because of the number of unmarried adults (roughly 60 million in North America), it is increasingly necessary to assess the consequences of this supposedly solitary lifestyle.

A questionnaire study was conducted to compare the physical wellbeing, frequency of depressive symptoms, happiness, and life satisfaction of 517 single adults with a matched sample of 521 married adults. Contrary to the findings of most previous studies, the married respondents did not report better physical health than the single respondents. The married respondents were, however, significantly happier, less frequently depressed and more satisfied with their lives. Further analyses showed that social support was a better predictor of life satisfaction and depressive symptomatology than marital status per se.

But being married is still a factor in psychological well-being, happiness, and life satisfaction, at least insofar as the primary affectional bond provides the requisite social support. Other factors which contribute to the quality of single life were assessed and discussed.

 PETER LANG PUBLISHING, INC.
62 West 45th Street
USA - New York, NY 10036